Cher

PRAISE FOR *CHEROKEE DNA STUDIES*

---

# Cherokee DNA Studies

*Real People Who Proved the Geneticists Wrong*

DONALD N. YATES and TERESA A. YATES

Panther's Lodge Publishers

Phoenix

LIBRARY OF CONGRESS CATALOGUING-IN-PUBLICATION DATA

Yates, Donald N., 1950– author
Cherokee DNA studies:  real people who proved the geneticists wrong
/ Donald N. Yates and Teresa A. Yates
p.      cm.
Includes bibliographical references and index.

**ISBN 978-0-6923-1370-1**
softcover : acid free paper ∞

1.  Cherokee Indians—History.   2.  Cherokee Indians—Migrations.
3.  Cherokee Indians—Alphabet.   4.  Cherokee language—Etymology.
5.  Indians of North America—Transatlantic influences.
6.  Human population genetics—Mediterranean Region.   I.  Title.  II. Series.
E99.C5Y39  2014        975.004'97557 — dc23       2012019546

BRITISH LIBRARY CATALOGUING DATA ARE AVAILABLE

DNA Consultants Series on Consumer Genetics 1

Manufactured in the United States of America

*Panther's Lodge Publishers*
*26438 N. 42nd Way, Phoenix, Arizona 85050*
*www.pantherslodge.com*

# CONTENTS

# ACKNOWLEDGMENTS

DeWayne Adamson, Judith Alef, Joseph F. Bailey, Michelle Baugh, Karen Beck, Sharon Crisp Bedzyk, Brent S. Vaughn Blount, Edith Breshears, Tatiana Brooks, Linda Burckhalter, Dawn Copeland, Bruce Linton Dean, Gail Lynn Dean, Edmund F. Durfee, Pamela G. Edwards, Tommy Doyle Fields, Beatrice L. Frost, Mary M. Garrabrant-Brower, Michael E. Gilbert, Cheryl Lynn Green, Chris Harmston, Barbara A. Henson, Kim M. Hill, Denise Holmes-Kennedy, John R. Ihlefeld, J. Jones, Ken Jordan, Miranda King, Eleanor M. Leonard, David E. Lewis, Kimberly Mebust, Karen Sue Mitchell, Debra Modrall, Michael W. Moore, Maxine Nethercutt, Warren D. Pearson, Gerald Potterf, Patrick Pynes, Jimi Riddle, JonLyn L. Roberts, Nadine Rosebush, Marie A. Rundquist, Larry Rutledge, Betty Sue Price Satterfield, Joy Shorkey, Donell Sigler, Billy Sinor, Phyllis E. Starnes, D.J. Thornton, Elizabeth Pearl Thurman, Malee Thomas, Edward Viera, La Nita Jordan Wacker, Paul Minus Williams, Dustin Blake Yates.

Aarian P. Afshari, Suzanne C. Allen, James R. Alvarez,, Theresa Bailey, Tiffany Baker, Tommy E. Barrios, Timothy Benjamin, Susan Benning, Pamela Bowman, John Michael Brill, Jackfay Poole Buitenhuis, Kari Carpenter, Tony Wardell Carter, Linda A. Carter, Paul Arnold Cazee, Sharon Rebecca Chatterton, Yvonne M. Clark, Connie Curry, Elizabeth Deland, Earl E. Dulaney, Mary Alice England, Madonna Jean Epstein, Brenda Joyce Espinoza, Mona Feirl, Lovancia Francisco, Sylvia J. Francisco, Jan Franz, Charles Robert Franz, Clinton E. Guillermo, Patricia Gurule, Christy Hall, Joel Kenneth Harris Sr., Gregory Damon Haynes, Leroy James, James C. Keating, Norma D. Kellam, Stephen D. Kubik, George S. Lambert, Leigh Lambert, Michael Joseph Little Bear Sr., Bettie Sue Cooper Melton, Milca Montanez, Jesse Montes, Patricia Elaine Murphy, Evie Nagy, Ashley Dawn Nielsen, Petra V. Perez, Gene K. Ponder, Mary Bee Poole, Ann Pyle, Chana Rahamim, Philomena Redding, Sonya Redding, Sterling Respass, Kathleen A. Rogalla, Carol Myers Rymes, Vivian A. Santos-Montanez, Donna Schalk, Pamela Dawn Sexton,, Victor Shipman, Joseph A. Shippley, Juanita L. Sims, Linda Sherril Sponenburgh, James Richard Stritzel, Alvin L. Stults, Easter Lorene Hall Swinney, Tino De La Luz Thundereagle, Neal Van Poperin, James Eric Walker, Charlotte Boyle Walker, Deann Ward, Maria Rosa Williams, Anthony Eric Wilson, Connie Ann Wilson, Shelia Maria Wilson, Juanita Wilson, Karen Worstell, Mary A. Young.

# INTRODUCTION

"If your ancestors didn't hang with us when it wasn't cool," said a spokesperson for the Eastern Band of Cherokee Indians, "you shouldn't be trying to hang with us now." What is wrong with this statement? A lot.

This is a book about genetic genealogy, not the rights of American Indians or indeed about Cherokee history, culture and society. It recounts the surprising experiences of 119 men and women who participated in DNA Consultants' Cherokee DNA Project from 2003 to 2014. Their motives for engaging in DNA testing were not those of the imaginary acolytes of coolness rebuffed by the executive director of cultural resources whom I have quoted.

These are all real people, Americans from every walk of life and of all ages and backgrounds, in places scattered across the country. What they have in common is they were rejected—by science, commercial firms, neighbors and other family members. In other words, to use a loaded expression, they were discriminated against. They were told they didn't belong. In the lyrics of John Trudell, the Lakota songwriter, they didn't "answer to their description."

Who hasn't heard about the Cherokee grandmother myth? According to one Internet oracle, "Let's just be honest here. Your great-grandmother was probably NOT a full blooded Cherokee Princess." Hundreds of sites and articles proliferating on the web politely or impolitely tell you why. Reason no. 1: The Cherokee didn't have princesses (it turns out they did and still do). Reason no. 2: "Unless your great-grandmother was living on the Cherokee Reservation in either Oklahoma or North Carolina, she probably wasn't a full blood (nor was anyone else). Reason no. 3: "The word Cherokee has become generic, like the word Kleenex" (really?).

Maybe I should have had a Kleenex when I went into the gym on the Hopi Indian Reservation. There were two admission prices, one for Indians and one for *bahanas* (white people). Although it was a pittance's difference, I asked for the former, telling the Hopi on guard I was Cherokee. "Don't get a nosebleed," he said.

Perhaps the deadliest arrow in the quiver of the grandma haters is the "old-wives' tale" explanation. "'Princess' was a popular term of endearment early in the 20th century," says one source. "Your great-grandfather may have called your great-grandmother his Cherokee princess, not because she was royalty, but because he loved her. Isn't that sweet?" Yes, but I do not think sweetness was why King James I recognized Pocahontas as a princess or why the War Department paid my 5th- great-grandfather an annuity in the name of "Black Fox, the Cherokee King." In multiply intertwined genealogies, my grandfather was descended from one of Black Fox's daughters and my grandmother from another. If their father was a "king," what did that make Nancy Blackfox and Mary Ann Black?

It gets even better. "Your white ancestor may just have told his family his wife was a Cherokee princess to alleviate racist tension." Or: "It's possible that your ancestor may not have been American Indian at all, but rather African-American."

There is no evidence beyond the anecdotal and theoretical to think our great-grandfathers and great-grandmothers got everything wrong. Despite its juggernaut march into popular belief, the phenomenon of the Cherokee Princess can be traced to a single article written in a forgotten book in 1996. The book was *Dressing in Feathers: The Construction of the Indian in American Popular Culture* and the article was "My Grandmother Was a Cherokee Princess: Representations of Indians in Southern History." In it, Joel W. Martin imagined, "Having hated and 'removed' most literal Indians, southerners fell in love with figurative ones . . . an astonishing number of southerners assert they have a grandmother or great-grandmother who was some kind of Cherokee, often a 'princess.'" More falling in love here.

## Maybe My Great-Grandmother Really Was a Cherokee Princess

Identity is one thing, DNA another. One is a construct, the other objective fact. Could DNA be used to prove or disprove the ubiquitous stories of Cherokee heritage that kept rearing their ugly heads on the reservation and genealogy forums? This book basically lets the study results and data speak for themselves.

Chapter One, "Trail of Fears," begins by reviewing scientists' attitudes and approach toward researching American Indians. Particular attention is paid to ethnographic and genetic studies of the Cherokee. We see that they are perhaps the least understood despite their prominence in American history and present-day status as the largest "nation." In DNA surveys as in anthropological studies Cherokees are sorely under-represented. Why? One reason is that they are thought to be so highly admixed and acculturated that what is quintessentially different and uniquely ethnic is at best a moot question.

We next look into a textbook case, "Nancy Cooper v. The Choctaw Nation" (Chapter Two). The plaintiff, a chief's daughter in Indian Territory, died before bitter victory came to the 135 relatives joining in the famous lawsuit. The decision was swiftly overturned in Federal court, later re-instated, annulled again, then in the short space of several months in 2013-2014 eased for a handful of enrollees but again overturned "forever" against all claimants.

In "Prelude 2003," we revisit what may be called Phase O, and in two subsequent chapters (4 and 6) Phase I and II of the house study published as "Anomalous Mitochondrial DNA Lineages in the Cherokee." Chapter 5 expands on the central finding with an examination of the meaning and time depth of admixture in the tribal histories of the Cherokee and Hopi.

Chapter 7 is devoted to my own explorations in the field of Cherokee genealogy, which began in the 1980s and accelerated with the advent of DNA in 2000.

In Chapter 8, we review a selection of posts that sprang forth as important news broke in genetics, archeology, anthropology and associated disciplines. The Cherokees are not alone in having an unusual population structure. Full genomic sequencing and autosomal DNA approaches will undoubtedly shed light on the mystery of the Navajo with their Chinese admixture, the Sioux with an unexplained high incidence of European male haplogroup R (like the 30,000-year-old Ma'lta boy in Siberia) and other groups.

"Where There's Smoke" is the perfect title for Chapter 9. Drawn largely from interviews conducted with participants, it tells their stories in their own words. Each of these is different, though they all share similar outcomes. Each is compelling testimony to the roles of fascination, fear, frustration, validation and triumph played by DNA and hard science in their lives.

Over the course of ten years both my wife and I got to know many of the subjects beyond a superficial administrative level. They became more than statistics as we learned we were actually related to them, unbeknownst to either party before. Some were enrolled members of federally recognized Cherokee tribes, some belonged to state Indian tribes, most were unaffiliated. While the majority identified as white, others were Hispanic or even American Indians by open declaration, even living on reservations. A surprising number were African Americans, well informed of their European and Native American roots.

Not a single participant went into the study for any other gain than the twin satisfaction of finding out the truth and serving the stated goals of the project. No one rushed out to get their Indian card. The Bureau of Indian Affairs doesn't regard DNA as material evidence in such matters anyway. Even if participants had tried to press newfound Cherokee connections, their quixotic actions would have come to naught. We've already seen the likely reception they would have been given by the cultural affairs department at Tahlequah, Oklahoma or Cherokee, North Carolina.

All of us are "anomalous" and "admixed." Our unique set of genes is precious. Even if we do not understand or accept everything strident headlines or private testing results tell us, the genetic heritage stretching back unbroken to our ancestors is what makes us tick. That is why when I started my company I pledged to treat everyone's ancestry as though it were my own. It has been our pleasure to help tell the stories of a hundred-plus passionate customers and share their ongoing journeys of discovery and self-awareness.

*Donald N. Yates*

# 1 TRAIL OF FEARS

The study of Cherokee DNA is a parlous endeavor. The combination of American Indian genetics and ethnic analysis is bound to be a sort of confusion compounded. Fear of the known and unknown. . . angst over conclusions and consequences . . . . xenophobia and misunderstanding everywhere. Modern-day genetic genealogy has deported thousands of unsuspecting seekers of the truth down a Trail of Fears.

Can we at least divest genetics of some of the fear? All DNA, or deoxyribonucleic acid, is nothing more than an arrangement of elements. Hydrogen, nitrogen oxygen and the all-important carbon join chemically in different ways to form four key molecules: adenine (A), guanine (G), thymine (T) and cytosine (C). These four molecules or bases, along with a sugar molecule and phosphate, are the building blocks of DNA, the genetic code that has been replicating and recombining since life on earth began. The specific arrangement of these molecules, packaged in perfect copies in every cell of our body, provides us with an ineluctable trail going back to the prototypes of our ancestors and passing through every subsequent descendant on down to us.

Only about 3% of the AGTC code actually is recognized as a gene that "does something," in other words, determine hair color or produce an enzyme. The rest either serves for "punctuation" or its purposes are unknown. But even "non-coding" DNA sequences obey the strict rules of heredity.

The genetic glossolalia spit out in lab reports may look like this: ...CCATGGTACTGAATCCTT.... It used to be called "junk DNA," until it was objected the Creator didn't make any junk. The variations and patterns geneticists and genealogists detect in the family tree are called haplogroups (branches), haplotypes (twigs), signatures, alleles (variants), markers or just plain "mutations." The latter term does not mean that you carry a risk for developing a rare genetic disease or giving birth to a two-headed calf, however. Most mutations are neutral in effect on our biology.

Analyses of American Indian DNA usually focus on mitochondrial haplogroups. Scientists zero in on a set of about 16,600 nucleotides stuck outside the cell nucleus (where the six billion nucleotides composing all the rest of our DNA reside). Males and females have mitochondrial DNA, but only mothers can pass it. Deep ancestry in an unbroken line of mothers and their children is inferred from a small control region of nucleotides. The target is uniparental inheritance, the transmission of genes from one parental type to all progeny. Mitochondrial DNA can trace your mother's mutations back to the "daughter of Eve" she descends from, just as Y chromosomal haplotypes can reveal what "son of Adam" your father is. But both are tools of limited usefulness in understanding the wide diversity of genotypes and complex process of change across what is much like geologic time, the long stretch of history. Moreover, these are just two approaches to the problem. No past society has been composed of women alone or only men, and the male and female roles in human migrations and population expansions never quite seem to match up. Y chromosomal Adam is a lot younger than mitochondrial Eve. Our uniparental ancestors were not alive at the same time.

The history of sex is hardly an open-and-shut book. Geneticists construct their pedigrees and phylogenies using evolutionary theorems of random mating and sexual selection. But throughout most of human history couples have married non-randomly and led lives more monogamous than polygamous. We sometimes hear that all people on earth can be traced back to a small group of "anatomically modern" humans, or that the genes of Jesus or Buddha or Alexander the Great live on in infinitesimally small amounts in all of us, no matter where or when we might have been born. That is not true, even on a statistical level. Neither Jesus nor Alexander the Great had any recorded "heirs of their body." Rahula was the historical Buddha's only child. He became a celibate and predeceased his father.

The English and American monarchists are probably not all dead who proudly trace their pedigree to William the Conqueror. But William's male line died out with his own son Henry I, who was plagued with girl-babies and was succeeded by his nephew, Stephen of Blois. The telephone books today are not replete with listings for Conqueror, William T. Perhaps those who joy in his royal haplotype got it from illegitimate offspring? That should not surprise us since William himself was called the Bastard.

Geneticists tackling the new Indian Problem resort to desperate sampling of willing or unwilling reservation or South and Central American Indians, rarely comparing whole-genome data or tendered genealogies (e.g., A. Achilli et al 2013). Though Cherokee Indians constitute one of the oldest, largest and best-documented Native American groups, at the time of writing only 60 Oklahoma Stillwell and Red Cross Cherokee individuals have been genotyped with tribally specific markers, this only on the basis of mtDNA HVR I (Smith et al 1999, Schurr 2000, Malhi 2001). Cultural resistance to DNA testing, extinction of male lines by warfare and government policy, unknown amounts of European admixture and the Cherokees' own particular problematical history of non-reservation life and assimilation have hampered genetic research and denied us all answers.

## Indian Groups in the U.S.

"There are many humorous things in the world," observed Mark Twain, "among them the white man's notion that he is less savage than the other savages." Since the beloved author of Tom Sawyer penned these words one might expect that knowledge of Native Americans would have become a dry and settled matter.

The United States contains some three hundred Indian reservations, covering more than fifty million acres of land in twenty-seven states (Pevar). Differences between Indian and Indian are as bewildering as their similarities. A famous book speaks of 500 nations while an encyclopedia enumerates 223 separate and distinct cultures (Josephy, Klein). Oklahoma alone has sixty-seven tribes. According to a U.S. government report, American Indians represent one percent of the population but fifty percent of its diversity (Hodgkinson et al.). They account for a large part of America's fascination in the eyes of tourists, especially Europeans, who often come without pre-conceived ideas.

Between the 1990 and 2000 federal censuses, the U.S. Indian population doubled from nearly two million to over four million. Most of the increase came from altered categories of reporting that allowed people to identify with more than one ethnic category, for instance "American Indian" and African American. Yet there was more behind this dramatic shift. Since about the 1920s American Indians were having more children. Their numbers have been rising rather than declining (McNickle). Undoubtedly, there is also an element of fashion in this trend. It is now more acceptable to be American Indian. But such groups as the Pan American Indian Association maintain that even these figures were low. Executive director Chief Piercing Eyes insists there are more than fifteen million U.S. citizens of Indian ancestry. As Indian blood becomes increasingly "watered down," the United States is witnessing an atavistic return of the Red Man.

Among the New Indians (Steiner's phrase) the Cherokee are perhaps the best educated, best organized and certainly most numerous. In the southern states it is hard to find an old family without some degree of Indian blood. Cherokee is the most common type mentioned. By a wide margin, the Cherokee today constitute the largest Indian group. The Navajo or Diné comprise a distant second. It is estimated there are nearly 500,000 or more self-identifying Cherokee Indians in the United States. These numbers include the three federal entities Cherokee Nation of Oklahoma, United Keetoowah Band and Eastern Band of Cherokee Indians in North Carolina, plus more than one hundred state tribes and untold unaffiliated Cherokees. Los Angeles has the largest concentration (Thornton).

Most people believe they "know" a lot about Indians. But what defines American Indians in the first place? A friend asked me, "What do you say to someone who tells you, 'Funny, you don't look like an Indian?'" I said I didn't know. He told me, "You ask them, 'What does an Indian look like?'" Fluctuating criteria cause a lot of fear and confusion. For instance, you can qualify as an Indian for educational or healthcare purposes but be rejected by anthropologists or geneticists (Pevar 12-13). Prehistoric and sometimes even historical Indian populations diverge significantly from modern-day populations.

## Who or What Are Indians?

A long list can be made of what Indians are *not*. On a sufficient cause basis, the list does not necessarily include belonging to a tribe, carrying an Indian card, being a full blood or having red skin. Some Indians do not belong to a tribe, carry an Indian card, are not full blood, do not have red skin, and so forth.

For the purposes of Indian treaties and acting as guardian of the "nations within a nation" that are its legal wards, the U.S. government defines Indians on a tribal basis, case by case. It registers individuals who can provide a paper trail documenting descent from a tribal member whose name appears on the final rolls of their tribe. A Certified Degree of Indian Blood is issued and the tribe enrolls the individual (and sometimes the family). The Dawes Rolls that form the crux of these decisions were prepared on the basis of male surnames in the years around 1900. Government policy at that time was to privatize any remaining communal lands, extinguish tribal governments and allot small parcels of land in severalty to qualified Indians. Congressional and agency actions pursued a long-held strategy of dealing once and for all with the Indian Question by administering it away. Federal recognition came to be predicated on prior recognition. The government became increasingly protective of "our Native Americans." In effect, Indians ceased to be Indians and became instead *descendants* of Indians, losing historicity. The BIA's Branch of Acknowledgement and Research denied even this status to hundreds of thousands of people, particularly in the Southeast. There were not supposed to be any Indians left there.

A further complication is that many states do not have federally recognized Indian tribes. By treaty, the chief of the Mattaponi Indians delivers a freshly killed deer to the front steps of the statehouse in Richmond each year. Virginia's Indian affairs go back to British treaties. But "Pocahontas' people" (as they are known today) continue to battle for their rights (Rountree). Significantly, at the Peace of Paris that concluded the Revolutionary War, both the new nation and Great Britain avoided the subject of "Americans," as Indians were then called. Native sovereignty was not mentioned by either our Founding Fathers or British negotiators. Indians were condemned to a legal limbo.

Neither Kentucky nor Tennessee, the original homelands of the Shawnee, Cherokee and other groups, has state-recognized tribes. During the period known as Termination (1953-1968), Congress voted to end federal services to Indians "at the earliest possible time" (McNickle 105). More than a hundred tribes were wiped out with the stroke of a pen. Under Republican administrations treaties were systematically disavowed and abrogated as an estimated 300 Indian groups sought recognition for the first time. The century-long scandal of the Individual Indian Money

Accounts continued, with billions of dollars owed to descendants of Indians cheated by the Dawes Act.

## Legal Definitions

In a broad definition expressed in the U.S. Federal Code, Indians are persons descended from the aboriginal inhabitants of the Americans who are at the same time recognized as members of some Indian community (Pevar). The U.S. Census Bureau ignores this distinction and regards anyone as Indian who says they are. Arguably, you either are or are not an Indian, in your own estimation as well as the eyes of others. As Lakota Sioux Chief Noble Red Man (Matthew King) says, "Our people don't come in parts" (Arden & Wall 34). The "one drop" rule of African American identity is notably denied to Native Americans.

America's indigenous peoples, then, remain ill defined. They are poorly understood, sometimes even by themselves. Xenophobia runs through all dialogues and disputations about the matter. Part of the reason is that indigenous people are habitually treated as objects of study. Rarely are they the ones looking on and scrutinizing with a privileged research methodology of their own (Smith). It is revealing that even the names of Indian tribes originate with Europeans: Cherokee (a Shawnee word applied by Carolina traders), Creek (after Ochese Creek in Georgia), Ft. Apache (those gathered around an American fort in Arizona), Delaware (after Lord Delaware), and so forth (Waldman). Many tribes never even encountered the Europeans, much less got "discovered." Some were extinguished before even being named or having their language recorded (e.g. the Yuchi). According to medico-historical experts, ninety percent or more of the population of North America succumbed to the onslaught of virulent European diseases in the sixteenth century (Churchill). The survivors blended and coalesced with others to form new mixtures and new entities.

Division into tribes was another European artifice. The first mention of an Indian "nation" occurs with the Cherokee about 1810.

In "Anthropologists and Other Friends," Lakota Sioux lawyer Vine Deloria, Jr. complains about the patronizing, anti-Indian attitudes of the scientific community. Indian history and prehistory have always been political dynamite. Johns Hopkins Ph.D. Stephen C. Jett criticizes the dogma entrenched in our universities that denies indigenous people writing, metal implements, stone buildings and transoceanic travel, calling it racism.

Are Native Americans, all Native Americans, even yet able to participate as equals in the debate?

## Living Stereotypes

Woefully typical of popular literature is a book in which Indians are identified on the first page with Mongolians (Crutchfield 13). Indians have short stature, stocky build, almond shaped eyes, off white to yellowish skin coloration, Asian shovel teeth and straight, black hair. "At some point in time," the reader is informed, "probably while chasing the great animal herds, a group of these Mongoloid people strayed across what is now the Bering Strait, but what was then a dry land bridge, and for the first time 'officially' people the New World" (13-14). Once the New World is wondrously peopled, there follow four periods of prehistory: 1) a Paleo-Indian culture of thinly scattered hunters and gatherers, defined by the so-called Clovis Point, a type of spearhead chipped from flint, 2) Archaic times, when "instead of bands forever on the move, the beginnings of settled life prevailed" (18), 3) the Woodland Period of pottery, agriculture, and the Mound Builders, and 4) the Mississippian Culture the Europeans found when they arrived after 1492.

All these multitudes descend from a very small group of original settlers who migrated out of Siberia as recently as three to four thousands years ago or as long ago as thirty to forty thousand years. "We can assume that several families of these people, representing probably twenty to thirty individuals at the most, made up a band, and that many of these bands wandered over the face of North America for thousands of years" (15).

Would the story of European prehistory ever be written like this? Hardly. For one thing, European prehistory is divided into a number of periods and sub-periods unfolding differently in different regions. America has only a single monolithic period, the Paleo-Indian age, where Europe enjoys a Paleolithic (Old Stone Age), Neolithic (New Stone Age), Acheulean, Upper and Middle Paleolithic, Solutrean, Magdalenian, Ausonian, Epigravettian and others.

## The Academic Version

But surely this version of history is a grossly oversimplified one. Let us then look at Crawford's more academic *Origins of Native Americans*. This work presents conclusions drawn from the fields of genetics, archeology, linguistics, medicine, demography, geography and history, as well as cultural anthropology. The facts have been attenuated in a post-genetics age.

The lineaments of age-old pseudo-anthropology are still plainly to be seen in textbooks and encyclopedias. Though some new pieces of evidence have come to light in the past few years, Crawford's synthesis can stand as a reliable guide. Read the Wikipedia article on American Indians—if you can wade through a disjointed morass of factoids and footnotes—and you will see what I mean.

Crawford begins with origins, that "battleground of the theorists" which in the words of another American Indian expert has "snared to their downfall not a few crackpots, mystics, 'linguistic acrobats,' racists and even famous institutions . . . [including] of course the anthropological profession itself"(Wauchope 12). Early theories like the "lost tribes" explanation are glossed over rather quickly. Crawford takes us almost immediately to today's generally accepted theory of Asiatic origin. This rests on the pillars of four similarities between Native Americans and arctic or sub-arctic Asian peoples: 1) shared genetic markers, 2) morphological resemblances in contemporary populations, 3) skull shapes and capacities as measured by the science of craniometry, and 4) common cultural trends.

Recalling geneticist Cavalli-Sforza's tree based on forty-two world populations, Crawford goes on to reaffirm the continent-specific definition of race. According to Cavalli-Sforza, the human tree has two main limbs, the African and non-African, with the North Eurasian limb branching off into Europeans (Caucasians) and Northeast Asians. Included in the last category are the Amerindians. Amerinds are closest in genetic distance to Northern Turkic, Chukchi and other Arctic peoples. They share a number of genetic markers with Northeast Asians, including a similar frequency of female lineages (viz., the mitochondrial haplogroups A, B, C, and D), immunoglobulins, human leukocyte antigens (HLAs) and a susceptibility to middle ear infections.

These sweeping generalizations are based on a comparison of contemporary populations. Were Mongolian and Native American populations the same as they are today? Have not numerous genetic types become extinct? Have not bottlenecks and genetic drift altered the profile of populations? What about ancient DNA samples? Pääbo et al. in 1988 proposed the existence of a previously unknown founding lineage on the basis of mitochondrial DNA extracted from a rare specimen of 7,000-year-old human brain matter in Florida. The new type, however, was almost immediately dismissed as extinct and "of no importance." Similarly, an analysis of the bone remains of 25 pre-Columbian Mayas by Gonzalez-Oliver's group produced one type of mitochondrial DNA that could not be classified. Its relative frequency was ten times the number of all ancient Tierra del Fuego DNA.

Human population structure can shift and re-align relatively rapidly. The effects of a "non-random event" such as an earthquake or crop failure can cast a long shadow. Massive gene flow is evident in the Norman invasion of Britain in 1066 CE, Within about a generation, virtually every Anglo-Saxon name on property and estate lists was replaced by that of a Norman. Today, easily 80 percent of British surnames can be traced to William the Conqueror's French retainers.

## Flawed Research

Most investigators have a definition of Native American that is circular and self-reinforcing. Conclusions are used to support premises, which are then applied to new conclusions. Such false logic is excused by a bias toward western "reservation Indians." Groundbreaking studies dividing Native Americans into four maternal lineages (later termed A, B, C and D) were founded entirely on small Pima, Maya, Ticuna, Mexican and South American Indian samples. The very first study of mitochondrial DNA in American Indian populations (Wallace) inferred an Asian correlation from small, over-worked samples of Pima and Papago Indians. Earlier blood marker studies by Salzano were confined to South American Indians. Salzano virtually ignored North American Indians. In a study reaching the same conclusions, frequencies of an enzyme known as UMPK were established on the basis of only six demographic groups: Cree, Athabaskan, Venezuelan Indians, Eskimos, Aleuts and Yupik.

Morphological resemblances between Asians and Amerindians comprise a second point emphasized by Crawford. These shared physical features include straight, black hair, sparse beards and body hair, the Mongoloid spot at the base of the spine, small brow ridges, and high cheekbones. Dental evidence in pronounced shovel teeth is also adduced, and craniometric studies (skull measurements) are said to clench the connection. A fourth category of evidence for Crawford is shared cultural traits, but he does not pretend to give an exhaustive list. He mentions only four: 1) animism, 2) shamanism, 3) tipis, and 4) calendar sticks.

13

Do all tribes have shamans? The Creek and Choctaw do not. Or calendar sticks? It is doubtful. Why do other Indians not have sand paintings like the Navajos? Unless these cultural affinities somehow form a unique and universal complex, this argument has little cogency.

Crawford next reviews the earliest estimated entry of Native Americans into the New World. From the dogmatic date of 12,000 years ago to the "new synthesis," which postulates successive waves beginning as early as 40,000 years ago, we move rapidly through the archeological finds of pre-Clovis sites like Pennsylvania's Meadowcroft rock shelter with its carbonized basket dated 19,600 ± 2,400 YBP to Chile's Monte Verde river settlement with its three apparent hearths radiocarbon dated close to 34,000 year ago.

Crawford next considers Greenberg's 1987 proposal of three macro-linguistic stocks corresponding to the same number of major migrations out of Asia. Amerind is the oldest and most prevalent. This is followed by Na-Dene, which includes Athabaskan (mostly Alaskan and Yukon) and Navajo/Apache (American Southwest). Aleut-Eskimo (extreme Arctic) is the most recent. As Crawford notes, however:

> The conclusions of Greenberg and his colleagues slowly unravel. . . . Some pertinent evidence from linguistics, ecology, genetics and archeology has been uncovered since the initial formulation of Greenberg's three-migration theory (p. 24).

## Jones' Critique of the Peopling of the Americas

In September of 2002 appeared an incisive study from the Bäuu Institute in Boulder, Colorado. Written by Peter N. Jones, it was titled, "American Indian Demographic History and Cultural Affiliation: A Discussion of Certain Limitations on the use of mtDNA and Y Chromosome Testing." Jones offered a critique of the controversies surrounding the origins of Native Americans. He claimed that "most studies have not used random samples, but instead have used convenience samples obtained from diabetic studies, rheumatic studies, and AIDS studies, as well as other studies" (p. 5). In addition to noting unreliable data and invalid methodologies, he faulted population geneticists and anthropologists for their poor knowledge of history. Scientists were blindly attached to the Clovis First and Bering land-bridge theories. They failed to imagine more complex scenarios. "Because of the high mobility of American Indian groups in the prehistoric [period], along with examples of intergroup marriage and non-random mating, there is ample reason to believe that the genetic history of American Indians is much more complex than the current five haplogroup frequencies lead us to believe" (p. 9). Among the horizons in American Indian genetics still awaiting exploration were "the possibility of future haplotypes being discovered" (p. 10), "the possibility of mutation addition or deletion, and other factors" (p. 19), and the use of corroborative techniques other than just mtDNA or Y chromosome testing, such as *alu*-insertion and human lymphocyte inheritance (p. 23).

According to the author of *American Discovery*, "Conventional anthropologists cannot yet envision habitation dates for America comparable to European sites" (Thompson 1994 p. 61). Nor can they admit that human beings might have crossed the ocean before Columbus. Dean R. Snow speaks of the "fantastic claims for pre-Columbian migration to the New World that plague archeologists periodically" (Kehoe 1981, p. 5). Anthropologists' enmity toward diffusionism is loud and plain beginning with Harold E. Driver, *Indians of North America* (Chicago, 1961).

Are there really "canoes, dugout, and kayak-type boats painted in red or black in Pleistocene Spanish caves at La Pasiege, Castillo, and La Pileta, including the midship peak distinctive of Beothuk boats" (p. 57)? No, not boats. And if so, not seaworthy. Elephant trunks appear to be sculpted in the ball court at Chichen Itza? No, parrot beaks. Evidence has accumulated of fire-rings, smashed skulls of extinct animals and primitive tools from 40,000 years ago—and even 400,000—in California? Natural lightning strikes.

Of the possibility of admixture, something systematically excluded from almost all the studies, one archeologist writes, "Today there is a scattering of both L (African) and H (European) in American Indian populations, but so little that it most likely represents intermarriage since Columbus's time" (Adovasio 2003, 240). All studies of Cherokee DNA have noted the presence of maternal haplogroups H and J. But these European haplogroups are dismissed as the product of European admixture after 1492, even though unmixed subjects were preferentially enrolled in the samples.

All "European" DNA is factored out on the American Indian side and all "Russian" DNA is ignored on the Siberian side of comparisons. Only 9.5

percent of Native American samples are judged "unmixed" (p. 193). Moreover:

> The Atlantic seaboard and several regions of the southeastern US have the highest admixture rates, which approximate 50% (Pollitzer et al 1967; Szathmary and Auguer 1983) (p. 185).

According to firmly established genealogies for the Navajo, even this tribe has "not inconsequential numbers of genes of European origin" (pp. 185-186).

A leading contemporary archeologist admits that modern North American archeology has not outgrown its nineteenth-century descriptive phase, as typified by the monumental series of publications brought out by the Smithsonian. Archeology is still fixated on publishing surveys and catalogues. . . as is apparently genetics, another science that seems stuck in description. Significantly, William Dancey's recent article on Hopewell culture (now dated *ca.* 400 BCE to 200 CE) concludes with a fundamental paradox: "We are left . . . with an enduring enigma, and a renewed challenge to a new generation of scholars and fieldworkers" (Pauketat and Loren 232).

Stinted in particular seem the Indians of the Eastern Seaboard and the Mississippi and the Ohio Valley. These tribes consistently fail to be included in genetics studies. Out of a total of 1,600 subjects, one major study uses only 37 Cherokee, 35 Creek, 27 Choctaw, and 35 Seminole, most of them from Oklahoma, to represent all Southeast Indians (Mahli et al. 2002). Another study has 500 subjects all together (Lorenz and Smith 1996). The Native American Molecular Anthropology Laboratory at the University of Rome has no new data on Southeast tribes.

Geneticists are clearly afraid of a large number of scenarios to entertain or investigate. Archeologists have few, if any, answers to important questions. How are modern-day Southeastern Indians related to the so-called Mound Builders? It is as though an American Middle Ages did not exist. "Fragments of pottery have been made the basis of our interpretation of history," according to Barry Fell (1980, 259-60):

> Adhering naively to the idea that all new developments are brought from another place by some footloose peoples, we have created a

host of different fictitious "Peoples" whose complex comings and goings fill the pages of American archeology texts but tell us absolutely nothing about the languages or places of origin of any one of them!

## Indian History Written by Europeans

There are 500 Indian Nations according to the title of a popular book. Not one of them has a satisfactory history, by which I mean competent written account of their past. Rather than tackle the particulars of a single tribe, their unique language or a distinct period in a tribe's history, scholars and scientists have preferred to author general histories or compilations . . . with titles like *500 Nations*. For a variety of reasons, none of these treatments can really be said to be satisfactory either. The encyclopedic approach suffers because of a dearth of individual studies, and local histories and "first-cut" journal articles that might be expected to contribute to a gradually accumulating body of knowledge about American Indians are stillborn for lack of a settled framework in the field as a whole.

Of the "500," it is the Cherokee who are most harmed by the confused state of things. They comprise the largest and therefore most important nation. If we cannot understand who the Cherokee are we are not very advanced in our knowledge about American Indians. One might think that the problem could be solved by having more Native authors writing history and doing research rather than allowing others to write it for them. That only compounds the confusion, because Native authors are often fighting old wars. At any rate, they founder like all the others. Either they are engulfed by the many-headed Scylla of case studies or wrecked on the Charybdis of the discipline itself.

The latest history of the Cherokee by Robert Conley was commissioned by the principal chief of the Cherokee Nation of Oklahoma. It is a general treatment of a particular subject and combines the failings inherent in both approaches. The Cherokee Nation of Oklahoma is not coterminous with the Cherokee people. There are more Cherokees that do not belong to the Cherokee Nation of Oklahoma than belong to it. Its history is neither comprehensive nor even representative of Cherokee history since it begins only in 1838, after the defeat of the Cherokee by the government and their removal on the Trail of Tears to Indian Territory. Conley's history has several axes to grind—one in particular aimed at decapitation of the rival

United Keetoowah Band. It glosses over the pre-1838 past and ignores most events that take place in the Cherokee homeland in the East, of which most Western Cherokee have little experience.

Cherokee historiography falls into the same periods as the history and development of Federal Indian policy, preceded by British Indian policy. Except for James Adair's *History of the American Indians*, published in London in 1775, no study of the subject of American Indians was attempted in monograph form during the Colonial Period in the English language. To be sure, several classic treatments existed in Spanish. One was Gregorio de Garcia's *Origen de los Indios del Nuevo Mundo e Indias Occidentales* (Valencia, 1607), a work that summarized all the learned hypotheses advanced to that day. It concluded that American Indians were human beings. Another was Bartolomé de las Casas' *Historia de las Indias,* so radical in its pleas for Indian rights that it was not published in its entirety until the nineteenth century.

In the Peace of Paris concluding the American Revolution in 1783, Native Americans were studiously ignored. The whole issue was tabled by both the British and the Colonials, as we have seen. The sovereignty of Indian tribes, validity of Indian treaties and status of Indians as individuals were simply not addressed, although some tribes (like the Iroquois) had fought on the side of the rebels and others (like the Cherokee) on the side of the British. Theoretically, reparations and damages might have been imposed. No peace treaty, at any rate, was signed with any Indians.

The new nation's Indian policies began to take shape after the election of the first president, George Washington, in 1792. The president emerged as the Great White Father, taking the place of King George and awarding medals of himself to what became "medal chiefs." The U.S. Senate took on the role of guarantor of Indian rights and treaties. During the interregnum, much encroachment had taken place on Indian lands. The states of Kentucky and Tennessee were carved out of Cherokee territory. The Great White Father was given a list of 500 names of white men settled illegally in the Cherokee Nation. He was given the list by white men lobbying the government to allow them to stay.

### War and Peace

There was every reason to place the Indians under the care of the Senate, for this chamber of government also had the authority to declare war and make peace. From 1790 until the 1860s, Indian affairs were regulated by the

War Department. Studies of Indians took on the character of language manuals, musters of soldiers, warrior counts, auditor's records and fatality lists. Henry R. Schoolcraft, an Indian agent, published his massive work, *Historical and Statistical Information Respecting...the Indian Tribes of the United States* in six volumes from 1851 to 1857. Portraits of chiefs were commissioned and displayed, somewhat like a baseball card collection, at the Indian Gallery of the Department of War in Washington. Constantine Rafinesque flourished during this period as a lone well-informed, well-trained and unprejudiced scholar in matters of Indian prehistory and the archeology of ancient Native America.

The last treaty with an Indian Nation was signed in 1867, after which treaty making was suspended. Two Indian wars ended without any treaty—the Second Seminole War (1835-1842) and the Sioux Wars (beginning 1854 and continuing with the Indian victory at the Battle of Little Big Horn in 1876 and U.S. army Massacre at Wounded Knee in 1890). The Seminole War was the most expensive Indian war fought by the United States, at a cost of $1 million for every Seminole killed. It lasted longer than any other war. The last Indian wars were fought with the Apaches and Utes and ended without any pretense of treaty making. Most information about American Indians appeared in newspapers, with the result that the "newspaper Indian" came into being.

By the 1880s all Indians within the bounds of the United States were situated on reservations. All of these were west of the Mississippi with the exception of a handful of tiny properties like those of the Iroquois and Cherokee Indians of North Carolina, both of which were salvaged by white citizens for the use of the red man. The next chapter in Indian policy is usually known as the Dawes Act years or period of severalty. Congress passed the Dawes Severalty Act in 1887. Among the measures in this act was one to terminate Indian communal ownership of the land on their reservations "as speedily as possible." Indian governments were also ended. This era also saw the rise of American Indian anthropology, spearheaded by the Bureau of American Ethnology at the Smithsonian Institution. The Bureau's founding director, John Wesley Powell, sought "to organize anthropologic research in America." At this time, there appeared James Mooney's *Sacred Formulas of the Cherokees* and *Myths of the Cherokee* (as the 7th and 19th annual reports of the Bureau). He also wrote *Historical Sketch of the Cherokee*, reissued in 1975 after the Cherokee Nation of Oklahoma regained its standing and began to function as a government again.

Much of Cherokee official history and its politicization can be glimpsed in the following chiefs' list. This list does not include the chiefs of the Western Cherokee and the Texas Cherokees (like John Bowles), the single Principal Chief of the Confederate Cherokee Nation, Stand Watie, the chiefs of the Eastern Band of the Cherokee Indians (which include the white man Colonel William Holland Thomas), or the chiefs of the United Keetoowah Band of Cherokee Indians, federally recognized since 1946 and situated in both Oklahoma and Arkansas. Also omitted are groups lacking federal recognition such as the Northern Cherokee Nation of the Old Southwestern Territory, as well as state-recognized groups such as the Echota Cherokee Nation of Alabama.

## Cherokee Principal Chiefs

Wrosetasetow, 1721-1735. This mangled name is probably the same as Outacite, or Mankiller. He was a headman from the Lower Town of Keowee, first to sign a treaty with the British, along with thirty-five other chiefs.

Ama-edohi, 1736-1741. Usually spelled Motoy. Meaning: Beaver (literally, "swims in water"). Chota becomes capital.

Ammouskossittee, 1741-1753. Often called Motoy II. Meaning: Bitter Water.

Guhna-gadoga, 1753-1760. Known to the English as Old Hop.

Ukah Ulah, 1760-1761. Said to be a son of Old Hop. For the title, see Chapter 7.

Ada-gal'kala, 1762-1778. Rendered in this book Attakullakulla. English, Little Carpenter. Referred to himself as "president." Admixed (?).

Agan'stat', 1778-1785. Oconostota (Ground Hog Sausage). Admixed.

Tassel, 1785-1788. Treacherously murdered by the Wataugans under a flag of truce.

Little Turkey, 1788-1804. First Chickamauga chief.

Blackfox, 1805-1811. Admixed. Also known as Henry White. Called by terms of his annuity from Washington "the Cherokee king." His seat was Creek Path.

Pathkiller, 1811-1827. Leader of a Ghost Dance movement. New

Echota becomes capital.

William Hicks, 1827. A mixed blood. Moravian convert and first Christian chief.

John Ross, 1828-1866. One-eighth blood. Grandson of Scottish trader John MacDonald. Chief during the Great Removal of 1838. Tahlequah, Indian Territory (Oklahoma) becomes capital.

William Potter Ross, 1866-1867. Nephew of former.

Lewis Downing, 1867-1872.

William Potter Ross, 1872-1875.

Charles Thompson (Oochelata), 1875-1879. Half-blood.

Dennis Wolf Bushyhead, 1879-1888. Three-quarters Cherokee, last chief of significant degree of Cherokee blood.

Joel Bryan Mayes, 1888-1891. Mixed blood.

Thomas Mitchell Buffington, 1891.

Colonel Johnson Harris, 1891-1895.

Samuel Houston Mayes, 1895-1899.

Thomas Mitchell Buffington, 1899-1903.

William Charles Rogers, 1903-1905. First "puppet" chief appointed by U.S. government, a usurpation of Cherokee sovereignty that was to last until Chief Keeler.

Frank Boudinot, 1905. Not accepted by U.S. government. Descendant of Elias Boudinot. With statehood of Oklahoma, the Western Cherokee become the Cherokee Nation of Oklahoma. Under continued action of the Dawes Commission, they lose all their reservations and communally owned land.

. . . [no chiefs]

William Wayne Keeler, 1971-1975. Since 1949 appointed chief and since 1968 chairman of the board and chief executive officer of Phillips Petroleum Corporation. Resigned after found guilty of illegal contributions to Richard Nixon's campaign during Watergate.

Ross O. Swimmer, 1975-1985. Resigned to accept appointment as head of Bureau of Indian Affairs.

Wilma P. Mankiller, 1985-1995. Said to be one-eighth degree of blood. Indian activist during the occupation of Alcatrez Island by AIM members in 1969. First female chief. Author of an autobiography.

Joe Byrd, 1995-1999. Not elected, court-ordered. George Bearpaw's name was stricken from the ballot.

Chad Smith,1999-2011.

Bill John Baker, 2011-present.

The government of the Cherokee Nation of Oklahoma (the only officially recognized Cherokee Indian group) was discontinued in 1903, and the Rolls were closed. There were to be no new Indians after this, maybe a few stragglers, for to be enrolled in a federally-recognized Indian tribe henceforth meant that one had to provide the Bureau of Indian Affairs (successor to the War Department) with a paper trail of birth and death certificates leading back to someone named on the final rolls. In the case of the Cherokee Nation of Oklahoma, this meant the Dawes Roll of 1898. For the belatedly recognized Eastern Band of Cherokee Indians in North Carolina—a tract of land around present-day Cherokee that had lain in receivership since its donor Col. Will Thomas forfeited on his taxes—it meant the Baker Roll of 1924. Most Cherokee genealogy today focuses on these two rolls.

Below, we list the official government rolls for the Cherokee, accompanied by our own historical annotations. The following warning appears below this list in the original publication: *If you are a descendant of any Cherokee on these rolls, then you are a Cherokee by blood. If not, then you are not a Cherokee. Just saying you are Cherokee will not suffice. You must be able to prove it.*

## Official United States Government Cherokee Rolls

**Source:** *Cherokee Observer*, **1998**

## THE ROLLS TAKEN EAST OF THE MISSISSIPPI

1. RESERVATION ROLLS IN 1817: A listing of those desiring a 640 tract in the east and permitted to reside there. All were subsequently barred from possessing their reservations.

2. EMIGRATION ROLLS 1817-35: Those who filed to emigrate to Arkansas country and after 1828, to Indian Territory (later called Oklahoma, meaning Land of the Red Man in Choctaw).

3. HENDERSON ROLL 1835: A census of over 16,000 residing in Alabama, Georgia, Tennessee, and North Carolina to be removed to Oklahoma under the illegal treaty of New Echota (1835).

4. MULLAY ROLL 1848: This was a census of 1,517 Cherokee people remaining in North Carolina after the removal of 1838. John C. Mullay took the census pursuant to an act of congress in 1848.

5. SILER ROLL 1851: A listing of some 1,700 Eastern Cherokee entitled to a per capita payment pursuant an act of congress in 1850.

6. CHAPMAN ROLL 1852: Prepared by Albert Chapman as a listing of those Cherokee actually receiving payment based on the Siler Roll.

7. SWETLAND ROLL 1869: Prepared by S.H. Swetland as a listing of those Cherokee, and their descendents, who were listed as remaining in North Carolina by Mullay in 1848. Made pursuant to an act of congress (1868) for a removal payment authorization.

8. HESTER ROLL 1883: Compiled by Joseph G. Hester as a roll of Eastern Band of Cherokee Indians in 1883. (This roll is an excellent source of information, including ancestors, Chapman Roll number, age, English name and Indian Name.

9. CHURCHILL ROLL 1908: By Inspector Frank C. Churchill to certify members of the Eastern Band of Cherokee Indians. Like the Hester Roll, includes a lot of information including degree of blood. Rejected applicants also are included.

10. GUION MILLER ROLL 1909: Compiled by Mr. Miller of all Eastern Cherokee, not Old Settlers, residing either east of west of the Mississippi. Ordered by Court of Claims as a result of suit won by the Eastern Cherokee. See Guion-Miller Roll West for more details.

11. BAKER ROLL 1924: This was supposed to be the final roll of the Eastern Cherokee. The land was to be allotted and all were to become regular citizens. Fortunately the Eastern Cherokee avoided the termination procedures, unlike their brothers of the Nation to the west. The Baker Roll revised the current

membership roll of the Eastern Band of Cherokee Indians in North Carolina.

## THE ROLLS TAKEN WEST OF THE MISSISSIPPI

1.     OLD SETTLER ROLL 1851: A listing of Cherokee still living in 1851 who were already residing in Oklahoma when the main body of the Cherokee arrived in the winter of 1839--as a result of the Treaty of New Echota (1835) Approximately one third of the Cherokee people at that time were Old Settlers and two thirds were new arrivals.

2.     DRENNEN ROLL 1852: The first census of the new arrivals of 1839. The New Echota Treaty group--"Trail of Tears."

3.     The DAWES ROLL 1898-1914: The final roll for allotting the land and terminating the Cherokee Nation of Oklahoma. Senator Henry L. Dawes was the commissioner's chairman, and consequently the name Dawes is associated with the final roll. The roll turned out not to be as final as it was expected to be. Upon the reorganization of the Cherokee Nation of Oklahoma in the 1970's the Dawes Roll became the only means of certifying membership. To be enrolled by the Cherokee Nation, one must prove ancestry to a person enrolled by Dawes. Information on enrollment with the Cherokee Nation may be obtained by writing to:

> Cherokee Nation of Oklahoma
> Tribal Registrar
> P.O. Box 948
> Tahlequah, Oklahoma 74465

4.     GUION-MILLER ROLL 1909: A court of claims suit resulted in members of the Eastern Cherokee living either east or west of the Mississippi, not including the Old Settlers, to be entitled to participate in a monetary award by the court, as a result of various treaty violations. In order to participate one had to be alive on May 28, 1906 and establish themselves as a member of the Eastern Cherokee, or a descendant of, at the time of the violated

treaties. 48,847 separate applications were filed, representing some 90,000 individuals. Out of this number, 3,436 Cherokee east of the Mississippi were certified by Mr. Miller as being eligible to participate in the award. One lucky enough to find an ancestor on this roll can find out a tremendous amount of information. Not only is the roll detailed, but copies of the actual applications are available, which in most cases, go back to the mid and early 1800s.

In 1924, U.S. citizenship was extended to all American Indians. For the first time, more American Indians were being born than were dying. Their population was slowly increasing. In 1922, the first advocacy group, the Association on American Indian Affairs, was founded. For the Cherokee, these years are marked by the publication, in 1921, of Emmet Starr's *History of the Cherokee Indians and Their Legends and Folklore*, still today the master compendium of Cherokee family history and clans.

Republican presidents ended a decade of supremacy in 1932. The New Deal under Democrat Franklin D. Roosevelt began. The Indian New Deal could be summed up in the single figure of John Collier, Commissioner of Indian Affairs, 1932-1945. He was the first high-ranking government official to conduct what we would call today a "needs assessment" of what was still seen as "the Indian problem." The result was a rejuvenation of Indian self-sufficiency and a thorough reorganization of the Bureau of Indian Affairs and reservation system. As Vine Deloria once remarked, the whole effort of Indians at that time was to learn administrative law. The rising stars on a reservation, if they escaped boarding school, read Felix Cohen's *Handbook of Federal Indian Law*, often with a flashlight in their tipis. Concurrently, many anthropologists of the John Wesley Powell and Franz Boas school were collecting the traditions of various tribes and putting them on the shelves of libraries for the first time. Unfortunately for Cherokee studies, there was not much activity on the part of scholars, anthropologists or administrative bodies during these years.

### Last Two Periods of Federal Policy

The period known as Termination and Relocation began in 1945 and lasted into the 1970s. Under Dillon Meyer, treaty rights and federal benefits to tribes were to be stopped. Reservation youth were to be relocated to urban centers where they could be schooled and find employment. It was a disastrous time for American Indians, including the Cherokee, for whom the watchword of the day was assimilation. Little interest was shown in Indian history until the efforts of the National Congress of American Indians (founded 1944) began to pay off. A pan-Indian political consciousness and self-determination movement came into being during the late 1960s and early 1970s.

A period known as Self-Recognition began with the American Indian occupation of Alcatraz Island (1969-1971), 1972 American Indian Movement occupation of BIA headquarters in Washington, D.C., and Wounded Knee Incident of 1973. It witnessed the achievement of civil rights by American Indians and a prolific output of literature, scholarship, journalism and political writings. The *Journal of Cherokee Studies* was founded. Dominant figures in American Indian letters were Vine Deloria, Jr., author of *Custer Died for Your Sins* and *God Is Red*; Angie Debo (*And Still the Waters Run,* 1973), and Dee Brown (*Buried My Heart at Wounded Knee*). Although these books set the tone for many subsequent historical works, they were far from objective and unbiased. They raised few historical problems that had to be worked out or worked on. They did not break any new ground.

The present period of American Indian studies may be called the Academic. In Cherokee studies, Mooney and Royce are reprinted. It has been marked by professionalism on many levels—professional teachers, professional artists, professional professors, professional journalists, professional gaming experts, professional musicians, professional administrators, on and on. It is not impossible that by now there exists something called a professional Indian.

General studies, it seems, went their own way with a profusion of coffee-table books. My favorite is the series by artist Ted Mails *The Mystic Warriors of the Plains*). The rest is bricolage. It is a ripe moment for harvesting innovative works of multi-disciplinary conception and listening to original new voices.

By the same token, a wave of political correctness and ethnic bias has swept over editors and academic institutions, so that American Indian studies by American Indians and American Indian studies by Americans are two different things. Under the circumstances, little collaboration on projects is fruitful. A true cross-pollinating or interdisciplinary effect is rare given the antipathy between the two (imagined) ethnicities and emphasis on different professions and specialties. Characteristic of the times are scholarly compendiums like the *Handbook of American Indians* and *American Indian Religious Traditions: An Encyclopedia.* Programs in universities are liable to be called Indigenous and Southwest Studies. They can be housed in English, sociology, anthropology, archeology, history or American studies departments.

For my part, I see no reason why an American Indian cannot go to Hollywood and get a part that is *not* one playing an American Indian. I think an American Indian choosing Victorian literature for their doctoral dissertation would not only be a boon to Victorian literary criticism but also a beneficial role model for other American Indians. I see no reason to shoo the anthropologists and "other friends" off the reservation or tell them fibs. As a mixed blood, I have sometimes felt compelled to fire bullets and race over to the other side to get hit. Telling me I can't have an Indian card and become a ward of the government is like forbidding me from joining the French Foreign Legion.

So where does this sketch of Indian studies leave us? Nature does not like a vacuum. The scientists and historians who study nature do not like one either. They have filled the gaps in our knowledge with fears, prejudice, misunderstanding and ignorance.

# 2 THE OLDEST CASE

Elephants and Indians have long memories. This chapter will acquaint readers with a jumbo-sized foul-up that still rankles among Oklahoma Choctaws, the story of Nancy Cooper v. The Choctaw Nation. It represents the longest running enrollment case in Federal Indian law. Nancy Cooper was the daughter of a Choctaw chief and is my first cousin five times removed (Donald Yates).

"Ever since we were kids," says Tom Estep, "my mother told us how we were the descendants of a Choctaw chief. "I thought, 'Ya, right, Mom,' but she was always telling it and how we were being denied our rights as descendants.

"When we asked why, there was no clear reason. One of the stories was there was a fire in the courthouse that destroyed all the records. Another was Grandpa was too drunk to make it to some government meeting. And finally there was the 'too proud to be put on a roll' explanation.

"One night I was watching a show on TV about AIM, the American Indian Movement, and was sitting there thinking about how the BIA and the Dawes Commission had really screwed over us Indians. I googled my grandfather's name, Oscar Peck, and lo and behold a document popped up from the Department of the Interior with his name on it in connection with the famous court case Nancy J. Cooper v. The Choctaw Nation. Nancy Cooper and others had fought to get the Cooper family name onto the Choctaw Rolls.

"This lit a fire under my mom, who is now seventy-six. Within days, she and my brother were on their way to file for their CDIB (Certificate of

Degree of Indian Blood)." Spoiler alert: it's not going to happen. Before revealing the outcome, however, it is necessary to provide some background on Nancy Cooper and her father, Capt. John Cooper.

John Cooper was the son of Henry Labon Cooper and brother of my ancestor Isaac Cooper. John fought in the Creek War with Andrew Jackson, attaining the rank of captain. His brother Isaac (whom family members called Zack) did similar duty in the Cherokee Wars, marrying Nancy, the daughter of Chief Black Fox, and carrying on the Cooper line with the Cherokees in East Tennessee and North Alabama. John, who was of equal degree Choctaw blood through their grandmother Malea Labon Cooper, walked the Choctaw path. He became a respected chief, building a home in West Tennessee and producing a large family after marrying his wife Nancy Ann Pyle, half Choctaw. The Pyle name today is well known among Oklahoma Choctaws. Gregory E. Pyle (born April 25, 1940) was elected as Principal Chief in 1997 and has been re-elected by wide margins ever since.

### John Cooper's Story

John Cooper was born in northern Mississippi in 1771, when the area known as San Esteban de Tombecbe (St. Stephens) was still ruled by the Spanish, if only in name. His father, a Portuguese mulatto named in Spanish archives as Enrico Labon Cooper was an important land developer, tobacco grower and road builder. The Coopers were British Jews with interests spread throughout Tennessee and beyond.

John Cooper's biography is found in the records of the Ohoyohoma Club in McAlester, Oklahoma:

> A man who cultivated his land, raising food for his family and livestock, Captain Cooper was surprised and shocked when the soldiers came in midwinter, January of 1836, and commanded an immediate removal of his family to the Indian Territory. They had only time to gather and pack a few necessities which the soldiers allowed to be tied on their horses' and mules' backs. They rode away toward their new home leaving behind their house, a structure of four rooms, a verandah separating the house from the smokehouse. They also left six cribs of corn and other important foods for their survival.
>
> When they arrived at the Mississippi River the ship or boats which they had been promised in writing were not there to take them across

this very cold water. The soldiers, who were driving them had not been told of this promise. They used their only means of crossing, riding their swimming animals across. Many of their party drowned and they also lost most of their food and other necessities.

[Capt.] Cooper's wife [Nancy Ann Pile or Pyle], who was ill when forced to start on the perilous journey, was physically unable to continue. A few miles from the Mississippi River in the state of Arkansas, the soldiers permitted the sick woman and their old mother [probably Molly Huston Cooper, wife of Henry Cooper] to be left in the wild and rugged country with her two daughters, Delitha and Narcissa. Gen. [sic] Cooper and his son and sons-in-law were made to continue their journey westward, driving their remaining cattle. There remains today a crossing in southeastern Oklahoma called Cooper's Landing, which was named for the courageous and faithful Choctaw husband and father. As soon as possible they escaped from the soldiers and made their way back to where the old mother and daughters were left. The mother had died two days after being abandoned. Delitha and Narcissa had survived by eating bark of trees and other plants and animals.

John Cooper was an educated Indian - spoke and wrote the English language. He fought in the war of 1812 with Andrew Jackson. The two men made a gentlemen's agreement that the Choctaws of Perry and Maury County, Tenn. were not to be moved to the Indian Territory until the spring of 1836. The two men continued to correspond and Andrew Jackson verified 'their promise in writing.' Our grandfather, John Cooper was deceived by this Democrat. He asked [*page torn*: that no one in the family would every vote for a Democrat again. They became staunch Republicans.] (*Pioneers of Oklahoma,* Oklahoma Hist. Socy.).

Before this John Cooper spent most of his life in Wayne County, Kentucky, parts of Alabama, parts of Mississippi and Perry, Davidson, Sumner, Rutherford and Lincoln counties in Tennessee. Members of his immediate family went over the Trail of Tears several times, some of them dividing off and managing to settle in Illinois, Missouri and Arkansas. He found refuge intermittently with relatives in Tishomongo County, Mississippi and Rutherford County, Tennessee, until they too were caught by the dragnet of Indian removal. At the end, he was living in a modest plantation on the west side of the Buffalo River near Linden in Tennessee.

There he died or was killed in 1839, as he attempted one last time to recover his confiscated possessions.

John's siblings adopted whatever strategies they could devise to escape the fell times. His elder brother Houston married an "octoroon woman" and established a plantation in Davidson County, Tennessee. Houston moved or fled there from Sumner County when the state of Tennessee extinguished all Cherokee claims reaching to Nashville. There Houston managed to buy 640 acres on the west side of the Harpeth River from John Nichols or Nicholas, one of the Cooper's business partners. The deed included "all advantages, ways, water courses, mines and minerals. John's sisters Nancy and Mary both married Nicholas men, as did his daughter Delitha, taking as her husband Wilson Nichols.

Then suddenly John Cooper disappears from the records. So do all the Nichols or Nicholas in-laws—either disappear or were disappeared. The same thing happened to John's brother James Cooper. Disappeared or was disappeared.

## William Cooper, Choctaw Trader

A variation on the disasters overtook their uncle William Cooper, who was born in North Carolina in 1753. William and Henry Cooper were two of the five sons of William Cooper and Malea Labon. William Cooper Sr. was a guide and scout for Daniel Boone. He was regarded as a Cherokee half-breed married to a Choctaw half-breed. William Jr. settled with other Coopers in Natchez District, becoming a *cabo* (corporal) in the tri-state area around the headwaters of Tombigbee River. He built several forts for the Spanish governor. He married a Choctaw woman of the family of Chief Homastubbee and conducted the Chickasaw and Choctaw trade between Natchez, Mobile, Pensacola and New Orleans. The names of his business partners make for a Who's Who of the great Indian trading companies—Panton and Leslie, John Turnbull, John Joyce, James Frazier, Arthur Carney.

In Spanish records, Guillermo Cooper is mentioned as "a colored man of Portuguese extraction" residing on the upper Tombigbee River.[1] The use of

---

[1] Kaye, Ward, and Neault, *By the Flow of the Inland River*, pp. 22-24, 67; Monroe County Deed Book 1, page 118, Monroe County Chancery Clerk's Office, Aberdeen, Mississippi. See Jack D. Elliott, Jr. (2000), "The Plymouth Fort and the

"colored man" does not indicate Negro admixture. It corresponds to Mulatto, the term used to describe William's brother Cornelius Cooper back in Granville County, North Carolina. Both terms were understood to refer to "one born of an Indian mother" (Hicks 1998 p xiii). Thus Malea Labon was regarded as Indian and her husband William Cooper as Portuguese.

In 1806, William Cooper returned to Mississippi Territory and got a grant on Big Black River. The next year, planters in West Florida declared their independence from Spain. From June to September 1810, many secret meetings were held, along with three open conventions in the new district of Feliciana. A contemporary writer described the breakaway state "much the most populous, wealthy and important district in the province." Out of those meetings grew the West Florida Rebellion.

William Cooper was not to meet with a pretty death. As a Choctaw he saw through the pretensions of the "rebellion" and stood fast with the Spanish. On September 23, before dawn, an armed group led by Philemon Thomas attacked and captured the ramshackle Spanish fort at Baton Rouge. Three days later the leading revolutionaries signed a declaration of independence, then delivered it to Governor David Holmes of Mississippi Territory and Governor Claiborne of Orleans Territory along with a request for annexation by the United States and protection from Spanish counterattacks. The "rebellion" proved nothing but naked land grab.

Philemon Thomas, who instigated the attack on the Spanish garrison at Baton Rouge, declared after the U.S. takeover that "the great object he had in view was now accomplished, and that he approved of the taking" (Sterkx and Thompson, 386). Thomas and his men had killed two Spaniards and wounded five when they stormed the fort at Baton Rouge. Now they also murdered William Cooper, (Arthur 1935, 110, 121).

William's son, also named William, married Susan King, the daughter of Chief Moshulatubbee by his favorite wife Malea, said to be half white. Their eleven children left a large number of descendants, who sometimes got on the Choctaw rolls, sometimes on the Chickasaw and sometimes on no roll. One of them was Israel Cooper (born about 1855, died April 2, 1929).

The Jewish roots of the Coopers persisted through the generations, as can be seen in the Hebrew and explicitly Jewish names given to children. In

Creek War. A Mystery Solved," *Journal of Mississippi History*, 62:328-70. We thank D.J. Thornton for this reference.

the Choctaw branch we find not only Israel and Malea but also Jacob, Hiram or Harmon, Benjamin, Samuel, Rachael, David, Isaac, Delitha, Narcissa, Kezziah, Rebecca, Oliver, Joseph, Caldwell, Arminda, Artemissa, Barthenia, Sarah, Eve, Lillie, Isaiah, Orin, Moses, Salathiel, Sophia, Solomon, Hulda, Jesse, Jeremiah, Elijah, Elia, Jasper, Jehu, Alexander and Levina. Not your run-of-the-mill English names.

Returning to Israel Cooper (who began to spell his name Isreal), his great-granddaughter in California found him on the Choctaw rolls, although married to a Chickasaw woman. "I have just begun trying to find more info on the ancestors of my father, George Isreal Mason," Patricia Lee Burleson wrote to us. "I have visited the Shady Grove Cemetery, Haskell County, near Kinta, Oklahoma, burial site of many of my relatives. Isreal Cooper, my great-grandfather, is buried there.

"The name of his daughter, my grandmother, is Lorinda Cooper Mason; I have a photo of her. You show the record of Isreal Cooper with several wives, but Sally 1857, the first wife, would be in my lineage. I have a copy of the original enrollment Choctaw Nation Roll record:

1. #613,Cooper, Isreal, age 44, Full Blood, San Bois County, Wm Cooper,Dead, Choctaw Roll, Susan Cooper, D,    Choctaw Roll

2. #614,Cooper, Lorinda, age 13, Full B, San Bois County, Number 1, mother, Sally Cooper, D, Choctaw Roll

3. #615,Cooper, Edmund, age 10, Full B.        " "          "            "
   "

4. #616,Cooper, Sam,      age  8,    "       " "          "            "
   "

She provided the following notes:

Number 1 Isreal Cooper, husband of Becky Cooper, Chickasaw Roll , Card #644

Number 1, 1896, San Bois County, 2074

Number 2, 1896        " , 2077, as Lorinda Cooper

*Capt. John Cooper*

Number 3, 1896       " , 2078

Number 4, 1896       " , 2079   as Samual Cooper

For Child of Number 2 see New Born (April 26, 1906) Card #57   My
    father George Isreal Mason

The majority of Chief Moshulatubbee's descendants gradually fell off the rolls, victims of assimilation, poverty or the steady inroads of government policy. Dr. Raymond Hurst, a college teacher and direct descendant of Austin Albro Cooper, rediscovered his heritage in 2005. The Cooper name had been lost in an adoption, but DNA testing of Hurst's Y chromosome verified his descent in the male line. In 2000, Ronald C. Martin, a California dentist, painstakingly reconstructed the family tree of his Choctaw Cooper ancestors, displaying vital records, family photographs and the entire legal docket on a genealogy website he created. He is descended from Mary Rebecca Cooper Martin, one of Capt. John Cooper's great-granddaughters.

John Cooper's children did not have easy lives. Greenberry never married. Henry moved to St. Tammany Parish in Louisiana. Isaac moved to Kansas. Narcissa, married to George Washington Taylor, stayed in Arkansas. The Civil War was harrowing, as Indians fatally switched sides and incurred a double despoliation from Union and Confederate troops and bushwackers. Delitha Cooper was the wife of Wilson Nichols, who met his death during these troubled years. It is said that when soldiers came to take the family's provisions in 1864 a young daughter killed one by hitting him over the head with an iron shovel. In retaliation, the soldiers executed the father and his three older boys. James Burton and Orin were the only boys to survive.

William Huston Cooper, John's eldest, was born in Maury County, Tennessee, during the family's hunted years and spent one step ahead of the swirling forces of violence. Huston and his Choctaw wife took their household from place to place in Arkansas, moving from Marion to Pope and finally Johnson County. Huston, known as Billy, died at the age of 59. Photographs show a bony, haunted face with deep-sunken eyes. "Billy was a tall blue-eyed man with high bridge nose, hair brown, neither black nor light and high cheekbones, I think as best I recollect," remembered William Thompson, a Choctaw official, in 1898. His wife Barthenia outlived all nine of their children and died at the age of 99 in Indian Territory.

Poor, alone, blind and never married, Nancy Cooper faced a destitute existence in the 1890s, when the Dawes Severalty Act took effect. Elders advised her to apply for tribal membership so she could receive a small government stipend. She became the title plaintiff in the case Nancy J. Cooper v. The Choctaw Nation. It was tried in the Southern Division of U.S. Court, Indian Territory, under Judge Hosea Townsend. On November 15, 1897, after more than a year of testimony was taken, the court issued its decision. Nancy Cooper and her relatives were enrolled in the Choctaw Nation.

### Two Days Too Late

But after more of the disenfranchised applied for tribal membership the Supreme Court overturned the case in 1909. "My husband and I talked to the BIA in Muskogee and found out about the 1909 ruling," wrote descendant Pam Hynson. "They told us the reason it was overturned was because the people named in the court ruling were not living in the Choctaw area when they were added to the Dawes rolls. They in fact were in the Chickasaw area of Duncan, Comanche area, now Stephens Co.. Aunt Artie Meecie was told that her family was too poor to be on the rolls. There were over forty Choctaws on the Nancy Cooper case. Nancy died and it was overturned after she fought so hard to win the case in Ardmore. Died thinking nieces and nephews would be taken care of and knowing their heritage would be confirmed. There were Browns, Coopers, Sanders, Nichols, Campbells, Bowens, Martins and Longs. The National Archives in Ft. Worth has the case and letter to Caswell Marion Brown, File no. 6022, June 29, 1909 titled 'Denied enrollment' from the Commissioner of Indian Affairs."

Nancy Cooper v. The Choctaw Nation turned into one of the classic cases of federal Indian policy. It continues to be studied in law schools, and there are hundreds of Choctaw descendants who have not given up seeking enrollment or re-enrollment. It was one of the meritorious cases championed by J. W. Howell, an Eastern Band of Cherokee attorney and assistant in the office of the Attorney General for the Department of the Interior.

Could some of the problem have been the way the Coopers "looked"? Consider this statement gathered from the affidavits given in 1897:

Testimony of William Thompson age 60. Lived in Ark. 51 years. "I lived in Davidson Co., Tenn. until one year before my father left for Ark. and that year I lived in Williamson Co., Tenn. just across Harpeth River. I knew a man named William Cooper and Berry Cooper said to be his brother. They said their father was named John Cooper. I knew a man named Houston Cooper, who looked like he was sixty-five or seventy years old, when I was about nine years old; he was said by my father and William Cooper to be John Cooper's brother. I did not know any of these parties in Tenn. except Houston Cooper. I knew the others of whom I have spoken in this, Pope Co., Arkansas... I know Billy and his family and Mrs. Taylor and her family well as close neighbors. Well, now they were different in general appearance as between Billy Cooper's and the Taylor family and Mrs. Nichols and her family... Narcissa Taylor was dark-skinned and jet black eyes and hair; and Mrs. Nichols was even darker in skin that the others, and she was very dark indeed. She looked like if she had been in the Choctaw and Cherokee and Chickasaw Nations, that she might have been taken as one of those tribes."

The legal details appear to be these. Although the names of all the claimants except the newborns began immediately to be registered by the Choctaw Nation, an adverse decision arose in the Choctaw-Chickasaw citizenship court. Subsequently, the Department of the Interior held that the citizenship court never acquired jurisdiction of the case and directed that enrollment proceed. But that did not hamper the foregone conclusion. The completion of the enrollment of claimants in the original case was prevented by a misconstruction of the Attorney General's decision of February 19, 1907. It then pleased the Department of the Interior to misconstrue the decision of the citizenship court rejecting the claimants as final. On March 4, 1907, the Attorney General repeated his opinion of February 19, 1907, reiterating that the claimants were entitled to enrollment. This latter brief, however, did not reach the Department of the Interior until March 6, 1907, two days after the rolls were closed by operation of law. There was no authority in the Secretary, under the law, to enroll them.

Nancy Cooper was laid in a pauper's grave. Her father John Cooper had been enrolled and un-enrolled. Not only was the family too poor to be Indian. It was two days too late.

*The opening page of Nancy J. Cooper v. The Choctaw Nation. Courtesy Ronald C. Martin.*

How many of my Choctaw cousins were mangled in this miscarriage of justice, now over a hundred years old? Here is a list I came up with, based on court records.

### Choctaw Enrollees, Dawes Commission Case Number 1418

1. Nancy Cooper – 1st cousin, 5 times removed, daughter of 4th great-granduncle Capt. John Cooper, bringer of suit Nancy J. Cooper v. The Choctaw Nation
2. Nancy A. Cooper Brown – 2nd cousin, 4 times removed
3. Rebecca Cooper Brown – 2nd cousin, 4 times removed
4. Jane Cooper Campbell – 2nd cousin, 4 times removed
5. Polly Cooper Bowen – 2nd cousin, 4 times removed
6. Polly Ann Brown Peck – 3rd cousin, 3 times removed
7. William Houston Bowen – 3rd cousin
8. George W. Bowen – 3rd cousin, W stands for Washington

9. Offalter, Arminda Jane Campbell – 3rd cousin
10. William Nighton Brown – 3rd cousin
11. Caswell M. Brown – aka Dan Casual Marion Brown
12. Arty M. Sanders –Arminda Mincey Nichols Sanders, 2nd cousin, 4 times removed
13. Jesse W. Sanders – son of former
14. John N. Sanders – brother of former
15. James B. Nichols – James Bruton Nichols, cousin
16. Orin M. Nichols – Orin Mayberry Nichols, cousin
17. Long, T. T. – husband of Nancy J. Bowen, 3rd cousin
18. William B. Brown – William Bluford Brown, husband of 3rd cousin
19. George G. Brown – Grant George Ulsis Brown, cousin
20. Mary R. Martin
21. Samuel H. Cooper – Samuel Houston, or Huston, Cooper, 2nd cousin, 4 times removed
22. Nancy Cooper = 1.
23. Rebecca Cooper Brown = 3.
24. James Bruton Nichols = 15.
25. George Washington Martin
26. William Knighten Brown =10.
27. Orin Mayberry Nicholsy = 16.
28. James Henry Martin
29. Caswell Marion Brown = 11.
30. Polly Ann Brown Peck = 6.
31. George G. Brown = 19.
32. Nancy Alice Brown = dau. of 3.
33. Bettie Brown – child of 3.
34. Becky Brown – child of 10./26.
35. Mary Brown – child of 10./26.
36. Mamie Brown – child of 10./26.
37. Alice Brown – child of 3.
38. Alice Brown – child of 10.
39. George Brown – child of 10.
40. Susie Brown – child of 10.
41. Maudie Brown – Mandie Brown, child of 11.
42. Willie Brown – child of 11.
43. Florence Peck
44. Oscar Peck
45. Benjamin Grant Peck
46. Andrew Peck
47. Willie Emma Brown
48. Arty Mincy Sanders = 12.
49. John Newton Sanders = 14.
50. Jessie Wilson Sanders = 13.
51. Joseph Monroe Sanders
52. Elijah McFadden Sanders
53. Mary Sanders

54. Monroe Sanders
55. Amanda Menirva Sanders
56. Joseph Ostin Sanders
57. William Newton Sanders
58. Thomas Wilson Sanders
59. Minnie Rachel Sanders
60. Nancy Ellen Sanders
61. James Sanders
62. John N. Sanders
63. Joseph M. Sanders
64. Ozey May Sanders
65. William Ercell Sanders
66. Mincy Reynolds Sanders
67. John William Nichols – s/o James Burton Nichols
68. Dell May Nichols – Della May Scott, d/o James Burton Nichols
69. Nancy Velmon Nichols – Nancy Velma Nichols d/o James Burton
70. James Willis Nichols – s/o Orin Mayberry Nichols
71. Maggie May Nichols = d/o Orin Mayberry Nichols
72. Myrtle Nichols – Mettie Myrtle Nichols, d/o Orin Mayberry Nichols
73. Lorrie Alta Nichols – Lonie Alta Nichols, d/o Orin Mayberry Nichols
74. Polly Cooper Bowen =5.
75. Jane Cooper Campbell = 4.
76. William Houston Bowen = 7.
77. George Washington Bowen = 8.
78. Rosa Isabel Bowen Higgins – child of 8.
79. Nancy Barthena Bowen
80. Jessie Anderson Bowen, Jr.
81. Elizabeth Jane Bowen
82. James Spencer Bowen
83. Eliza Jane Bowen
84. Leona May Bowen
85. Rosa Evelin Bowen
86. Jessie Anderson Bowen
87. William Quitman Bowen
88. Nancy J. Brown Long – Nancy J. Bowen Long
89. Mandie Long
90. William Long
91. George Long
92. Sidney Long
93. Pearley Long
94. Unknown Long
95. James Salathol Campbell – Dr. James Solathiel Campbell, cousin
96. Leona Isabel Campbell
97. Lucinda Lonella Campbell
98. Walter Scotto Campbell
99. Amanda Jane Campbell Ofolter
100. Charlie J. Campbell

101. John F. Campbell
102. Amanda M. Campbell
103. Mary Rebecca Cooper Martin
104. Caldonia Martin
105. James Henry Martin
106. Rosa Clemy Martin
107. Nancy Cooper = 1.
108. Samuel H. Cooper = 21.
109. William Houston Cooper = 2nd cousin, d. Nov. 9, 1942
110. John Cooper, Jr. – John Willis Cooper, 2nd cousin, d. Jan. 1, 1944
111. Dora Ann Cooper – Dona Ann Cooper Worsham, 2nd cousin
112. William Bluford Brown – husband of Rebecca Cooper Brown, 3.
113. Andrew Jackson Peck
114. Nancy Caroline Nichols
115. Rebecca Cooper Brown = 3.
116. Susie Brown
117. William Ercell Sanders
118. Mincy Reynolds Sanders
119. Martha Jane Sanders
120. Louisa Higgins
121. John Ray Sanders
122. Nancy Jane Boen
123. Sallie Sanders
124. Bettie Brown
125. Becky Brown
126. Nancy J. Long
127. Rosa Boen
128. Earl Long
129. Sarah Boen
130. Nancy Jane Brown
131. Sarah Brown
132. Julia Ann Boen
133. Amanda Brown
134. Lizzie Sanders
135. Amanda M. Nichols
136. Mary Boen
137. Robert Lawrence Martin
138. Rebecca E. Brown
139. Rebecca C. Brown – Rebecca Catherine Cooper Brown = 3.

In the aftermath of the fait accompli, disappointment settled into the ranks. But the Cooper Choctaws were not giving up or in. With dogged determination—one might say proverbial cussedness—descendants kept pursuing the case. One of their most redoubtable advocates was Aunt Artie Meecy. She was born Artimissa Cooper on November 29, 1833, just before the Trail of Tears, at her grandfather Capt. John Cooper's home in Perry

County, Tennessee. Her mother was Delitha (Dilly) Cooper (1817-1875), John and Nancy's fifth child, who married Wilson L. Nichols. Arty Mincy, as she was nicknamed, was one of thirteen children: a younger sister killed a Civil War soldier by hitting him on the head with a shovel, as we saw above. Aunt Mint, as she was also called, married Samuel Newton Sanders and raised five boys and one girl. She died in Terral, Jefferson County, Oklahoma in December 1924 at the age of ninety-one.

From time to time, I would hear from Cooper Choctaw cousins in Oklahoma. There would be good news, followed after an interval by bad. The people at the enrollment office were invariably polite and sympathetic, but their hands were tied by the federal agency. Once, I know, a truck-driving cousin pulled her rig up in front of tribal headquarters, left the motor running and emerged an hour later with her enrollment papers. She drove off into the sunset in a cloud of diesel. Usually, however, the tales ran to frustration and outrage.

Imagine my surprise when I opened an email from cousin Pam, now living in Okemah, Oklahoma, to find that the tribal enrollment board of the Choctaw Nation had rethought the issue and granted citizenship retrospectively again after 115 years. "They're welcoming everybody home," said Pam, who attributed the landmark reversal to a 50-year-old class action suit, emerging genealogy technology on the Internet and the persistence of her brother, Johnny Hynson, age 65.

"Johnny started talking to one of the ladies at tribal headquarters in Durant last September," she told us. "He went back time and time again with documentation and the names of relatives who could bear testimony, some of whom he hadn't spoken with in 50 years." At last, in a decision pointedly side-stepping the role of the Federal government, the Nation re-admitted the whole family. Descendants of William Buford Brown and others named in the case Nancy Cooper v. The Choctaw Nation got their Choctaw tribal membership cards and benefits.

Yet it was not to be. Just in time to ruin people's holiday hopes in December of the same, the Choctaw Nation of Oklahoma sent one of the recent Cooper enrollees a letter telling him he could keep his enrollment card, but "there will be no more of the Cooper families allowed to be placed in the Choctaw Tribe." And as Pam informed us, this time "the doors are closed FOREVER."

There's an update, however. A webpage dedicated to reopening the case (cooperchoctaw.com) reports that the BIA Muscogee office has a new standby statement. "This is going to take an act of Congress to get this correct," according to a spokeswoman.

We do not know if by "act of Congress," the agency was using figurative or literal language. Given the difficulty of passing any new legislation, I hope it was the former. The latter would be in in my candid opinion a totally futile exercise. At least, being proud of your Choctaw ancestry and fighting to be recognized by geneticists and genealogists is far less frustrating and can in fact be positive and rewarding.

So the Choctaw Coopers were Indian enough to be removed, but after the survivors got to their new homes not Indian enough to be recognized. One expert, Ward Churchill, refers to such a an operation of history as "paper genocide." Hoping against hope for attention, maybe these personae non gratae besieging the gates of officialdom are suffering from the Southeast Syndrome?

## The Southeast Syndrome

The federal government's playbook for the continuing dispossession of Indians and extinguishment of rights was revealed in an article in the *American Indian Quarterly* in 1990. BIA veteran William Quinn distilled years of employment as an "ethnohistorian" at the Bureau of Indian Affairs in a sort of legal brief on what he scornfully called Wannabe Indians. "The Southeast Syndrome: Notes on Indian Descendant Recruitment Organizations" argued that Native American cultural associations in that region of the country are *not* Indian tribes; they do not deserve federal recognition and in fact do not even qualify as "authentic."

In this position lurks a denial of Indian historicity similar to the disbelief some anti-Semites choose to vaunt about the Jewish Holocaust. All Indians must "vanish" as though they had never existed. Quinn has a deep-seated antipathy toward any ethnicity that does not conform to the dominant, white, Anglo-Saxon, Protestant, male technocracy of contemporary America.

Quinn defines the Southeast Syndrome in a very precise way. It is a resurgence of Indian identity or "pan-Indianism" among descendants "and others" in the former territories of the Five Civilized Tribes. The brief historical background he gives by way of a lead-in is not very sympathetic to Indians real or imagined. We encounter the same truisms found in most

U.S. history textbooks. What is original on Quinn's part is the sleight of hand that comes next. The Indians who remain behind after the forced removals of the 1830s suddenly become *descendants of Indians*, not actual Indians per se. True Indians have been relegated to history, at least in the reservation-free (we are tempted to say *judenrein*) Southern states.

> Not all the Indians of the southeastern tribes, however, went west. Small bands of Cherokee, Creek, and other tribes either hid in the hills, swamps, or similarly remote places or obtained official permission to remain. Others, mostly individuals of mixed blood, simply relocated to the next county or area where they were not known as Indian and homesteaded or otherwise established themselves as white by repudiating, at least publicly, their Indian heritage.

Note that in the eyes of the government, these "individuals of mixed blood" cease to be Indians once they are separated from their tribe. Their children and grandchildren are merely "descendants," some of them only alleged and unproved at that. These watered down versions of the Indians of history strive for a legitimate status they will never obtain. Since they do not live in Indian Country they cannot be Indian. Because they are modern and contemporary they cannot be granted any historicity. Ultimately, all Indians are illusions. If we rub our eyes they may disappear. The land will be free of any encumbrance.

There are disturbing subtexts of a racist nature here. Quinn hints that the mixed bloods were the result of miscegenation in the first place. Some white men will always want to "turn Injun" on you! Even though the mixed bloods were once valued members of Indian communities, at a time when Indian nations enjoyed autonomy and power, their descendants are to be repudiated and rejected.

To Quinn's horror, these "descendant organizations" actively recruit members, apply for federal and state recognition as Indian tribes (a process which if it is successful brings entitlements such as educational assistance) and promote what he judges to be a phony, unfounded culture, one based on books and media images. He describes the movement in alarmist words:

> First, it has given rise to individuals identifying themselves as Indian whose ancestry has no documentable Indian heritage or whose claim to

Indian ancestry is simply bogus. Such people are usually enamored of a romantic image of the noble Indian, so they applicably identify with this image and usually assume an Indian name, certain costume and ornamental trappings. Second, whether there is any Indian blood in their family lines or not, most of the culturally non-Indian people identifying as Indian have distorted notions of Indian cultures, issues, and history— notions which have their bases more in films and novels than in fact . . . . Related to these common images of the Indian stereotype is an ideology best described as a belief in the "Indian way." Analogous to the teachings, or general philosophy of fraternal organizations, the "Indian way" among members of these groups is used in the sense of propriety in their behavior toward one another.

According to Quinn, the requirements for an American Indian group to exist as a "tribe" presuppose:

. . . that a single Indian group has existed since its first sustained contact with European cultures on a continuous basis to the present; that its members live in a distinct autonomous community perceived by others as Indian; that it has maintained some sort of authority with a governing system by which its members abide; that all its members can be traced genealogically to an historic tribe; and that it can provide evidence to substantiate all of this.

What seems to worry Quinn most are the ridiculous lengths to which Wannabes will go to give themselves the appearance of being Indian. He describes specifically the horrors of "reverse acculturation":

While the usual pattern of acculturation among members of more traditional Indian tribes has been to assume gradually the technologic material culture of modernity, these individuals in organizations epitomizing the Southeast Syndrome reverse this process. With their cultural starting points being indigenes of our modern, technologic society, they aspire retrochronologically [sic] to their images of pan-Indian culture wherein chiefs wear war bonnets, everyone wears moccasins, naturalism is sacrosanct, and the "Indian way" is practiced. This is often accompanied by an apparently perfunctory depreciation of modern material culture.

About the best Quinn can make of this behavior is that the "descendants" suffer from a form of "selective perception." Having played lawyer, he will now play psychologist. These illegitimate groups are probably "harmless and may indeed serve as a method for the externalization of unconscious archetypes or suppressed elements within the psyche." But they still constitute a serious burden to "the solemn guardians of Indian rights and dedicated champions of Indian causes."

### The Oldest Scandal

In recent times the solemn guardians of Indian rights have not received a a very good report card for public service. During the years when they were busy launching the inquisitorial Office of Recognition, a young woman on the Blackfoot Reservation in Browning, Montana started asking difficult questions about her tribe's trust accounts. Elouise Cobell's initial inquiries were blown off by the BIA, which informed her that she did not know how to read the reports. In 1987, Cobell started the first Native-owned bank in the United States. She then went on to become the lead plaintiff in suit that makes Nancy Cooper v. The Choctaw Nation look like an undeserved parking ticket.

Cobell v. Babbitt (as it was first named, after Secretary of the Interior Bruce Babbitt) was filed in June 1996 in U.S. District Court to compel an accounting and adjustment of the Individual Indian Monies, going back to 1887, unsuccessfully reformed and audited in 1992, and described by one reporter as "the world's sloppiest banking record keeping" According to Bruce E. Johansen, the IIM case "has become the stuff of political and legal legend . . . with half a million plaintiffs . . . it is the largest class action ever filed against the U.S. government . . . the largest single employer of federal legal talent in the history of the United States."

As the case dragged on for more than two decades, systemic, if not precisely systematic malfeasance and larceny unfolded in the headlines. The government had never established an accounts receivable system, not since the Indian Department was created in 1823, so it never knew how much money it was handling at any given time.

Partial records indicated that more than $50 million was never paid because the BIA had lost track of account holders. About 21,000 accounts were listed in the names of people who were dead. Large numbers of records had been stored in cardboard boxes, left to soak (and smear) in leaky warehouses. About $695 million had been paid— but to the wrong people or Native governmental entities. One property record valued chain saws at $99 million each. Some of the records were contaminated with asbestos, and others had been paved over by a parking lot.

Of the 238,000 individual trusts . . . 118,000 were missing crucial papers, 50,000 had no addresses, and 16,000 had no documents at all (Johansen).

Supervisors appointed to clean up the mess quit in disgust. Federal judges were removed. The blue-chip accounting firm of Arthur Andersen went down in defeat, failing to reconcile 2,000 tribal accounts, to say nothing of the 17,000 individual ones—and that for the relatively short span of the past 20 years. The Departments of the Interior and Treasury "inadvertently" destroyed 162 boxes of vital trust records during the course of the trial. In 2003, the Bush administration proposed a legal bill of over half a billion dollars to hire more attorneys to defend itself. Cobell was quoted on "Native America Calling" as saying, "Just by not settling the case, it's costing the government and taxpayers $160,000 an hour, $7 million a day, $2.5 billion a year." The Bureau of Indian Affairs website was closed for a period of eight years.

The bottom line was "the BIA and Treasury Department never built a record-keeping system capable of tracking the money owed to Native Americans based on income from its superintendency of their resources" (Johansen). A Republican-controlled Congress was unwilling to seriously consider paying hundred-year-old arrears that could cost as much as $40 billion. In March 2005, Attorney General Alberto Gonzales stated, "The United States' potential exposure in these cases is more than $200 billion."

The case was settled for $3.4 billion in 2009, with $1.4 billion going to the plaintiffs and $2 billion allocated to repurchase land that was distributed under the Dawes Act of 1887 and return it to the tribes. But as of August 5, 2014 the settlement had still not been paid to beneficiaries (Wikipedia article).

It seems Nancy Cooper et al. and Elouise Cobell et al. will have to continue to wait.

# 3 PRELUDE 2003

*"DNA Testing of Southeastern American Indian Families to Confirm Jewish Ethnicity," Paper Delivered by Donald Panther-Yates at the Society for Crypto Judaic Studies Conference, San Antonio, August 3, 2003. This paper, which could be called Phase 0, was the first inkling I had that Cherokee descendants today carried a lot of European-seeming genes that were really probably as original as Asiatic ones to the multi-ethnic origins of the tribe.*

The project I will be speaking about today is the first of its kind I am aware of. It grew out of the Melungeon Surname DNA Project started by Beth Hirschman, who was generous enough to pay for some of the tests. I want to begin by thanking both Beth and Bennett Greenspan of Family Tree DNA for their amazing help and support. At one point in the project, when the results were beginning to roll in, I was pleased to see that both Bennett's son Elliott and Abe Lavender matched mitochondrial DNA results of several of our participants. Beth was able to e-mail Bennett with the message, "Welcome to Melungeon-land!"

The project called for volunteers to take either a female descent or male descent genetic test if they could provide reasonable genealogical proof that they were descended either from an early Indian trader or a Native American woman who married or had children with one. The odds were all against us. In order to qualify, the descent of the trader or his wife could not cross from the male to the female line; it had to be either the outside male line, father to son, father to son, or the outside female line, mother-daughter, mother-daughter. We could not, for instance, test one individual who claimed, very eloquently and convincingly, to be descended from both Pocahontas and her sister-cousin Princess Cleopatra. I received a fair measure of hate mail from professors of Indigenous Studies. One volunteer, a Collins in Kentucky, wrote to me about Torah study in her local band of the Saponi, though she assured me they were all good Christians. I also got an interesting letter from the chief of a Tennessee band of the Cherokee who lamented the fact that the tribe members were going through their fourth round of DNA testing without proving much Indian blood. They *had* found so much Jewish types among them that one of them decided to adopt the name "Rolling Bagel."

Some of the test subjects invariably got cold feet and bowed out. I am particularly sorry to have missed the linear descendant of James Adair (author of the first anthropological study of American Indians), the linear descendant of Abraham Mordecai (founder of the town of Montgomery, Alabama), and the linear descendant of Cherokee Chief John Looney (whose ancestors were the famous Luna family of Portugal, among them "the Woman Who Defied Kings"). On the positive side, though, we hit pay-dirt by locating people with the right credentials and level of cooperation for a number of important historical figures. These included Nancy Ward, the Beloved Woman of the Cherokee Nation, who has more than 12,000 known descendants alive today; Col. William Holland Thomas, the Welsh trader who founded the Eastern Band of Cherokee Indians in North Carolina; Chief John Bowles, the leader of the Texas Band of Cherokees; and Elizabeth Tassel, said to be the first Cherokee to marry a white man, (Ludovic Grant, a Scottish trader). To these may be added an ancestor both Beth and I have in common—William Cooper, an explorer and trader who was the scout for Daniel Boone.

What I'm going to do is run through the numbers first, then talk about a few of the genetic types on both the female (mostly Indian) side and white (mostly male) side, then sum up with some observations about the early mixing of Indians and Jews in the Colonial period. You will see that admixture between Jews and Indians is a sort of Eastern parallel to the experiences you are probably more familiar with in the American Southwest. I've brought all my files with me on a laptop if anyone is interested in seeing specific data or is curious about pursuing a connection after the lecture.

First, the numbers. There were 9 persons, mostly females, who took the Native Match test, and 12 persons, necessarily males, who took the Y chromosome test. Only one test result came back Unknown. Many of the haplotypes were unique, meaning they matched no sample in either Bennett's clientele at Family Tree DNA or the larger databases he cross-indexes to, including Michael Hammer's. This shouldn't surprise us because the DNA testing of Native Americans has been very limited, controversial, concentrated in any event on Navajos and other Western reservation tribes. Peter Jones of the Bäuu Institute in Boulder, Colorado, recently published an important paper criticizing the whole state of anthropological genetics and calling for an entirely new beginning. Of the five lineages the current state of scholarship classifies as Native American—haplogroups A, B, C, D and X—our project found 2 Cs and one B, no A, no D, and one X, the latter in an uncle of one of our participants. The majority of those hoping to authenticate their female Indian ancestry (5 out of 9) proved to be H, the most common European haplogroup. One was J, the classic Jewish/Semitic haplogroup. As for the Y chromosome haplogroups, half (6 out of 12) were R1b (sometimes called the Atlantic Modal Haplogroup), 2 (17%) were E3b, one of two well-studied Jewish haplogroups, and one was J2, the second well-established type. There were also single entries in the categories of Viking (Locklear, a Lumbee Indian name), Native American (Sizemore), and as I mentioned, one sample that turned out to be a "big unknown."

So those are the results we are dealing with. Both Beth and I—I'm not sure about Bennett—were impressed with the fact that, though this was just a small sample, it produced the same proportion of what we might call male Jewish DNA, roughly 20 percent, vis à vis 80 percent male non-Jewish DNA, as is the proportion in most studies of both Sephardic and Ashkenazi populations. On the female side, the most startling result was a strong hint that there were females carrying Middle Eastern genes among the Cherokees even before so-called "white contact" in the eighteenth century.

For our first break-out, let's talk about the results for a woman whom I shall Jasmine, for she showed the J haplogroup in her female line. Jasmine was very forthcoming with documentation, names, dates and a lot of family history that would probably not have been shared and made available under other circumstances. She claimed strict matrilineal descent from Betsy

Walker Hyde, a native girl born about 1718, who was captured in a military attack by the English and raised by Sen. Felix Walker. Her descendant, Catherine Hyde, was remembered as a "full blood Cherokee." Catherine became the mistress of Col. Will Thomas and bore him several children. Jasmine put me in touch with the last, lone descendant of one of Col. Will's other daughters, whom he fathered with another native woman, Demarius Angeline Thomas Sherril. The mtDNA there was haplogroup X, a rare Native American lineage which may have come from Europe or the Middle East, not Asia. There are many reasons to think Col. Thomas himself was a crypto-Jew. His mother was a Calvert, and the Holland surname is often associated with Jews from the Netherlands. Supporting the suspicion these people were crypto-Jewish culture are the names they gave their children: Demarius (Tamar), Darthelia, Joshua, Parmelia and (my favorite) Docie Beatrice.

Let us go now to the man who turned out to bear Jewish male DNA. I was extremely pleased to get correspondence from the descendants of Col. John Bowles, the founder of the Texas Band of the Cherokee. Chief Bowles died leading a war party, shot in the back by a white man near Redlands, Texas, in 1839. We located two elderly brothers in Oklahoma who were great-great-great grandsons of the legendary chief. To everyone's surprise Bowles DNA came back J2, with a two-step mutation matching a person identified as Ashkenazi from the Ukraine. How could this be? Bowles was similar to other Cherokee chiefs of his day in being a half-breed. His father was a Scottish trader and his mother a full-blood Cherokee. When his father was killed and robbed by two North Carolinians in 1768, John was only twelve years old, but within two years the fair-complexioned, auburn haired boy had killed both his father's slayers. After that, he became a Chickamauga warrior. He was called The Bowl (in Cherokee, Duwali). And he was not the only "white chief." Another during the same period was The Glass, whose name in the North Carolina settlements was originally Thomas Glass. Chief Black Fox, my ancestor, was a Scotsman descended from Blacks and Foxes. I believe all these families were Scottish crypto-Jews. They were heavily intermarried, generation after generation.

I ran a search for matches on Bowles DNA in the Y-STR Haplotype Reference Database. There were 17 matches in Europe—Albania, Berlin, Budapest, Bulgaria, Bydgoszcz in northern Poland, Cologne, Colombia (2), Freiburg, Latium, Pomerania, Stuttgart, Sweden, Tyrol, Umbria, Warsaw and Westphaia. A "one-off" mutation produced Freiburg and Lombardy. The picture that emerged was one that closely echoed the distribution pattern for the Gothic invasions that re-peopled Italy, France and Spain. To the contrary, the predominant matches in our Melungeon surname study have led to the Iberian Peninsula and to places like Antioquia, Colombia, where Marranos and crypto-Jews emigrated. Here was a Jewish haplotype that, historically speaking, seemed to have traveled out of Scandinavia and the Baltic region, passed through Italy to Spain and Scotland and migrated on to the Americas, where it mingled with the Indians.

In another of our surnames, Rogers, one can also trace the footsteps of the Goths.

How about Wales as an unlikely place to find Jews? Our project established the Jewish origins of another great pioneer family of the South who intermarried with Cherokees, the Blevinses. Two of our Blevins test subjects were found to have E3b genes, which even Bennett admits are Ashkenazic. The name Blevins originates in Britain and by the seventeenth century was associated with the little port town of Formby. It may be derived from *(a)b* (Welsh for "son of") and Levin (meaning Levite). William Blevins, born in Rhode Island, was a Long Hunter who explored Kentucky and Tennessee with Elisha Wallen in 1734. His son had two Cherokee wives, sisters, and a multitude of Blevinses appear on the Cherokee rolls. All are my cousins, as my great-great-grandmother was Mahala Jane Blevins. The Blevins family has occasionally shown itself to be openly Jewish. Bertha Blevins, a declared Jewess, married Moses H. Cone, who was born in Jonesboro, Tennessee, in 1857. She endowed the Greensboro (N.C.) Health Care System upon her death in 1947.

Now it is time to look at the American Indian results. We were fortunate in being able to sample the DNA of two key female figures in Cherokee history. Elizabeth Tassel (we might as well call her a "princess" as long as the American Indian Movement or sticklers in the BIA are not listening), married Ludovic Grant, a Scottish trader about 1720. His name probably comes from French *Grand*, German *Gross*. The couple's descendants are the oldest of the bloodlines studied in a definitive fashion by Emmett Starr, whose genealogies were the basis for government blood quantums and tribal membership. One of Elizabeth Grant's eleventh-generation descendants, with a long Dutch name, joined our study and her DNA proved to be haplogroup C. This was also the haplogroup of an Oklahoma descendant of Nancy Ward, the famous Beloved Woman. Both participants preserve their clan affiliation, which is Wolf Clan.

Does this tell us anything? I think it does. One's clan was passed from the mother to her children in a strict matrilineal fashion, just like mitochondrial DNA.

Another test subject, a San Francisco man, matched a woman of Hispanic descent with a crypto-Jewish surname. He carried B lineage and the family still preserved the fact they were Long Hair Clan.

Haplogroup C, notably, has a large "cline" in the southern Appalachians. The B haplogroup, concentrated in the Southwest, appears to fit the Pueblo Indians.

Let me mention a "Big Unknown," before concluding. This was an 80-year-old gentleman in California by the Scottish-sounding name of McAbee who generously joined our study, with the help of his niece. Their family had a sturdy tradition of crypto-Jewish practices in Kentucky, including opening the door for the prophet Elijah on special days. Everybody at Family Tree DNA drew a blank over his DNA, which was finally classified as "Unknown." It was described by all the rest of us as "eerie." The family claimed they were descended from Judas Macabbaeus. Could it be true? As I learned, it is indeed a very rare haplotype. The closest matches in the Y-user database in Berlin were in Albania, Bulgaria/Romani, London and with a Bulgarian Turk. If surviving descendants of the Hasmonean Jews, the first convert population, lived anywhere it would likely be in those places.

The last DNA test results I would like to talk about were those of a verifiable crypto-Jewish family among the Choctaw and Chickasaw Indians. This was a male paternal-line descendant of Louis LeFleur/LeFlore, a French Canadian trader who married Rebecca Cravat, said to be an "Indian princess." He introduced the first cattle, hogs, keel boats, cotton and tobacco crops to the Choctaw. LeFlore thus occupies the same position of Culture Bearer as Nancy Ward holds among the Cherokee. His son Greenwood became the principal chief of the Choctaw, married a Jewish Cherokee woman named Elizabeth Coody and managed to stay in Mississippi after Indian removal. One branch of the family in modern times changed its name to Flores, which seems to be the original Portuguese form. Flores is a big Marrano surname. A run through the Y-STR database confirmed numerous Iberian and Latin American matches, with Asturias and Central East Spain being the strongest hits.

One of the really cool things about DNA analysis is finding a match and making contact with people you would never have dreamed you are related to. When we got the results for Gayl Wilson, an enrolled Cherokee in Oklahoma, and found out she carried the Nancy Ward gene, a young schoolteacher in California by the name of Juan Madrid wrote to us inquiring how he could have matched her. Madrid, of course, is a fairly common Marrano name. But he had no tradition of being Cherokee. His grandmother lived among the Comanches, and all the family would talk about is "some Indian blood somewhere," without being specific. Juan definitely had the Cherokee Wolf Clan gene, and he is now pursuing tribal enrollment. I found out he already had an Indian name. Significantly, he is called Two Hearts.

It is time to draw some conclusions and end. Bennett has repeatedly assured both Beth and me that there is no such thing as "Jewish DNA." Strictly speaking, it's true. There are haplogroups into which the DNA of people known to be Jewish today fall. But even some Arabs and Muslims test positive for the Cohen gene. So how can we be so sure the Y chromosomal haplotypes we are studying are Jewish? The answer lies in a chain of circumstantial evidence. The overwhelming preponderance of surnames with Hebrew and Sephardic Jewish roots, combined with multigenerational cousin marriage and other historical factors, cannot be ignored. Genetics without a good genealogical chart is useless. Even the charts can sometimes be misleading unless one has access to death-bed confessions and whispered family traditions.

Only in the last two years did I find out my family was Jewish, or perhaps better said, crypto-Jewish. There is not a single surname in my family tree, which I have traced back more than 700 years in some lines, that defies the pattern. Despite all this, though, I always wanted to find something concrete and unequivocal, something of the vanished past I could touch with my hands and cling to in my thoughts. So this spring I made a pilgrimage to New Hope Cemetery on Sand Mountain in Tennessee where my great-great-great grandmother Mahala Jane Blevins Cooper is said to be buried.

New Hope is a beautiful, forgotten place. The dogwoods and redbuds were in flower; it was Sunday morning. The Cooper-Blevins burial plot was on the edge of the cemetery with the oldest stones, rough unmarked header and footer rocks, unlike the rest of the graves. I took a picture of my great-uncle Harmon Cooper's memorial. It had the Freemason or Templar cross and showed a hand pointing to the sky, with the words GONE HOME. I was thrilled, satisfied at last I had concrete proof, for I'd seen similar designs in the crypto-Jewish burials at Purrysburg, South Carolina. I cleaned the graves ... put down a tobacco offering in the Indian manner ... and said Jewish prayers. I finally experienced what I think I had been looking for all along ... a strong feeling that the ancestors were placated and pleased. If I have accomplished nothing else, I would like to leave you with this. We all have a moral imperative to uncover our families' past. They would have been proud of us.

# 4 ANOMALOUS MITOCHONDRIAL DNA LINEAGES IN THE CHEROKEE (PHASE I)

**Abstract.** A sample of 52 individuals who purchased mitochondrial DNA testing to determine their female lineage was assembled after the fact from the customer files of DNA Consultants. All claim matrilineal descent from a Native American woman, usually named as Cherokee. The main criterion for inclusion in the study is that test subjects must have obtained results *not* placing them in the standard Native American haplogroups A, B, C or D, hence the use of the word "anomalous." Most subjects reveal haplotypes that were unmatched anywhere else except among other participants. There proves to be a high degree of interrelatedness and common ancestral lines. Haplogroup T emerges as the largest lineage, followed by U, X, J and H. Similar proportions of these haplogroups are noted in the populations of Egypt, Israel and other parts of the East Mediterranean.

## The Cherokee

The Cherokee Indians are a Southeast U.S. indigenous people traced by anthropological science to at least the sixteenth century, when Spanish conquistador Hernando de Soto invaded the region. Archeological excavations have established continuity between today's Eastern Band of Cherokee Indians in North Carolina and the Qualla Phase of occupation of the Appalachian Mountains from 1450 CE, "or earlier," i.e., the Pisgah Phase (Fogelson 2003:338). According to Cherokee elders and keepers of their traditions, notably Keetoowah priests, their age is much more ancient, and their origins and migrations before settling in the Great Smoky

Mountains quite complex. Their pre-contact population may have been as high as 30,000 (Thornton 1992:17), and although their numbers dwindled in the aftermath of European contact, typhoid, smallpox and warfare, they were the most numerous of the so-called Five Civilized Tribes of Indians displaced across the Mississippi in the years before 1838. After removal, about 1,500 remained to be registered on Indian census rolls in the East (Fogelson 2003:341), while many more doubtless were in hiding or were sufficiently assimilated to go unnoticed. According to a 2007 report from the U.S. Census Bureau, the Cherokee are the largest tribal group today, with a population of 331,000 or 15% of all American Indians. This figure seems to reflect mostly or exclusively those enrolled in the three federally recognized tribes of the Cherokee Nation of Oklahoma, United Keetoowah Band in Arkansas and Oklahoma and Eastern Band of Cherokee Indians in North Carolina, not Cherokees or their descendants who have never been placed on a U.S. government roll. No Cherokees live on reservations. The most numerous community, in fact, resides in the Greater Los Angeles area.

Despite their numbers, the Cherokee have had few DNA studies conducted on them. There are only three known reports on Cherokee mitochondrial DNA. A total of 60 subjects are involved, all from Oklahoma. Possibly the reason the Cherokee are not recruited for more studies stems from their being perceived as admixed in comparison with other Indians. Accordingly, they are deemed less worthy of study. Yet only 9.5 percent of Native American samples are judged "unmixed" in the first place. One study that maintains the "Atlantic seaboard and several regions of the Southeastern US have the highest admixture rates, which approximate 50%," also admits that firmly established genealogies for the Navajo, believed to be one of the most unmixed tribes, show that even they have "not inconsequential numbers of genes of European origin" (Crawford 1998:134-35). No matter how you look at it admixture is a problem in the study of American Indians. When geneticists use the word it designates lineages that do not belong to one of the five generally accepted American Indian mitochondrial DNA haplogroups A, B, C, D and X. This is true of the two examples of H and one of J reported in Cherokee descendants by Schurr (2000:253). Schurr takes these exceptions to prove the rule and regards them as instances of European admixture.

## DNA Studies That Include Southeastern Indians

| mtDNA Haplogroup | n= | A | B | C | D |
|---|---|---|---|---|---|
| **Cherokee** | | | | | |
| Oklahoma Stillwell (Malhi 2001)* | 37 | 10.8 | 45.9 | 43.3 | 0.0 |
| Oklahoma Red Cross (Mahli 2001)* | 19 | 21.1 | 21.1 | 52.5 | 5.3 |
| Smith et al. 1999 (and Schurr 2000) | 4 | 0.0 | 0.0 | 25.0 | 0.0 |
| Total | 60 | 13.3 | 35.0 | 45.0 | 1.7 |
| **Choctaw** | | | | | |
| Weis 2001 (and Bolnick & Smith 2003) | 27 | 74.1 | 18.5 | 3.7 | 0.0 |
| **Chickasaw** | | | | | |
| Bolnick & Smith | 8 | 12.5 | 75.0 | 12.5 | 0.0 |
| **Creek** | | | | | |
| Weis; Lorenz & Smith; Bolnick & Smith | 39 | 35.9 | 15.4 | 20.5 | 28.2 |
| Merriwether & Ferrell; Bolnick & Smith | 71 | 36.6 | 15.5 | 9.9 | 38.0 |
| Total | 110 | 36.4 | 15.5 | 13.6 | 34.5 |
| **Seminole** | | | | | |
| Huoponen (1997), incl. Bolnick & Smith | 40 | 62.5 | 25.0 | 7.5 | 5.0 |
| **Grand Total** | **257** | **36.6** | **23.7** | **19.1** | **16.0** |

*Includes Lorenz & Smith (1996); repeated in Bolnick & Smith (2001).

The logic governing American Indian sample selection seems to go as follows:

Lineage A, B, C, D and X are American Indian.

*Therefore*, all American Indians are lineage A, B, C, D and X.

If any haplogroups are discovered that are *not* A, B, C, D or X, they are rejected from the study (as evidently in Bolnick and Smith 2003). The reasoning of many anthropologists and geneticists can be summarized as: "All men are two-legged creatures; therefore since the skeleton we dug up has two legs, it is human." It might be a kangaroo.

## Description of This Study

The present study concentrates on the "kangaroos"—the documented or self-identifying Cherokee descendants whose haplotypes do not fit the current orthodoxy in American Indian population genetics. Cases come from the customer files of DNA Consultants, a testing service founded in 2003. The method used is the standard one adopted for differentiating mitochondrial DNA lineages by characteristic mutations on a control sequence known as the D loop, which contains two segments called Hypervariable Region (or Section) I and Hypervariable Region (or Section) II (Richards and Macaulay 2000). Included are 52 individuals who ordered a Native American mitochondrial DNA test, and whose matrilineal ancestry, as it was determined in testing, happens to fall outside the haplogroups A, B, C and D. (Additionally, seven instances are adduced of X , which can be Native American or Eurasian.) Comparisons were made to the databases known as Richards, Cambridge Concordance and Mitosearch. Raw data appears at the end of this book. All test subjects have given permission for their names and results to be published in this article. All have submitted detailed genealogies naming, insofar as was known to them, a Cherokee female ancestor. A list of haplotypes and earliest known female ancestors follows.

### List of Phase I Participants by Ancestry

|   | Hg | Genealogy |
|---|-----|-----------|
| 1 | H   | New England Indian, Norse? |
| 2 | X2  | Annie L. Garrett, b. 1846, Miss. |
| 3 | J*  | Native American |
| 4 | H   | Native American |
| 5 | X2  | Native American |
| 6 | H   | Cherokee |
| 7 | X2  | Agnes Weldy b. ~1707 |
| 8 | H   | Canadian? |

| 9  | J*     | Cherokee, Emily Glover 1837-1903, Tenn. |
|----|--------|------------------------------------------|
| 10 | X2     | Seyinus from Qualla Boundary, N.C., b. 1862 |
| 11 | U2e*   | Cherokee wife of Jewish trader Enoch Jordan, b. 1790 Ga. |
| 12 | U2e*   | Susanna Owens, Cherokee, b. 1760, Granville Co., N.C. |
| 13 | U2e*   | Rosannah Alexander, b. 1749, Mecklenburg Co., N.C. |
| 14 | U2e*   | Susannah Wallen or Waldon |
| 15 | U5b*   | Wife of George Culver, b. 1775, d. 1830, Hancock Co., Ga. |
| 16 | U2e*   | Cherokee, N.C. |
| 17 | U5a1a  | Ann Dreaweah, Cherokee |
| 18 | U5*    | Adopted, Okla. |
| 19 | U5a1a* | Jane Rose of the Eastern Band of Cherokee Indians |
| 20 | U5a1a* | Clarissa Green, wife of John Hodge, b. 1846, Wolf Clan |
| 21 | U4*    | Lillie C. Wilson-Field, 1857-1937, b. Catawba, N.C. |
| 22 | U5b2   | Wilma Nell Atchison, wife of Gilbert, Blackfoot (?), b. Kansas |
| 23 | K2     | Sarah Ann Rose, b. Rock Creek, N.C. |
| 24 | T1*    | Ann Houston, b. Va., mother of Susannah Walker |
| 25 | T1*    | Native American (surrogate mother?) |
| 26 | T1*    | Melungeon and Cherokee |
| 27 | X2     | Mother of Ollie McCorkle, b. 1906, I.T. |
| 28 | T*     | Melungeon |
| 29 | T2*    | Native American |
| 30 | K      | Mother of Linna Mitchell, born 1779, Choctaw Nation |
| 31 | T2*    | Cherokee |
| 32 | T*     | Sully Firebush, daughter of a Cherokee chief |
| 33 | Unk.   | Unknown Bermuda |
| 34 | T5     | Choctaw-Cherokee |
| 35 | T*     | Zella Hand Rogers, adopted 1901, Red Lake Band of Chippewa |
| 36 | Unk.   | |
| 37 | Unk.   | Hurley Choctaw or Pitchlynn on Armstrong Rolls (?) |
| 38 | L1b1   | |
| 39 | T4     | Choctaw-Cherokee |
| 40 | Unk.   | |
| 41 | T*     | Cherokee |
| 42 | L1c2   | Subject identifies as Native American |

| 43 | L3 | Juanita Pratts, b. Mexico 1885; Comanche or Mexican |
| 44 | J* | Betsy Walker, Cherokee, adopted by Sen. Felix Walker |
| 45 | J* | Myra Jarvis, Melungeon, b. 1815, Ga. |
| 46 | J* | Betsy Walker, Cherokee, adopted by Sen. Felix Walker |
| 47 | X2 | Polly, wife of Col. Will Thomas |
| 48 | X2 | Cherokee woman married to Longhunter Wallen (Walden) |
| 49 | U2e* | Jane Campbell, b. 1828, Choctaw Co., Miss. |
| 50 | T* | Native American |
| 51 | T* | Cherokee Gentry sisters |
| 52 | T* | Cherokee Gentry sisters |

## Haplogroup H

Let us examine these anomalous haplotypes starting with haplogroup H, the most characteristically European. H is termed Helena in the scheme of Seven Daughters of Eve (Sykes 2001). Its highest frequency occurs in Spain and France, where Europeans wintered the last Ice Age (Achilli et al. 2004; Loogväli et al. 2004; Pereira et al. 2005). It was probably the predominant maternal lineage that gave rise to the hunter-gatherer Magdalenian culture of cave art made famous by the paintings at Lascaux and elsewhere in southern France and northern Spain and Portugal. When agriculture spread to Europe from the Middle East some 7,000 to 9,000 years ago, H was either among the recipients or bearers. It is the most common female lineage throughout Europe, accounting for approximately half the population. It is the haplogroup, in fact, of the British man whose DNA was selected as the Cambridge Reference Sequence, the norm against which mutations and other haplogroups are measured (Anderson 1981; Andrews 1999). The exact same sequence makes an early European appearance in a skeleton excavated from the Paglicci Cave in Apulia in the heel of the Italian Peninsula, dated to 28,000 years ago (Caramelli et al. 2008). Historically, H is the maternal line of French queens and kings. Marie Antoinette, whose mitochondrial DNA has been reconstructed in two modern-day forensic cases (Jehaes 2001), descends from Frederuna of France, consort of Charles the Simple, a descendant of the emperor Charlemagne. H is also the haplogroup of Queen Victoria, Prince Philip and Russian Czarina Alexandra (Gill et al. 1994).

Although this quintessentially European haplogroup would seem to be the most likely suspect if admixture were responsible for anomalous haplogroups, it plays only a minor role in our study. There are but four cases of H. **Case 1** is a Rhode Island woman who claims descent from New England Indians. Her profile matches no other in the Cambridge Concordance, FBI database (Monson 2002) or Mitosearch, although there is a one-step mutation to an individual classified as Amerind in the Cambridge Concordance. **Case 4** is unusual for a mutation at nucleotide site 16362C. This woman lives in Georgia and claims descent from a Cherokee woman. Her mutations are matched by descendants of women born in the 1860s in Wisconsin and Arkansas but by no others. There are also close but not exact matches with Korea, Japan and Mongolia. The mutation 16362C occurs in four out of five of the classic Native American haplogroups. Because Case 4's mutations are only reported in people born in North America, it seems appropriate, particularly in conjunction with a suitable oral tradition, to regard her lineage as indigenous to North America, not as admixture arriving recently from Europe. **Case 6** is marked by a mutation at 93G not instanced anywhere else. According to the subject's daughter, Joy Shorkey, the line can be traced to Sarah Smith, born 16 August 1806 in Georgia, suspected to be Cherokee. **Case 8** falls in the same category.

## Haplogroup X

Haplogroup X is a latecomer to the received set of Native American haplogroups. Sykes names it Xenia ("foreign woman"), which is a good choice given its mysterious origins and world travels. Its relative absence in Mongolia and Siberia and a recently proven center of diffusion in Lebanon and Israel (Brown et al. 1998, Malhi and Smith 2002; Smith et al. 1999; Reidla 2003; Shlush et al. 2009) pose problems for the standard account of the peopling of the Americas. Today, haplogroup X accounts for about 2% of the population of Europe, the Middle East (Near East in British usage) and North Africa. It is more characteristic of the East Mediterranean and Caucasus than other parts of Europe. Particular concentrations appear in Georgia (8%), Orkney Islands (7%) and Israeli Druze (28%, Shlush et al. 2009). Among Native American groups, it has been reported in high frequencies among the Ojibwe and other northern tribes, where it comprises up to 25% of mtDNA lineages. Among the Micmac of the northeastern U.S. and adjacent Canadian provinces, its frequency attains 50%. It is also present in lesser percentages in the West among the Sioux

(15%), the Nuu-Chah-Nulth (11%–13%), the Navajo (7%) and the Yakima (5%). Two clades have been proposed. Rare X1 is predominately North African, associated with Afro-Asiatic language speakers. X2, conventionally divided into a Native American branch (X2a) and all others (X2b-f), is much more common (van Oven and Kayser 2008).

We have seven instances of haplogroup X. They all belong to X2, but it is not possible to assign them all to subclade X2a. (If we compare our own and other known X2a haplotypes with the X2's reported in Shlush et al.'s study of the Israeli and Lebanese Druze, the same common mutations are observed. It would appear that the demarcation between Native American and Old World forms of X2 is an artificial one.) Significantly, both "branches" have the same estimated time to coalescence, 20,000 to 30,000 years before present. But usually, if an X2 is found in the New World it is automatically assigned to X2a. No two haplotypes are exactly alike, although the shared motifs 153G, 195C and 225A in HVS2 are recurrent. All genealogies reported lead to a Cherokee woman. **Case 2** derives from Annie L. Garrett, born 1846 in Mississippi; there is an oral tradition in the family of her being Cherokee. **Case 7** is the mitochondrial DNA of Michelle Baugh of Hazel Green, Alabama, traced to Agnes Weldy, born about 1707. Descendants include enrolled members of the Eastern Band of Cherokee Indians. **Case 10** goes back to Seyinus, a Cherokee woman born on or near the Qualla Boundary in North Carolina in 1862. **Case 27** is the son of Gladys Lulu Sutton, born in Indian Territory in 1906; her birth certificate specifically states that she was a Cherokee Indian. Her mother was Olivia McCorkle Walker Ginn, born in West Virginia in 1865. This line matches that of Penelope Greene Fraser, born 1779, in Walton County, Georgia (Mitosearch ID 3M6H6). **Case 47,** James Stiles Riddle, has a genealogy descending directly from the Cherokee woman called Polly, who had a daughter out of wedlock, Angelina Demarius (born 1827, married Sherrill), with Col. Will Thomas, the founder of the Eastern Band of Cherokee Indians in North Carolina. Polly was the namesake for the Qualla reservation (the sound *p* lacking in the Cherokee language and being rendered with *qu*). **Cases 44** and **46** below also have a connection to Col. Thomas through another paramour of his who was evidently of haplogroup J. Finally, **Case 48** reflects descent from a Cherokee woman who married a Walden/Wallen of the same surname as Longhunter Elisha Wallen, one of the first white explorers of Tennessee, and a member of the Melungeons, a mixed ethnic group of East Tennessee. **Case 5** has unknown antecedents, believed, however, to have been Native American.

### Haplogroup J

The most common forms of J, termed Jasmine in the scheme of Oxford Ancestors, seem to have originated in present-day Lebanon approximately 10,000 years before present and to have moved north and west into Europe. Views about J are still evolving. Previously restricted to theories based on HVS1 sequences, its phylogeny continues to be articulated with the benefit of full genome sequencing (Logan 2008). All four of our J's are to be classified as J* (all J not otherwise characterized and subdivided). The overall haplogroup is found throughout Europe with particularly high concentrations around the eastern Baltic Sea, Russia and among the Bedouins and Yemeni, where it reaches frequencies of 25% or higher. It is a major Jewish female lineage (Thomas 2002), and it is a strong contributor to Arab, Greek and Italian populations as well. It is also relatively common in India. Along with male haplogroup J, it is believed to have been instrumental in spreading agriculture from the Middle East about 7,000 years ago. Haplogroup J has been linked to longevity and a certain form of hereditary blindness.

**Case 9** has a J haplotype distinguished by the unusual mutation 16162C. The subject's mutations are also associated with Native American lineages A and D (Comas 1996). Like the others in this study the specific haplotype is matched or nearly matched only with rare mitochondrial lineages reported in people born in the Americas. And like all the others, too, it goes back to a Cherokee source. Case 9 is Jerry W. Moore, the father of Michael Wayne Moore, who has traced the line to Emily Glover, born in Tennessee in 1837, reportedly a Cherokee. Both **Case 44** and **Case 46** trace their line back to Betsy Walker, a Cherokee woman born about 1720 in Soco (One-Town). Betsy was given as a child to Sen. Felix Walker to raise. While he was an apprentice for the Walkers, young Will Thomas (later chief of the Eastern Cherokees) fell in love with Catherine Hyde, her descendant. Catherine Hyde is the 6th-great-grandmother of test subject Kimberly McFadden Hill. Her sister Annie Hyde married Holloman Battle and produced the other instance of Betsy Walker's mitochondrial haplotype in modern-day descendant Sharon Crisp Bedzyk. The fourth example of J*, Judith Alef (**Case 45)**, is a descendant of presumed Cherokee Myra Jarvis, a

Melungeon woman born in 1815 in Georgia.

### Haplogroup U

Haplogroup U is a complex mega-lineage with an estimated age of more than 50,000 years. It is the oldest European haplogroup that is Homo sapiens rather than Homo erectus or Neanderthal, representing the first colonization of Europe by its present inhabitants. Human societies with haplogroup U4, U5 and U5a may have come into contact with Neanderthals living in Europe at the time. U shows up in the archeological record in Delphi and Spain around 50,000 years ago. Today U5, the most common clade, accounts for about 10% of matrilineal types in Europeans. Other clades of U are responsible for about five and a half percent, making U the second largest haplogroup after H. It has been found in high frequencies in the Indian subcontinent and at a low frequency in the Japanese, the North African Berber population, Ethiopians and Senegalese (Torroni et al. 1996, Passarino et al. 1998, Macaulay et al. 1999). In Finland, a population with a relatively small number of founder types, it has been associated with several rare medical conditions (Finnilä et al. 2000). One important divide in subcluster U2 goes back to the earliest millennia of the migrations of humans out of Africa, with U2e splitting off and expanding north into Europe, probably traveling along the Zagros Mountains, and U2i settling in India, where it reaches frequencies of around 25% today. With the exception of a single instance of U6 in a study of Mexican Indians, where it is attributed to European admixture (Green et al. 2000), haplogroup U has never been reported in American Indians to my knowledge. In our sample it covers 13 cases or 25% of the total, second in frequency only to haplogroup T.

Let us first describe the U5's. **Case 20** is Mary M. Garrabrant-Brower. She belongs to U5a1a* but has no close matches anywhere, unless a one-step mutation on HVS2 with an Asian and two Chinese samples are to be taken into account. Her great-grandmother was Clarissa Green of the Cherokee Wolf Clan, born 1846. Clarissa Green's grandfather was remembered as a Cherokee chief. Mary's mother Mary M. Lounsbury maintained the Cherokee language and rituals. **Case 19**, Bruce Dean, another U5a1a*, matches only one other person on both sectors, Marie Eastman, born 1901 in Indian Territory (Mitosearch EDCCB). Because of the precision of the match, he and the descendant of Marie Eastman who was tested and made the entry in Mitosearch are almost certainly cousins in a genealogical, as well as genetic sense. His descent is from Jane Rose, a member of the Eastern Cherokee Band whose family is listed on the Baker Rolls, the final arbiter of enrollment established by the U.S. government. **Case 22** is Michael Gilbert, who was given little information about his mother, Wilma Nell Atchison, beyond the fact that she was Blackfoot – probably the Virginia/North Carolina tribe by this name, also called Saponi, Sissipah and Haliwah. His haplotype is U5b2. Although there are four exact matches on both sectors, two of these are in the Old World (Ireland and Denmark), one is of unknown origin but American, and one leads to Arpahia Finley, born about 1827 in Albemarle County, Va. The latter location is the traditional homeland of the Blackfoot Indians. Because of the division of the matches, one could speculate that in this instance we may be dealing with a lineage that came over from northwestern Europe and *became* American Indian, only in all likelihood long before Columbus. **Case 15** is that of my wife, Teresa Panther-Yates, whose mtDNA can be designated as U5b*. It has no matches remotely close to it in either the Concordance or Mitosearch. Teresa has traced her maternal line back to Isabel Culver, who married Levin Ellis in Hancock County, Georgia, and died about 1838. There is a tradition in her family that this line was Cherokee. **Case 17**, an example of U5a1a, does have two matches – South Carolina and Norway – but the subject claims that the line goes back to Ann Dreaweah, a Cherokee woman married to a half blood Cherokee man. It may be another bifurcated lineage with representatives on both sides of the Atlantic. **Case 18** has no close matches at all and may be placed in the category of U5*. The subject was adopted in Oklahoma and knows nothing of his mother's ancestry. **Case 21** is Gerald Potterf, a U4* who traces his mother's line to Lillie C. Wilson-Field, born in 1857, Catawba County, North Carolina. She was probably Cherokee, although her ancestors may have been Catawba, a Siouan tribe from the Carolinas who joined the Cherokee in great numbers during the eighteenth century. U4 is associated with North Africa and the Middle East.

Our survey of U's leaves the five haplotypes classified U2e*. **Case 11** is my own, for which there are no close matches. This line evidently arose from a Jewish Indian trader and a Cherokee woman. My fifth-great-grandmother was born about 1790 on the northern Georgia and southwestern North Carolina frontier and had a relationship with a trader named Enoch Jordan. The trader's male line descendants from his white family in North Carolina possess Y chromosomal J, a common Jewish type. Some Jordans, in fact, bear the Cohen Modal Haplotype that has been suggested to be the genetic signature of Old Testament priests (Thomas et al. 1998). Enoch Jordan was born about 1768 in Scotland of forbears from Russia or the Ukraine. My mother, Bessie Cooper, was a double descendant of Cherokee chief Black Fox and was born on Sand Mountain in northeastern Alabama near Black Fox's former seat at Creek Path (and who was Paint Clan). The Cooper line goes back to William Cooper, a scout and road builder for Daniel Boone, who married Malea Labon (Hebrew first and last name), the daughter of a Choctaw woman and a French trader. The Cooper surname often appears in lists of common Melungeon names. I said there were no close matches for my mtDNA, but **Case 12**, Phyllis LaForce Starnes of Harriman, Tennessee, turned out to match perfectly with mine on HVS2. She traces her maternal line to Susanna Owens, born about 1760, probably in Granville County, North Carolina. The family is Melungeon like the Coopers, and Starnes suffers from a disease common among Melungeons and Sephardic Jews. Both Starnes' and my haplotypes share several motifs with three other cases of U2e*. **Case 13** is a near match with **Case 16**. The former's maternal line reportedly goes back to Rosannah Alexander, born about 1749 in Mecklenburg County, North Carolina, believed to be Cherokee. **Case 14** is a descendant of Mahalia Waldon (her surname coming from a famous Longhunter and Melungeon family). Mahalia was born in 1834 in Hancock County, Tennessee, in the Melungeon population center. All U2e* cases appear to have Melungeon, Cherokee and Jewish connections. The most frequent Cherokee clan mentioned in their genealogies is Paint Clan.

## Haplogroup T

Maternal lineage T ("Tara") is believed to have originated in Mesopotamia approximately 10,000 to 12,000 years ago and to have moved northwards through the Caucasus and westwards from Anatolia into Europe. It shares a common source with haplogroup J in parent haplogroup JT (Finnilä et al. 2001). Ancient people with haplogroup T were likely some of the first agriculturalists and probably comprised the group which first brought agriculture to Europe with the Neolithic Revolution. T is the same haplogroup as Sykes's, who named it Tara after the ancient center and capital of Ireland. The matches with the Russian Tsar Nicholas in a famous case (Gill 1994) prove that T was the matrilineal line of much aristocracy (along with H, above). Maurice, prince of Nassau, England's Charles I and King George I of Great Britain were all apparently T. The haplogroup includes slightly fewer than 10% of modern Europeans. The closer one goes to its origin in the Fertile Crescent the more likely T is to be found in higher frequencies.

All our T's are unmatched except in some cases with each other. **Case 35**, Jonlyn L. Roberts, has a puzzling, but typical genealogy that led her to embark on a lifelong quest for answers. Her mother, Zella, was adopted by the George and Mary Hand family of Hand County, South Dakota in 1901. Little information was passed down, but piecing together clues from her childhood, Roberts believes that her mother's original family might have come from the Red Lake Ojibwe Indian Reservation or one of the North or South Dakota reservations. At any rate, her mtDNA haplotype is a unique form of T*, one similar to others in this study. **Case 32**, another T*, leads to an unknown ancestor in Oklahoma. **Case 28**, also T*, is an individual reporting Melungeon ancestry. His mtDNA matched four people on both sectors in Mitosearch. All these were born in the United States; one traces back to Birdie Burns, born 1889 in Arkansas, the daughter of Alice Cook, a Cherokee (ID AB3YK). **Case 41**, Gail Lynn Dean, is the wife of Case 19; both claim Cherokee (among other) ancestries. No near match has her mutation 236C. **Case 32,** Linda Burckhalter, is the great-great-granddaughter of Sully Firebush, the daughter of a Cherokee chief who married Solomon Sutton, the stowaway son of a London merchant, in what would seem to be another variation of the "Jewish trader marries chief's daughter" pattern. Rounding out our T* haplotypes are the two matching **Cases 51 and 52**, both descended in different lines from the historically documented Gentry sisters.

**Cases 24, 25** and **26** are perfectly matching T1* individuals completely unknown to one another before testing. Two of them claim Melungeon ancestry; the other's is unknown. Case 26 is a distant cousin of mine with the same surname whom I did not know before he became a customer. Case 24 is the aunt of Case 12. **Cases 29** and **31** are examples of unique T2*'s. Both were ignorant of the origins of their maternal line, suspecting only that they were Native American. **Case 29**, which is T4, is from an extended family that claims Choctaw-Cherokee ancestry (like my own). The sole instance of T5, **Case 34**, took not only the mitochondrial test but also our CODIS-marker-based population matching ancestry test, DNA Fingerprint, to validate "Cherokee or Jewish ancestry" from her mother. She has scattered matches but none on both sectors. The results of her DNA Fingerprint Test show Ashkenazi Jewish in the No. 1 position, as well as American Indian admixture.

## Discussion and Conclusion

Our small survey shows a great deal of diversity both of haplogroups and haplotypes. It contains several examples of people who discovered through testing they are related and share the same Cherokee ancestry and even the identical matrilineal clan. It cannot be emphasized enough that our sample was assembled after the fact from individuals who did not know each other, and who came from all over the country. Unlike the U.S. majority population, the sample exhibits a mix of haplogroups that turns the usual pattern on its head. Haplogroup H, instead of an expected 50% dominant position, is one of the smallest, with only 7.7%. Haplogroup U, an older lineage representing the first wave of colonization of Europe before the ascendency of H, is numerous and highly diversified at 25% of the total number of participants. Haplogroup X, marked by an exiguous presence in the Old as well as New World (where it is found in large numbers only in select groups), attains a frequency more than tenfold that of Eurasia or Native America (13.5%). But the most startling statistic is the frequency of occurrence of T haplotypes. At 26.9 %, they figure as the leading haplogroup, with 14 individuals. Several of these evidently come from the same Cherokee family or clan, although they have been separated and scattered from their original home by circumstances and the events of history. The many interrelationships noted above reinforce the conclusion that this is a faithful cross-section of a population. No such mix could have resulted from post-1492 European gene flow into the Cherokee Nation. That would have required a large influx of non-European women marrying Cherokee men. The anomalous types of mitochondrial DNA (added to already documented examples of A, B, C and D haplotypes that are not part of this article) must reflect a pre-Columbian population structure.

If not from sources in Siberia, Mongolia and Asia, where do our non-European, non-Indian-appearing elements come from? The level of haplogroup T in the Cherokee (26.9%) approximates the percentage for

Egypt (25%), one of the only lands where T attains a major position among the various mitochondrial lineages. In Egypt, T is three times what it is in Europe. Haplogroup U in our sample is about the same as the Middle East in general. Its frequency is similar to that of Turkey and Greece. J has a frequency not unlike Europe (a little less than 10%). Our five instances of J sometimes have matches or near matches with European Jews.

But the most telling evidence in my opinion concerns haplogroup X. This, as we have seen, ranks as the third largest haplogroup. The only other place on earth where it is found at an elevated level apart from other American Indian groups like the Ojibwe is among the Druze, an endogamous population living for thousands of years with little genetic influx in the Hills of Galilee in northern Israel and Lebanon. The work of Shlush et al. (2009) demonstrates that the homeland of the Druze, because of the diversity of X haplotypes in it as well as their high frequency, is the center of a worldwide diffusion for X. It is the hallmark of a population of which the Druze are the lasting surviving heirs. The region acted as a refugium for humans during the last Ice Age much as the Iberian Peninsula did for other lineages (chiefly H). Haplogroup X (and to a lesser extent, K) is one of the distinctive signatures of the first out-of-Africa settlers in the land of Canaan (present-day Israel and Lebanon). In other words, the peculiar Druze sect preserves the genetics of the bedrock population.

In the case of this genetic refugium, however, I propose that since there is no star-like population expansion driving haplogroup X outward into Europe and to other parts of the Middle East, the lineage can only have spread in discontinuous fashion to the Americas and to other places where it has been noted such as North Africa, England, South America and Papua New Guinea. It must have arrived by sea. There are no genetic footsteps of haplogroup X leading to the New World across Europe, nor in Siberia or along a circumpolar route, as has been variously argued. From a genetic perspective, X survives at elevated frequencies in two separate places, Canaan or Palestine and Native North America. Its presence is particularly noteworthy in the tribes situated around the Great Lakes and Saint Lawrence Seaway like the Ojibwe and Micmac—and in the Cherokee .

On the Y chromosome side of Shlush et al.'s study, male haplogroup K was found to have a relatively high frequency of 11% in the Galilee region (2008:2). K (renamed T in the revised YCC nomenclature) has long been suspected to be the genetic signature of the Phoenicians (*Who Were the*

*Phoenicians?*). This early seafaring people originated in the interior of Lebanon after 1200 BCE (Aubet 2001:13-16) and spread later to Asia Minor, North Africa, Sicily and Spain, creating a mining and mercantile empire. Notably, they served as mariners for the Egyptians. Herodotus, moreover, has the following account of their trade activities with "a race of men who live . . . beyond the Pillars of Hercules":

> On reaching this country, they unload their goods, arrange them tidily along the beach, and then, returning to their boats, raise a smoke. Seeing the smoke, the natives come down to the beach, place on the ground a certain quantity of gold in exchange for the goods, and go off again to a distance. The Carthaginians then come ashore and take a look at the gold; and if they think it represents a fair price for their wares, they collect it and go away; if, on the other hand, it seems too little, they go back aboard and wait, and the natives come and add to the gold until they are satisfied. Their is perfect honesty on both sides; the Carthaginians never touch the gold until it equals in value what they have offered for sale, and the natives never touch the goods until the gold has been taken away (IV.196:279).

Some readers will immediately recognize in Herodotus' account a description of the Sacred Trade Circle of American Indians. No word was ever exchanged. The principal was "what you see is what you get." Barter alone was used. The exchange could be evened out to make it acceptable to one or another of the two parties if they were hesitant to accept it, as the Phoenicians were in the passage given above. All "sales" were final, since in the nature of things they were mutually satisfactory or else the deal would not have been consummated.

The most complete written description of the custom of the trade circle I can think of appears in a book that I wrote some years ago, as follows:

> To my knowledge, no one has ever successfully explained the origin of the term Indian giver. Was it the Indians who took back or the white man? The question is important if we are to know what to do with the Indian gift today. Seer tradition unravels the mystery as follows.
>
> When the white man first appeared in his sailing ships he left strange gifts on the shore. These were treated as goods placed on a trade blanket. It was normal for no verbal communication to take place in the

sacred trade circle, though it was unusual for the two parties not to be present at the same time. Our people understood the gesture and honored it with equal return gifts. Perhaps the pile they left on the shore exceeded the value of the white man's gifts. Maybe it was too little. It was hard to tell, nor did it matter. They were accepted. All gifting is final. *The Eighth Arrow: Right, Wrong and Confused Paths According to Tihanama Elder Wisdom* (e-book). Marion: Standing Bear Press, 2007:169.

Without a doubt it was the Phoenicians, whose name unto themselves was *Cana'ni* or KHNAI 'Canaanites', not *Phoenikoi* 'red paint people' (Aubet 2001:9-12; cf. *Oxford Classical Dictionary* s.v. "Phoenicians" ). They are referenced by James Adair when he observes that "several old American towns are called Kanāai," and suggests that the Conoy Indians of Pennsylvania and Maryland were Canaanites and their tribal name a corruption of the word Canaan. The Conoy Indians are the same Indians William Penn around 1700 described as resembling Italians, Jews and Greeks. By about 1735 they had dwindled to a "remnant of a nation, or subdivided tribe, of Indians," according to Adair (1930:56, 67, 68). One of the oldest Cherokee clans is called Red Paint Clan (*Ani-wodi*).

The next chapter will analyze Cherokee traditions about Egypt, Greece, Cyrene, Israel and Phoenicia and present links and alignments involving language, epigraphy, culture and historical accounts in addition to the genetics reported here.

## Haplogroup Distribution of Anomalous Types versus Europe and Other Populations

| Hg | N | % | Europe | Mid-dle East | Egypt | Druze | Eastern Med. |
|----|----|------|--------|--------------|-------|-------|--------------|
| H | 4 | 7.7 | 53.5 | 36.8 | | | |
| J | 5 | 9.6 | 9.5 | 11.4 | 6.3 | 7.0 | 12.7 |
| X | 7 | 13.5 | 1.5 | 3.5 | 1.6 | 27.9 | 4.8 |
| U | 13 | 25 | 22.2 | 26.3 | 7.8 | 11.6 | 16.4 |
| K | 2 | 3.8 | 5.8 | 6.2 | 3 | 16.3 | 3.6 |
| T | 14 | 26.9 | 8.4 | 11.9 | 25 | 4.7 | 6.0 |
| L | 3 | 5.8 | | | | | |
| Unk. | 4 | 7.7 | | | | | |
| Total | 52 | 100 | n=1021 | n=2736 | n=64 | n=43 | n=165 |

*Source: Suppl. data from Richards et al. (2000); this study.*

# 5 THE OLD WORLD ORIGINS THESIS

"We cannot solve our problems with the same thinking we used when we created them," remarked Albert Einstein. Applying that dictum to Cherokee DNA studies, we can easily suspect that the Cherokee people have been "problematized" with outmoded, colonialist thinking. DNA, that great arbiter of collective and personal mysteries, has failed to cut the Gordian knot not because its tools lack effectiveness, but because they have not been applied. The knot itself is an unreal phantom of myths and illusions, prejudice and superstition, politics and propaganda.

DNA Consultants' Cherokee investigations over more than ten years consistently produced a picture of Cherokee genetic diversity that seemed to have an ancient source, one split between the Old and New Worlds. There were Asiatic types (notably haplogroup B) alongside East Mediterranean haplogroups J, T and U, all with impeccable credentials. In 2012, I published *Old World Roots of the Cherokee*, which presented all the intertwining and converging linguistic, genetic, anthropological, archeological and historical arguments why I posited that the origins of the Cherokees rested at least partially on a 3rd century BCE. expedition across the Pacific from Ptolemaic Egypt. Appendix E contained the haplogroups and genealogy of Phase I participants, supporting an "anomalous" origin for non-ABCDX Cherokees. Appendix H listed evidence assembled from various modern and ancient references pointing to a Greek presence in North and South America, including two important inscriptions made public for the first time, the Possum Creek Stone and Clay County cave entrance falsely reported as historical and "Sequoyan" but actually at least a thousand years older. I also re-examined the Thruston Tablet, which shows a Cherokee chief in a Greek hoplite's stallion-crested helmet and carrying a spear giving away his daughter (a large silver Star of David around her neck) in a Morganatic marriage ceremony to another chief.

It was a bold explanation for what Mack Bettis has described as "the Cherokee enigma." Let us call it the "Old World Origins Thesis." But judgment of the whole must flow from acceptance or rejection of the constituent parts. Unfortunately, one of the first reviewers seemed willing to reject the "Old World Origins Thesis" without evaluating the many pieces of evidence and arguments upon which it was predicated. Jessica Bardill of Stanford University wrote a long review in *American Indian Culture and Research Journal* (2013, 37/4:199-202, in which she concluded:

> Many readers throughout American Indian studies, ethnic studies, and interdisciplinary studies in general will find writing in this intersection of science, history, language, and religion engaging and useful for the future of the fields; however, while interdisciplinary approaches such as those that Yates presents here deserve further exploration, this text ultimately fails to contribute a coherent or reliable analysis to the discussion (202).

So the whole was dismissed with little or no attention paid to the individual "exhibits" in the case or to chain of arguments. It is as though a court was assembled but the judge allowed neither side to call any witnesses. Or produce evidence. Does the oldest national narrative of the Cherokee not tell of a migration across the Pacific Ocean (*Red Man's Origin*)? The reviewer did not think it worthwhile to even mention this crucial text apart from my summary. Does the Cherokee language not contain relics of Greek? If it does, there must be a historical reason. Was Tsalagi an offshoot of an Iroquoian language or an accommodation to it replacing an older language? The former opinion is assumed, and a gallery of witnesses is told to go home. Did Cherokee music and musicology incorporate elements of Egyptian, Greek and Middle Eastern music? No one seems inclined to study stomp dance melodies except as impenetrable, primitive mysteries.

For the benefit of those who do not read long, academic monographs bristling with footnotes (which would seem to include reviewers of long, academic monographs), let us reprise here some of the main arguments and pieces of individual evidence behind the Old World Origins Thesis, especially as they may bear on and be supported by DNA.

*First known portrait of Cherokees: Seven Cherokees in London 1730 in an engraving by Isaac Basire: Onanconoa, Skalilosken Ketagustah, Kollannah, Oukah Ulah, Tathtowe, Clogoittah and Ukwaneequa. The last is my ancestor, Attakullakulla. Hargrett Rare Book Room and Manuscript Library, Georgiana Collection, University of Georgia.*

### The Clan Argument

The Cherokee Seven Clans are unique, specific only to that tribe. They are Wolf (Ani-Wahiya), Bird (Ani-Tiskwa), Deer (Ani-Kawi), Twister (Ani-Gilohi), Wild Potato (Ani-Gotegewi), Panther (Ani-Sahoni) and Paint (Ani-Wodi). *Old World Roots* relied heavily on a dusty resource in the Smithsonian, "Notes on Six Cherokee Gentes." The original card files were started by Albert S. Gatschet and include notations by James Mooney and J.N.B. Hewitt recording information from Cherokee medicine man John Ax, among others. The holding also incorporates manuscript materials by J. T. Garrett, interpreted by John D. Strange, Allogan Slagle and Mack Bettis. Photocopies were kindly shared with me by Bettis. Also having a hand in this priceless resource for Cherokee history was Herman Viola, director of the Smithsonian's Anthropological Archives, who facilitated access of these materials for Bettis in 1974. Of these "gentes," the people of the bird, wolf and deer are all traced to an original bird clan. The original name of this clan was Red Flicker, Sapsucker, Woodpecker or Ani-Tsaliena or Tsunilyana, meaning Deaf Clan. Cherokees testing as being A, C and D often have matches to Mexico, Central America and the U.S. Southwest—testimony to the Asiatic roots of these clans.

*Resemblance to a Cherokee? Portrait of a Woman of Cyrene, ca. 1935-1940. Luce Institute/Alinari Archive Management, Florence.*

Although Wolf is the largest clan today, that position was occupied by the Paint Clan before the large-scale disruptions beginning at the end of the eighteenth century (Anderson et al. 2010, p. 354, n. 84). Traditionally, war chiefs came from the Wolf Clan and peace chiefs or second chiefs from the Paint. Bird Clan members often provided priests, medicine men, speakers and ceremonial officiants, while Deer Clan members seem to be prominent among the scribes and intellectuals of the tribe. Chief John Ross (1790-1866) was Bird Clan, descended in the strict female line from Ghi-goo-ie (Ghigau, Beloved or War Woman), wife of William Shorey, a Scotsman. He was only one-eighth American Indian, though he became the Cherokees' longest serving principal chief. Sickatower, the oldest and one of the most important informants in the Payne-Butrick Papers, was also Bird Clan.

The other clans have divergent histories. We will not review the arguments identifying the Twister or Longhair Clan with B lineages and Polynesian origins, as they are hard to do justice to in summaries. Suffice it to say that the clan name literally commemorates Gi-lolo, the land where the earliest ancestors of the Hawaiians came from, identified by later Spanish, Dutch and English navigators as the Moluccas in the Indonesian Archipelago. Elizabeth Tassel was one of the first Cherokee women to wed an English frontier official, Scottish trader Ludovic Grant, about 1726. Several of our Cherokee subjects traced their mitochondrial DNA back to her. More than one of them remember the original Bird Clan affiliation, which their family never lost.

It seems that the Ani-Gotigewi, or Wild Potato Clan, just like the Twister Clan, exists only among the Cherokee. This clan seems to reflect Cherokee migrations through South America. The name of this clan, Gotigewa, pronounced approximately K'tigwa, appears to be a corruption of Quechua, the original name of the Andean people we know today as the Incas. Cornelius Dougherty, an Indian trader at Keowee in Lower Cherokee Country, married Ah-nee-wa-kee, a daughter of Chief Moytoy II (Amadohiyi) of the Wild Potato Clan. Another Wild Potato Clan matriarch was Susannah or Sonicooie, who married Thomas Cordery. Their descendants included Sarah Cordery, who married John Rogers, and many enrolled Cherokees by the names Vickery, Harris, McNair, Mosley, and Collins. The Nighthawk Society of Redbird Smith emphasized genealogies and traditions of the Wild Potato Clan.

What about the Paint Clan, Ani-Wodi? "Paint People" seems, without question, to be the customary term for Phoenicians, whose ethnonym or word for themselves was *Knai* "Canaanites." This name is rendered in Native America as Kanawa, a tributary of the Ohio. By tradition, Paint Clan members were doctors and hunters (*kanati*, from Greek *gennadi* "noblemen"), keepers of history (*tikano*, from Greek *tynchana* "events") and prophecy, and masters of protocol, diplomacy, and ceremony. Peace chiefs and Ukus ("owls," or wise men, in the Greek model; cf. Hopi *mongwi* "owl, chief") were often chosen from their ranks.

The Paint Clan was never called anything but by its true name, Paint (*wodi*). No other clans were combined with it, and it alone had the privilege of intermarriage between clan members. One of its trademarks was mask making, a sign of its origins in the ancient Mediterranean world of theatrical performances and religious spectacles. In Phase I and II of "Anomalous Cherokee Mitochondrial DNA Lineages," many Paint Clan descendants proved to be haplogroup U2e* or X. Cooper relatives of mine in North Carolina still speak of belonging to the Paint Clan.

By all accounts, the Panther or Blue Paint clan is almost extinct. Its members were known as "Dangerous Men" and "Night People." Its Cherokee name is Ani-Sahoni or Sakanike ("purple"), which means "They sit in the ashes until they turn blue-gray." Because West African medicine men are distinguished by white or blue face paint created from ashes, one might speculate that this minor clan could represent the African component in the Cherokee melting pot. Tribal traditions emphasize that the Cherokee include black people as well as white, red, and yellow. There are two paint clans, and it may be that the larger Red Paint Clan represents the original Phoenicians and the lesser Blue Paint fellow travelers that accompanied them, drawn from the teeming interior of the Carthaginian state.

*Red Man's Origin* tells of twelve original clans, five of whom became separated from the Cherokee in their crossing of the Great Waters and subsequently lost. It would be jumping to an unwarranted conclusion to equate these with the Twelve Tribes of Israel. But Greek mythology is replete with dodecads, notably in the Twelve Olympians. Greek and other Eastern Mediterranean societies used a duodecimal system of genealogies to account for one's personal lineage or clan descent.

Another echo of Greek or Phoenician legends is contained in the account of how the white man hoodwinked the Cherokee and cheated them out of their land:

> Then the white strangers, which were supposed to be visitors from heaven and who were supposed to be such on account of their white skins, as the idea and emblem of white was purity and spirituality among the Cherokees, these strangers were taken to be such, asked that they be allowed a small piece of ground upon which to camp, cook and sleep; it was charitably granted. These strangers were entertained by the Cherokee clans very charitably and food and other articles of comfort freely given to them. Then these strangers made known their desire and

willingness to remain with the native Cherokee clans if they were allowed to purchase a small piece of ground upon which to camp and sleep. They made known to the tribe that they only needed a small piece of land about the size of a bull hide. This modest request was freely granted to the strangers and sold to them for a trifling consideration. The supposed heavenly strangers then cut one of the ox hides which they had brought with them into a small string which they stretched around a square enclosing several hundred square yards. This they claimed to be in accordance with the purchase agreement to which the tribe finally agreed, saying at the same time that they had been deceived. Other purchases of land were made for which a consideration was always given by the white heavenly strangers, after the cession of which the tribe always acknowledged that they had been deceived. Then the tribe finally came to the conclusion that this white stranger was from the opposite pole of the heavens and put on his white skin for the purpose of deceiving.

Before coinage of currency (3rd cent. BCE) ancient peoples either used barter or trade tokens, a standard type being the oxhide-shaped copper ingots or reel-shaped metal pieces of the Phoenicians. The point of the story seems to be that the white invaders offered the Indians money and inflated the value of it. The same legend was told by the Phoenicians about their success in gaining the hinterlands of Carthage from the original native owners.

### The Linguistic Argument

Language shift is an unreliable guide to demographic and genetic change. But the same cannot be said of its importance in genealogies. Several of the participants in our project remark that as late as their parents' and grandparents' generation the Cherokee language was spoken in the household. We see that as a sign of Cherokee culture and genetics surviving in those lines, despite the fact that they were no longer living with other Cherokees and in fact, may have been unacknowledged by other Cherokees. It would also seem to imply a relatively low level of admixture.

A participant in Phase I was Mary M. Garrabrant-Brower, one of the 13 U haplogroup subjects who had been told by other DNA testing companies they were plainly *not* of Cherokee descent because they didn't have the right haplogroup. "My great-grandmother was Clarissa Green of the Cherokee

Wolf Clan," said Garrabrant-Brower. "Her grandfather was a Cherokee chief and my mother maintained the Cherokee language and rituals, even though we moved to the Northeast."

Is Cherokee the tribe's original language? Tsalagi, the name both of the tribe and language, has never been satisfactorily etymologized. According to the author of a recent grammatical study of Oklahoma Cherokee, Brad Montgomery-Anderson, "There are several beliefs about the origin of the name *jalagi*, but it appears that the word itself is not a native Cherokee word. In *Old World Roots*, we derived the word from corrupted Greek, along with a long list of other names, proper nouns and verbs. Like all the other arguments in the book the evidence for Greek words embedded in Cherokee must either be true or false. If such words as Tsalagi, Amoytoy, Koranu, Kanati, anetcha, Tlanua, tilihi and the rest are not Greek, what are they?

The first descriptions recorded by American traders, agents and missionaries often compared the Cherokee they heard to the Greek language. The field ethnographer John McIntosh reported that Huron, a language related to Cherokee, shared grammatical peculiarities with Greek. "As to the number and tenses, they have the same differences, as the Greek and some languages spoken in the north east of Asia . . . The action is expressed differently in respect to anything that has life, and an inanimate thing; thus, *to see a man*, and *to see a stone*, are two different verbs; and to make use of a thing that belongs to him who uses it, or to him to whom we speak, are also two different verbs." Cherokee makes many of the same syntactical distinctions.

Most people today regard Cherokee as "the sole representative of the Southern branch of the Iroquoian family of languages (Montgomery-Anderson, 4)." But why are Cherokee and Mohawk not mutually intelligible? Why does Mohawk have two or three times as many words as Cherokee? Why does Cherokee have a radically different syntax and grammar from Mohawk? Compared to Mohawk, Cherokee is so stripped down and simple it comes across as pidgin English. Are we misled by the fact that it is spoken so poorly and sporadically now as a second language? Why is two-thirds of its vocabulary non-cognate, not sharing the same roots as Mohawk? The lack of overlap extends to basic words like the names of numbers. In Mohawk, seven is *tsjada*. In Cherokee it is *gahlgwogi*.

The Oneida scholar Floyd G. Lounsbury undertook pioneering work in descriptive and comparative Iroquoian linguistics in the 1960s. Using a list of 200 common words he found only one-third inherited by Cherokee from a putative common ancestor. Because of linguistic anomalies, Lounsbury thought Cherokee "widely separate" from the others in its language family. Its divergence "must be ascribed to a more complete, *though not earlier*, separation." Until these fundamental questions are answered it does not make sense to regard Cherokee as a descendant of proto-Iroquoian and strict cousin to Mohawk.

We suggested, and continue to believe, that present-day Cherokee is rather a result of a historically fixed relexification process similar to that which gave birth to Yiddish in the Middle Ages. No one would claim that Yiddish, with its pervasive Hebrew vocabulary and Semitic pronunciation, is just another Germanic language like Dutch or Frisian or Anglo-Saxon. Nor would anyone theorize on the basis of linguistics alone that Central European Jews are primarily descended from Germanic tribes.

## The Archeology Argument

In comparison with other American Indian groups, the Cherokee possess no archeology to speak of. The Pisgah phase, generally dated to between 1000 and 1500 CE,, is the name assigned by archaeologists to prehistoric Cherokee culture in western North Carolina, but entries in handbooks are reluctant to see too much in the handful of sites excavated such as the Warren Wilson and Garden sites. Following the Pisgah is the Qualla phase (1500 - 1850 CE,). Even this, however, does not yield a definite "horizon" for what is distinctively Cherokee. Whatever else they are, the Cherokee are an old tribe and were living somewhere continuously (if not where history discovered them in the 16th century). But archeology is blind to any material trace of them before 1000.

In *Old World Roots* we draw attention to several signs of Cherokee antiquity in the records of excavations and rock inscriptions. These include the Thruston Tablet (Mississippian Era or before), the Bat Creek Stone and associated Roman coins (2nd century CE,), Possum Creek Stone (BCE), Sosorra drawings in a New Guinea cave (3rd century BCE.), Santiago inscription in Chile (dated internally August 5 of the 16th regnal year of Egyptian pharaoh Ptolemy Euergetes III, or 230 BCE) and extensive inscriptions in Greek and Hebrew on a Clay County, Kentucky cave entrance (perhaps 2nd century CE). Space forbids revisiting each of these key pieces of evidence for the long history of the Cherokee. To single out only one of them, though, is the Bat Creek Stone authentic and does it tell the story of a Jewish zealot entombed in a Cherokee burial? Or is it a fake? Or has it been misinterpreted? Does it tell us anything about the Cherokees? When I went to see it in Knoxville, the museum staff in Knoxville would only hand you a photocopied list of articles about it and say its status along with the writing on it was controversial. Most of the other ancient inscriptions in my list fail even to achieve that obscurantist position. But they are not going away!

*Bat Creek Stone. Catalogue No. AB4902, Department of Anthropology, Smithsonian Institution.*

*Senior tribal elders Bob Blankenship (left) and Donald Rose with his daughter Leslie Kalen and researcher Scott Wolter in Cherokee, October 27, 2010.*

In an update on the Bat Creek Stone, thanks to the activism of Leslie Rose Kalen and others in the Eastern Band of Cherokee Indians, this vital Jewish monument of Cherokee archeology was returned to the tribe, where it is on display at the museum and being studied anew unencumbered by preconceived theories (Cherokee Council House Resolution/Ordinance No. 794, dated August 4, 2011; Wolter 2013, pp. 117-27). The tribe also filed a formal request asking the Smithsonian to return the human jawbone reportedly found by the excavator for DNA analysis, but the authorities said they "couldn't find it" (Wolter 124).

## The Cultural Anthropology Argument

As with archeology, so with anthropology. The Cherokee are accorded extremely short shrift, especially in the branch of anthropology focused on the study of cultural variation. The ignorance and neglect begins with their tribal name, clan system and language and goes on to a sweeping non-engagement on similarities and dissimilarities between them and other Indians in traits, social customs, religious ceremonies and beliefs, political organization, material culture and lifeways.

What is the meaning of the chunkey stones prized by Cherokees and other Southeastern Indians? Or the Cherokee ballplay? Why are the Little People alive in Cherokee folk belief as in no other tribe? Why do the Cherokee habitually and ritualistically "go to water" or sweat in winter lodges? Did a historical Cherokee known as Sequoyah invent their syllabary? If he did, he is the only person in world history to have fathered a writing system singlehandedly. What is the Phoenix doing on the seal of the Cherokee nation? Isn't it time to at least ask the questions, even if they are difficult of solution?

When I published *Old Souls in a New World* as an abridgement of my work for a more general audience, I raised the possibility that "the history of America's largest Indian nation is actually a polite modern fiction, one invented by 'anthropologists and other friends.'" I subtitled the book "The Secret History of the Cherokee Indians." But the facts surrounding the Cherokee are not secret at all. They are as plain and obvious as the observations and opinions anyone makes and forms who gets to know the Cherokee people, or has more than a passing acquaintance with one of them, or *is* one of them, or has some of their blood flowing in their veins. Mack Bettis speaks of this eloquently in his foreword to *Old World Roots*.

*Possum Creek Stone, the earliest example of the Sequoyan syllabary. Photograph by Gloria Farley courtesy of Bart Torbert. © Gloria Farley Publications Incorporated.*

### The Hopi Analogy

Thomas Mills lived for many years on the Hopi Indian Reservation in Northern Arizona, where he and his mother opened and operated the Cultural Center at Second Mesa. A close friend was White Bear, the traditionalist who helped Frank Waters compile *The Book of the Hopi* in 1963. Mills was on familiar terms with other elders, kiva chiefs and artisans. In 2001, he wrote a little book of his own called *The Truth*. It was an attempt to reconcile some of the conflicting answers he had received from his sources.

How did a desert-dwelling, isolated people know of the earth's spherical shape and rotation in space? What was the long journey in boats from across the sea they spoke of? And who were the Ant People they took refuge with after the destruction of the first, second and third worlds? Eventually, Mills felt he had some answers from Egyptian religion. He came to believe that the Hopi *were* Egyptians, old souls in Native America, charged with the task of praying for the safety of the world. The delicate balance of affairs in human destiny depended on a Hopi prayer feather or *paho*.

*Paho* seems to be an Egyptian word (*pw*). Embedded in Hopi customs and rituals are apparently many traces of ancient Old World civilizations. I thought of a time several years ago when Hopi elders David Mowa and

Ronald Wadsworth came to give a talk at the university where I was teaching. I noticed David preferred to sleep on the floor in our guest room instead of the pullout bed. That was quite Indian, of course, but his act of leaving a crust of bread on the piano bench when he departed was not. This practice is rooted in the ancient Greek religious gesture of offering bread and milk to the household gods in a strange home.

Author Hamilton Tyler noted several Greek customs among the Pueblo Indians. The plinth-like figure of Masaw evokes the armless guardian statues or herms used by the Greeks as boundary markers. Hermes is both god of roads and boundaries and conductor of the dead to the underworld. "A number of students of Pueblo religion," Tyler admitted, "have remarked that it was something like Greek religion." Yet after uncovering astonishing analogies between the two religions, he concluded that "there is no actual connection between these two gods who lived centuries apart and on different sides of the globe."

Other parallels Tyler dismissed which seem compelling to me are: 1) the Zunis' harlequin-like Mudheads or Koyemshi, who arrive across bridges to taunt and harass people at the ceremony, just as did the clowns released on the Sacred Way between Athens and Eleusis at comic festivals (the word Koyemshi seems indeed to be a corruption of the Greek for "comedians," Latin *comici*), 2) Hermes' and Masaw's playing of tricks on other gods, 3) their gift of song, 4) a body of tales about them as thieves, 5) their status as the inventors of firemaking and as fire gods, 6) their common role of leading the host to war and 7) their respective positions as fertility gods.

In addition to these correspondences, I propose there is an echo of a Greek religious rite in the Zunis' Shalako, the ghostly ancestral figure who initiates reentry of the katsinas into the village at the winter solstice. Shalakos are costumed as luminous white armless figures ten feet high, similar in appearance to the Hopi depiction of Masaw. The Zuni Shalako seems to me to evoke the Egyptian god Osiris, a symbol of regeneration often portrayed as a linen-wrapped mummy. During the Shalako ceremony, the Koyemshi act up and poke fun at the spectators. In the Greek ritual, the maenads and bacchae roam around the crowd and feign tearing to pieces beasts and even humans who come in their way. Their counterparts at Zuni rend to bits live mice and rabbits and carry the small creatures about in their mouths.

## Egyptians Abroad

Egyptians have long been suspected of visiting the shores of America and even planting colonies here. Whether reached by east or west, the other hemisphere was regarded by them as the realm of Osiris, god of the underworld, as explained by Gunnar Thompson:

> From the vantage point of Egypt, the western Atlantic lies on the opposite side of the globe . . . . [Their] expression "inverted waters" is an accurate description of the western Atlantic, and it confirms Egyptian knowledge of the Earth's spherical shape. Likewise, the realm of Osiris was known as "The Underworld" because it was located beneath Egypt on the spherical Earth . . . Between both worlds flowed the "Two-Ways" ocean river . . . . Egyptian mariners traveled west to the realm of Osiris and returned to the Mediterranean via a "two-ways" ocean river [flowing both directions]—the North Atlantic current.

Could the Egyptians have traveled to the realm of Osiris also by crossing the Pacific from Asia?

Excited by the thought that there might be a real connection between the Hopi and Egyptians, I compiled a list of Hopi words that seem to have the same sound and meaning in Egyptian. Nearly all prove to be archaic terms relating to tribal ceremonies and religious history. The Hopi's main language is classified as Uto-Aztecan, a Native American linguistic phylum, but the formation of plurals with –*n* and –*m* points to Semitic or Afro-Asiatic affinities. Specialized religious terms in Hopi are relics or intrusions comparable evidently to fossilized words in the "old language" of the Cherokee. Such vocabulary evokes hieratic or priestly languages like Sanskrit in India or Latin in Western Europe.

With this daring key, events recounted in *The Book of the Hopi* became crystal-clear. Of the various former world ages or epochs recalled by the Hopi, one of them, Kuskurza, is specifically said to be "an ancient name for which there is no modern meaning." Reading the names of these epochs in Ancient Egyptian gives them true significance. They are: 1) World Destroyed by Fire (Tokpela), 2) Time Long Ago (Tokpa), 3) Age of Abandon (Kuzkurza), and 4) Age of the Strangers from Afar, the Fourth World or Present (Tuwaqachi). Thus, the creator Taiowa (Uto-Aztecan or Tanoan for "man, human, people," as in today's Tewa, Tiwa and Towa) has his nephew Sotuknang and Spider Woman give life to the innocent First

People in an Eden called Tokpela. They are led astray by the Talker and Katoya the handsome one (Satan the deceiver). The animals draw apart in fear and they begin to fight one another, in neglect of the Creator's plan. Sotuknang decides to annihilate the world by opening up the volcanoes and raining fire upon it, but not before saving some of the faithful by leading them to a big mound where the Ant People live. The Egyptian word for this refuge the Hopi will use to survive two further holocausts translates literally as "subsistence in the pyramid of the ants." Pyramid, in fact, means "anthill."

### Egyptian Words in Hopi
*Sources: Book of the Hopi; Beinlich Word-List .*

| Hopi | Meaning | Egyptian | Meaning |
|---|---|---|---|
| al(o) | horn, spirit | halos* | halo (horns of Ammon) |
| ankinamuru | house of Ant People | anx+jn+maA+mr | ants' pyramid (anthill) |
| bahanna | white brother in East | wbnw | Easterners |
| Bakabi | Place of Jointed Reed | sbA + kAp | Flute Palace |
| Betatakin | place-name | Abet-Ahken** | house of sun's glory |
| chua | snake | twA | snake |
| dicha | katsina | didaka* | lesson, teaching |
| Hohokam | ancient ones | hhkm** | Sea People |
| Hoki | original name of tribe | HkAw | magicians |
| Hopi | "Peaceful People" | hp | people of the law |
| -hoya | son (in names) | huios* | son |
| kachada | younger brother | kA + Xrdw | young soul |
| katsina | Spirit Beings | kA + xsn | life-force (ka) gods |
| koko | stick | knkw | wooden object |
| Kokopauli | Humpback Flute Player | knkw + fAj | flute carrier |

| Kuskurza | Third Age | khsks | wicked ruin |
| Lenyam | Flute Clan | hni + plural** | reed people |
| Masaw | original black inhabitant | msw | Libyan |
| Mishongnovi | Place of the Black Man | mSwS | Libyan |
| Moencopi | Place of Flowing Stream | mwjn +kAp | Palace of the Fountain |
| mongwi | chief | mn | exalted |
| Moqui | name of Hopi | magi* | magicians |
| Oraibi | Rock on High | oros* | boundary stone |
| paho | prayer feather or stick | pw | pray, do ceremony |
| paso | where land meets the sea | pHww | land's end |
| piki | tablet of cornbread | ptyka* | tablet |
| (S)hungnopavi | Reed Spring | hnj + baH | well watered, field of reeds |
| sipapi | kiva opening | sbA | gate, door |
| songoqaki | reed covering | hnj + kaj | reed ship |
| Tokpa | Second World | dakpat | bygone original age |
| Tokpela | First World | dapaw | destroyed by fire |
| Tuwaqachi | Fourth World | tawqat | people from foreign lands |
| wuya | clan object | wjA | amulet |

*Ptolemaic Greek
**Libyan

After the end of Tokpela, World Destroyed by Fire, the people emerge to the Second World, called Dark Midnight, but they begin to become preoccupied with materialistic concerns as before. They ignore once again the commandments of the Creator. Sotuknang and Spider Woman seal a select few in the underground world of the Ant People and direct the celestial Twins to leave their posts at the north and south poles. The earth spins around off its axis, rolls over twice and freezes into solid ice. After it warms and the earth and seas are revived, Sotuknang brings the remnants of mankind out of the Ant kiva to emerge into the third world, Kuskurza.

True to its name, Kuskurza is full of big cities, jewels, copper, tobacco and speeding vessels called *patuwvota*. The Bow Clan behind these marvels corrupts everybody with wickedness until finally Sotuknang and Spider Woman intervene and put an end to the Age of Abandon with a devastating flood. This time the faithful are loaded onto reed boats. Spider Woman guides them to the Fourth World (Age of the Strangers from Afar). They dwell in stages on a succession of islands and continue to travel toward the northeast until they reach the new Place of Emergence. Hopi elders believe this to have been the coast of California, but it may have been at the mouth of the Colorado River on the Sea of Cortez, for the Hopi enact a coming-of-age ritual each year by sending youths on a footrace to collect salt here from a site associated with their ancestors. In former times, there were several large inland seas and the river system of the region was different.

> Looking to the west and the south, the people could see sticking out the water the islands upon which they had rested.
>
> "They are the footprints of your journey," continued Sotuknang, "the tops of the high mountains of the Third World, which I destroyed. Now watch."
>
> As the people watched them, the closest one sank under the water, then the next, until all were gone, and they could see only water.
>
> "See," said Sotuknang, "I have washed away even the footprints of your Emergence, the stepping-stones which I left for you. Down on the bottom of the seas lie all the proud cities, the flying *pátuwvotas*, and the worldly treasures corrupted with evil, and those people who found no time to sing praises to the Creator from the tops of their hills."

### Grandmother Spider

Once the people make landfall in their new home, the old gods Sotuknang and Spider Woman depart and leave the emergent Hopi to their own devices. This is a clue to the origin of this cosmic tale, which must have arisen in Sundaland, or Island Indonesia, among what the Cherokee called the "wise ones of Seg." Indeed, throughout the entire Southwest

Pacific Ocean, cosmologies focus on the figures of the Father Sky (Sotuknang) and Earth Mother (Spider Woman), the former usually portrayed as warlike and destructive, the latter as the creator of all the arts of civilization that sustain and nourish the people, as, for instance, weaving, basket-making and agriculture.

*Mimbres bowl shows men with feathers and women wearing gold hoop-style earrings and traditional African multi-strand necklaces. Women in other paintings wear veils and kufis. Source: Fewkes.*

The central role of the Spider as the helper of mankind is preserved in two Cherokee tales. In one, Grandmother Spider Steals the Sun, it is the tiny water spider who swims across the water to an island where the fire burns in order to bring warmth and comfort to her freezing people. In another, the same water spider dives deep under the waves to bring up dirt and form the new country inhabited by the people.

We may therefore best understand *The Book of the Hopi* as codifying a sweeping vision of world history created by a founder civilization that came from Eden in the East (to use Stephen Oppenheimer's term). In the mythic underpinnings of this society, there had been an age of man destroyed by volcanic eruptions (Tokpela) followed by global darkness, undoubtedly the fallout of such a cataclysm (Tokpa, the Second World). This age, too, is destroyed, this time by ice, with the Celestial Twins forsaking their axes: Scientists today acknowledge the effect of the poles in causing Ice Ages. Kurskurza, the Third World of Abandon, ensues after the melting of the ice, but it quickly ends in floods. Its trademark is the boat (*patuwvota*). The old worlds having been destroyed by fire, by icy darkness and by rising waters, the survivors make their way to the Fourth, and Present, World, where they are called, in Egyptian, the People from Foreign Lands. Hohokam, the name of the Southwest's "mother civilization," means People from the Sea in Ancient Egyptian. From this, we may surmise that Egyptian boats made of reed conveyed the Islanders to their new home.

*Greek hoplite.*

There the people meet Masaw, who becomes their guardian and protector. He is described as black and ugly, scratching out a humble existence in Oraibi ("Cliff Town" in ancient Greek) on Second Mesa. He declines to be their leader but gives them permission to stay. First, however, they must start their migrations to the ends of the earth (*paso*, another Egyptian word).

The name Masaw is the same as Ancient Egyptian *msw* "Libyan." The Hopi say Oraibi was his original home, which they translate as Rock on High, but which is formed apparently from a Greek word meaning "boundary, landmark, covenant stone." Inasmuch as "fire" has the sense of "a group of Indian people," their discovery of Masaw sitting with his back to them around a fire implies not just one black man or Libyan but a nation of them. Another Second Mesa town, Shungnopavi, is translated as Place of the Black Man, although in Egyptian it means "fertile land, field of reeds," this being the main metaphor in their religion for the afterlife, or paradise. That these Libyans were of the same stock as ancient soldiers and mariners from the Old World is supported by the fact that a later character in *The Book of the Hopi*, Horny Toad Woman, tells Masaw, "I too have a metal helmet," in other words, armor.

The various names of the Hopi are also informative. These are Hoki, the secret original ethnonym, which seems to come from the Egyptian word for "magicians"; Hopi, the Peaceful Ones, Egyptian for "people of the law"; and Moqui, erroneously glossed as neighboring tribes' derogatory reference to them as "despicable people." In actuality Moqui is probably derived from Magi.

### Acoma and Zuni

Aside from Oraibi, another trace of the Greek language comes to us from Acoma. A legend there tells of the arrival of its first inhabitants. The story goes that there once lived a boy all by himself on Enchanted Mesa. One day he heard the shouts of a strange people. A town was founded in the spot where the echo was heard. The word Acoma is garbled Spanish, but in the Acoma language Haku'uw is very close to the Greek word *echo*, related to English "acoustic."

If Acoma has a hint of Greek, Zuni is pure Libyan. Its very form Ashiwi refers to the Oasis of Siwa in the land the ancients called Ammonia after its patron god of the sun, Ammon. Barry Fell sees the Zuni language as having "a large Libyo-Egyptian element similar to Coptic, to which have been added Ptolemaic roots brought to the Egyptian and Libyan lands by Greek settlers in the wake of the Spartan colonization of Libya in the eight century B.C. and the conquest of Egypt by . . . the Ptolemies, during the last four centuries B.C." There are also roots of Nilotic origin, he adds, introduced by Nubian slaves—perhaps a reason why the Zunis traditionally divide themselves into a red and black half in their village. Zuni religion owes much to the worship of Ammon as practiced in the land of Ammonia with its capital of Siwa.

An early observer of the Zuni, Herman Ten Kate, found the tribe to "have been familiar with the art of silversmithing for some time" and highly skilled at polishing shells and turquoise to make necklaces. Moreover, they "surpass all other North American tribes in making of pottery," especially large ollas for holding water. Their painting was black on while and their decorations ran to meanders, spirals and wavy lines, he said.

Other signs of Zuni's Old World origins are found in the name of its priesthood, Shi'wanikwe ("people of Siwa") and the place-name of an outlying village where apparently the Canaanite element among them settled, Kia'anaän. The Zunis' tribal name is Children of the Sun. Ten Kate notes, "In addition to their everyday spoken language, the Zunis have a more ancient language, known only to the highest priests, in which the prayers of their order are recited." He also reports that in Zuni traditions their ancestors came from the West in boats:

> That they were aware of the sea during their earlier wanderings seems to be the case not only because they worship it but because they are at the same time familiar with the octopus or one of the other cephalopods . . . . Through tradition they are also familiar with earthquakes. They are labeled with the name of "the sound from the shell of the gods" . . . the tradition in this respect refers to how "the ocean was whipped to a fury" by "the sound of the shell of the gods." Moreover, in former times they undertook pilgrimages to the coast of the Pacific Ocean for the purpose of collecting sacred shells . . . just as the Moquis [Hopis] did.

In Greek mythology, Poseidon, the god of oceans, creates earthquakes. Triton, a fish-tailed demigod worshiped in particular in Cyrene, blows the conch trumpet that controls the waves and sounds the approach of an earthquake. It is hard to imagine a better set of clues.

Libyan settlement in North America is apparent from North African writing systems, building styles and languages. The evidence for it ranges from a famous *tholos*-shaped subterranean stone chamber in Upton, Massachusetts to pre-alphabetic writing in a stick-script called ogam scattered across the American West. Inscriptions in ogam, Greek, Kufic Arabic, Phoenician, Tifanag (a Berber alphabet), Celto-Iberian and Egyptian all point to the Libyans. Many of the remains of the mixed Berber/Semitic/Greek/Egyptian peoples in the rock record have been identified and deciphered but many more have been overlooked or explained away. The monumental New England beehive chambers Fell believed to be in the style of Berber kivas were dismissed as colonial root cellars!

## In Plain Sight

In 1994, Gloria Farley, an epigrapher, published the results of nearly fifty years of exploration in and around her native state of Oklahoma. The massive book was titled *In Plain Sight;* a second volume was anticipated at the time of her death in 2006. *In Plain Sight* provides a good look at these Native Americans who were not who they were supposed to be, who used metal when they ought to have been still in the Stone Age, and who had writing despite the denial of it to them by modern-day anthropology. Chapter titles tell it all: They Came in Ships. . . They Signed Their Names . . . They Claimed the Land . . . The Trail of the Egyptians . . . They Knew the Sky . . . They Mourned Their Dead.

In the fourteenth century, impelled by years of drought, civil and political turmoil and invasions by Athabaskan and Aztec hordes from the north, the Hopi retreated to Oraibi and the three mesas in northern Arizona where they are now. The earliest date for Old Oraibi as established by tree ring chronology performed on its wooden timbers is 1150 CE. Elders quoted in *The Book of the Hopi* speak of the 1200s and 1300s as a time when other groups such as the Badger Clan were gathered in after petitioning for admittance. They say that the Navajos and Apaches did not arrive in Hopi territory until one generation before the Spanish (1580).

## Enter the Elder White Brother

According to tradition, Masaw gave the Hopi four tablets to safeguard as their original instructions. The Sun Clan tablet applies primarily to the members of that clan. The Hopi are mostly silent about the symbols on it but they insist that a now-lost Elder White Brother was given a corner and charged with returning after being sent to the East.

I believe the headless person they interpret as a wicked chief beheaded as a warning not to disobey their covenant is not that at all. In ancient Libya, rulers were buried without their heads; it was a sign of royalty and even divine status. Surely, this is a depiction of a Libyan expedition's leader or governor. Note that the figure is within a cartouche, the shape reserved for a pharaoh's name.

In ancient times, a bargain or promise was sealed by breaking a tablet, stick or other object so that a later match between the two parts would identify the rightful partners when the contract was fulfilled. Elder Brother was sent with instructions to look for the missing members of the original migration, those whom history would know as the Cherokee. We lose track of them somewhere about Oklahoma.

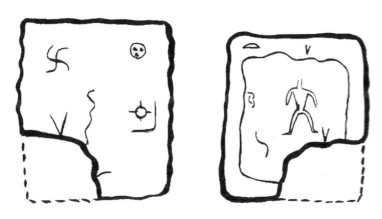

*Hopi Sun Clan Tablet.*

Among the unusual finds Gloria Farley describes in her book *In Plain Sight* is a stone pulled out of the family's farmland by curious eleven-year-old Brent Gorman of Warner, Oklahoma, in 1971. It was identified by Barry Fell as a Libyan boundary stone in the Numidian alphabet. His translation of its script, which resembles that of the Sun Clan tablet, was: Land Belonging to Rata. A discussion of the Warner Stone was published in Fell's book *America B.C.* and its Numidian writing system and the interpretation of the latter were confirmed by visits from surprised scholars at the Universities of Tripoli and Benghazi in Libya. The stone is now in the permanent collection of the Kerr Museum in Poteau, Oklahoma.

John RedHat Duke (1930-2002) was a Cherokee elder enrolled both with the United Keetoowah Band and Cherokee Nation of Oklahoma. A member also of the Keetoowah Society, he converted to Judaism as a teen-ager and became a Levite priest, making his *aliyah* and achieving Israeli citizenship under the "Law of Return."

Both full-blood grandmothers spoke the old Southern Keetoowah dialect. He was a strong believer in the Lost Tribes of Israel theory of American Indian origins.

RedHat came to the attention of Hopi Elders at Oraibi in the 1960s because he apparently fulfilled Hopi prophecy, which stated that one day the True White Brother would arrive from the largest Indian nation bringing a new religion from the east and wearing a red hat or cloak. The Cherokee are the most populous Indian nation, and they are located east of the Hopi. The last *kykmongwe*, or high chief, Mike Lansa, declared the prophecy fulfilled except for one detail. The Bahana was to return the missing corner of the Sun Clan tablet, which John Duke failed to do.

Whenever we attempt to introduce such subjects as those covered in this chapter into intelligent conversation with others we are invariably met with the rejoinder that they are controversial. But in the world of science it is only opinions that are controversial. Facts are facts. The Bat Creek Stone, the Possum Creek Stone, the Thruston Tablet, the Hopi Sun Clan Tablet, stallion-crest helmets, chunkey stones, anhemitonic scales in music, Middle Eastern haplogroups, ogam and a host of other anomalies are facts. What is inferred from each piece of evidence or the whole circumstantial lot is opinion.

In conclusion, the Cherokee like the Hopi are old souls, Old World peoples in the New World. For the modern Cherokee, life still proceeds to the rhythms of drums, rattles, flutes and ancestral voices. Stoneclad, their armored culture hero, still sings the stirring tales of the past. We hear the dying echoes of a former age that created that ancient music.

# 6 MORE ANOMALOUS MITOCHONDRIAL DNA LINEAGES IN THE CHEROKEE (PHASE II)

**Abstract.** A sample of individuals who took a mitochondrial DNA test to determine female lineage (n=67) was created from participants in DNA Consultants' Cherokee DNA Project Phase II. Almost all beforehand claimed matrilineal descent from a Native American woman, usually believed to be Cherokee, and often named in genealogy research undertaken by the customer. The majority of subjects revealed "anomalous" haplotypes not previously classified as American Indian. Many matched others in Phase I. Several individuals overcame the barrier of a sealed adoption to find biological relationships, often to other participants. As in Phase I, a Middle Eastern type, haplogroup T, emerged as the most common lineage (19.4% in Phase II, 22.7% overall in the project), followed by H, U and J, all Eurasian types. Sub-Saharan African haplogroup L (9%) was prominent as a minor category. Old Europe haplogroups I, N, V and W occurred in small amounts and should be considered strikingly new, unreported signals of authentic Cherokee ancestry.

## Background

Ever since the pioneering work of Douglas C. Wallace, Rebecca L. Cann and others on the use of human mitochondrial DNA as a marker for genetic ancestry and disease, scientists have insisted on a very limited and rigid number of ancient Asian female founders for present-day American Indian populations. In 1993, Satoshi Horai of the National Institute of Genetics in Mishima, Japan was the lead author in a study with the agenda-setting title, "Peopling of the Americas, Founded by Four Major Lineages of Mitochondrial DNA." That same year, Antonio Torroni of the University of Pavia coined the term haplogroup in a publication in the *American Journal of Human Genetics* in which he and his co-authors postulated but four lineages, A, B, C and D to account for mitochondrial ancestries in their sample. Also in 1993, Anne C. Stone (Arizona State University) and Mark Stoneking (Max Planck Institute for Evolutionary Anthropology) confirmed the four haplogroups in a 1300 CE burial ground in central Illinois, the Norris Farms site. The year 1993 was truly an *annus mirabilis* in American Indian genetics. It remained only for the minor haplogroup X to be added to the original four lineages (Brown et al. 1998, Malhi and Smith 2002; Smith et al. 1999).

In the ensuing twenty years, academic studies, textbooks, the popular media and governmental policies fell into lockstep about the "peopling of the Americas." Despite a number of voices being raised in criticism (Jones; Guthrie; Jett), the model restricting American Indian ancestry to mitochondrial lineages A, B, C, D and X has remained intact. When direct-to-the-consumer DNA testing became available in 2000, commercial companies hopped on the abecedarian bandwagon. To paraphrase Henry Ford, you could have an Indian DNA test say anything you wanted as long as it was A, B, C, D and sometimes X. But were these haplogroup rules possibly equivocal and not conclusively decidable anyway?

Etched in stone along with the five classic Native American mitochondrial haplogroups has emerged a belief that all American Indians can be traced to a single entry from Siberia roughly 10,000 years ago across the Bering Strait, supposed at that time to have formed a land bridge. This prevailing notion was summarized and defended by Kemp and Schurr (2010). According to University of Florida doctoral dissertation writer Joseph Andrew Park Wilson, "Today it is rare to find a molecular anthropologist who favors more than two distinct migration events, and a majority of researchers are enamored with the single-origin hypothesis, which postulates just one founding group ancestral to all Native Americans." Wilson cites the following studies in support of this observation: Bonatto and Salzano 1997; Fagundes et al. 2008; Goebel et al. 2008; Kolman et al. 1996; Merriwether et al. 1995; Mulligan et al. 2004; Rubicz et al. 2002; Stone and Stoneking 1998; Tamm et al. 2007; Tarazona-Santos and Santos 2002; Zegura et al. 2004 (p. 102).

## *Band-aids on the Battleship*

This "A-D" thesis continues to stand with minor alterations. Perego et al. (2009) proposed on the basis of phylogeographic analysis of 69 mitochondrial types a "simultaneous but independent Asian source populations for early American colonists." But this modification of the theory involving "two roads taken" still kept within the A-D canon and maintained the primacy of the Bering land bridge (aided in a minor way by a seaborne route from Asia using the "kelp road"). Eventually, the lineup consisted of nine usual suspects: A2, B2, C1, C4c, D1, D2a, D3, D4h3 and X2a (Achilli et al. 2008).

After extensive examination of the subject Wilson concludes that the five mtDNA haplogroups actually have complex, multilayered histories. Moreover, the genetic story represents only one of the pieces of the puzzle; other evidence to be harmonized into a coherent "archeogenetic narrative" are languages and material culture (pp. 141-42).

Torroni and Wallace (then at Emory and La Sapienza in Rome, respectively) were apparently the first to use the term "anomalous" of mitochondrial types. However, in their important letter to the editor of the *American Journal of Human Genetics* in May 1995, they applied it rather narrowly to "a heterogeneous set of mtDNAs due either to recent genetic admixture or to new mutations that have abolished a preexisting primary marker," in other words to non-conforming types *within* the A-D paradigm.

Utterly "foreign" anomalies only came within the sights of geneticists in 2013, when a devastating shockwave hit the archeological establishment. At the epicenter was Danish researcher Eske Willerslev, who reported on two 24,000-year-old Siberian skeletons at the "First Americans Archeology" conference in Santa Fe, New Mexico. The fullest sequencing of ancient human DNA to date suggested that the people who lived near Lake Baikal at the dawn of human civilizations, and who later developed into the Native Americans of the New World, came more proximately from a westernly direction in Europe, not from Asia. Moreover, the mitochondrial haplogroup of the so-called Mal'ta boy the Danish team sequenced was U, a "non-Indian" type (M. Raghavan et al. 2014). The term anomalous now extended to entire haplogroups that did not fit the mold.

On the face of it, no haplotyping study can distinguish between deep ancestry and more recent admixture as the cause of unusual variations in DNA. Whereas tools like "time to coalescence," bootstrapping and phylogenetic trees can be used to compare types and estimate genetic distance, no logarithm can tell the geneticist *where* any given haplotype may have arisen and become characteristic. Projections of the source, spread, mutation and survival of uni-parental haplotypes can be deceptive, especially when they telescope tens of thousands and sometimes hundreds of thousands of years.

### Navajo Puzzles

To consider an apposite question from Navajo research, we might ask when did certain Asian genes in the modern-day Diné matching 4000-year-old DNA from Siberia and the Tarim Basin travel to the Americas? It could have been 20,000 years ago or it could have been in the 16th century. The "genetic signature" could have arrived by gradual "star-like" diffusion or through one or more discontinuous movements, some possibly seaborne, some repetitive, some marked by diversity of types, some non-diverse, some minor, some major, some conceivably separated from each other by centuries or millennia. Similar problems beset any modeling of tribally-specific genetic scenarios. As the Jones white paper pointed out long ago, geneticists have a tendency to take the long view and telescope genetic incidents. They often rely solely on statistical modeling applying classical evolutionary components like random mating and natural selection and do not take concerted account of histories, archeology, cultural baggage like myth and religion, and family or clan genealogies.

So far, autosomal DNA analysis has not assumed a large role in elucidating haplogroup history and the subject of admixture. The Centre for GeoGenetics at the University of Copenhagen's Natural History Museum of Denmark has led the way with a new "dual ancestry" model augmenting the A-D thesis. The current issue of *Archaeology* contains the heretical suggestion that "the earliest travelers to the New World made their way more than 20,000 years ago from what is now the west coast of France and northern Spain" (Swaminathan, p. 25), but this seems to be just another shot in the dark. A quite recent autosomal study of European DNA headed by Harvard's David Reich identified three ancestral populations on the basis of ancient DNA, one of which is Willerslev's "ancient North Eurasians related to Upper Palaeolithic Siberians," called ANE (Lazaridis et al. 2014). Belonging to haplogroup U, and sharing some alleles with 8,000-year-old Scandinavian hunter-gatherers, ANE is thus an ancient link between

Europeans and Native Americans, one quite separate incidentally from Turkic Chuvash and N-dominated Saami, both of which "are more related to east Asians than can be explained by ANE admixture" (p. 412). Haplogroup U has thus been established as an ancient founding haplogroup in Native American populations, dating back 24,000 years ago to the same time period as the A-D canon.

With the blossoming of phylogenetic and phylogeographic studies utilizing complete mtDNA sequences (Torroni et al. 2006), it is to be hoped that genetics will embark on a fundamental new approach to the study of American Indian haplotypes. Promisingly for Cherokee research, Willerslev's team in Denmark has included several participants in the present ongoing project as part of a larger study. The Danish initiative has sampled the 35,000 members of the Echota Cherokee Tribe of Alabama: Dr. Joel E. Harris, Sr. maintains a communication page.

## Procedure and Methodology

The purpose of the Cherokee DNA Project is to sample and investigate the genetic heritage of persons who may be of Cherokee descent and establish a reference collection of their DNA results and genealogies. Enrollment in Phase II began in October 2009 following the release of Phase I results in the blog post "Anomalous Mitochondrial DNA Lineages in the Cherokee" (August 31, 2009). Data were published in Yates (2012) pp. 161-62.

As in Phase I, a notice of the search for volunteers was publicly displayed on the company's website. Holli Starnes has acted as administrator throughout. All candidates signed up when they purchased either a mitochondrial DNA HVS1+2 ancestry test or a mitochondrial "report only" based on previous testing. After receiving fulfillment of their personal order, they were requested to execute and mail back a standard informed consent form. Participation was at no extra cost. Open enrollment via the website lasted until August 31, 2014, at which time 67 candidates were verified and accepted into the final sample. All had learned in their personal report that they probably had direct female descent through mitochondrial DNA from a Native American woman.

The sample selected for Phase II is composed of 39 female (58%) and 28 male (42%) subjects. Two husband-wife couples enrolled. Sometimes the subject's test was ordered by a family member, but no participants knew they were closely related *a priori*. Ages varied from 30 to 90. Participants mostly lived in the United States and Canada, where they were residents of scattered locations, from New Hampshire and Florida to California, Texas and Hawaii. One joined from as far away as New Zealand. No single state (such as Oklahoma or Tennessee) stood out in the demography.

Of the 67 subjects, eleven of them (16%) tested with other companies first, including Family Tree DNA, Ancestry.com and DNA Diagnostics Center. About half (47%) got first-time test results from DNA Consultants' service lab, Genex Diagnostics of Vancouver, British Columbia, and about one-third tested with Sorenson Genomics of Salt Lake City, Utah. Two participants did not want to reveal the identity of their lab. Enrollment was fairly evenly distributed over five years. The largest number of tests (27) was taken in 2010, at the beginning of the study.

The numbers above are provided to emphasize that though the study is purposive in nature, its scope has proved random with regard to geographical location, date, age, sex and other factors. The sample size (n=67) is similar to that of Phase I (n=52). There are no known biases in the sample. No public or private funding was sought or obtained, no volunteer was paid, and no commercial interests were involved.

## Motives, Customer Profiles and Report Fulfillment

Typical in respect to approach, background, motives and process was Sharon Benning of Roseburg, Oregon. "My grandmother and her family always said we were Cherokee and I know that they were afraid of looking too brown and would always stay out of the sun," wrote Benning in a customer inquiry on April 4, 2010. "They didn't want to be connected to Native Americans at all. I feel like I have missed part of my heritage and would like to know if this story is true." After purchasing a Native American DNA Test on April 5, she received and returned her sample collection kit. Sorenson Genomics of Salt Lake City, our service lab at the time, released her results to us in a "Certificate of Mitochondrial DNA Analysis," dated April 29, 2010. Staff then fulfilled her Native American DNA Report, which was signed by Donald N. Yates, Ph.D., Principal Investigator, on June 16, 2010.

In it, the customer was informed of hypervariable region sector 1 and 2 or control region mutations, matched to other instances of her haplotype and provided with an evaluation of its origin, history and distribution.

Standard databases consulted were the Cambridge Mitochondrial DNA Concordance (version 2.0, 1998), Richards et al. (2000), mtDNA Population Database, incorporating "sequence data from the scientific literature and the GenBank and European Molecular Biology Laboratory (EMBL) genetic databases (Monson et al. 2002, also known as Swygdam and FBI) and Mitosearch, a free online research tool from Family Tree DNA, Houston, Texas.

One limitation of the study is that coding region polymorphisms were not investigated. Nor were HVR3 mutations available.

The basis for all testing and comparisons was the revised Cambridge Reference Sequence of the Human Mitochondrial DNA, described in Anderson et al. (1981) and Andrews et al. (1999).

In the evaluation section of the report on page 3, this customer (whose haplogroup proved to be H, a "non-Indian type") could read:

> Haplogroup H is not one of the six classic Native American female lineages A, B, C, E, and X, although it has been identified in the Cherokee, where it is usually ascribed to admixture with Europeans (Schurr). Haplogroups T, J, K and U have also been found in Southeastern tribes (data on file, Bolnick). The subject's particular haplotype, with one exception, only matches descendants of women born in North America. It is probable, although still ambiguous, then, that it is Native American or indigenous to North America. In conjunction with a family tradition that the maternal line was Native American, it should be considered Native American. The subject is encouraged to join Phase II of our Cherokee DNA Studies.

Benning volunteered for Phase II and became participant No. 43. Pending the completion of the project, she was issued a certificate that specified "Female Lineage: H, Prob. Native American."

Typical of participants who submitted previous mitochondrial results for evaluation and possible inclusion, in other words who tested with another lab, was Juanita Sims. Her niece, Elizabeth DeLand, contacted Dr. Yates in July of 2014 and succeeded in enrolling her aunt as participant No. 67—one of the last to be accepted in Phase II. "Aunt Juanita originally had the test done because her grandmother and great-grandmother spoke Cherokee and she is trying to find it in her DNA," wrote DeLand. "She is U5 haplogroup and was told it was not Native American." Sims became one of six U5's in the second phase, joining six others in Phase I. Additionally, 9 of 135 in the old Family Tree DNA Cherokee Project were U5's. Sims' form of U5 exhibited two unmatched single nucleotide polymorphisms (SNPs), 16291T and 272G, although it loosely matched four other U5's in the study.

Juanita Sims was originally tested by Family Tree DNA and thus received no certificate from DNA Consultants, as hers was a "report only." Family Tree DNA did not certify her mitochondrial line as Native American but as Eurasian. Under its rules at the time, "Native American mtDNA Haplogroups are A, B, C, D and X," *tout court*. The Federal Bureau of Indian Affairs, Cherokee Nation of Oklahoma, Eastern Band of Cherokee Indians and United Keetoowah Band adopt similar definitions for what they consider "true" American Indian DNA types. Our study made no presumptions about the ethnicity or affiliation of haplogroups.

In addition to cross-references within the project, all participants were compared to 135 mitochondrial records from the Cherokee DNA project begun in 2002 under the late Chief Joe White of the Central Band of Cherokee of Lawrenceburg, Tennessee. The project met with a large response and remained active until 2011 under longtime administrators June Hurd, Marcy Palmer and Holli Starnes. It was closed for unknown reasons in 2011. Members' records and administrators' names were all peremptorily removed. Its replacement project at Family Tree DNA shows 51 records, has the same name and lists Roberta Estes as administrator, but is not to be confused with the original project. Fortunately, the CBC generously gave access and granted permission to DNA Consultants to make a study of this valuable collection before it was taken offline.

## Summary of Phase II Results

To tabulate haplogroup assignments, 56 individuals from Phase II (83.5%) proved to have anomalous haplogroups and 11 (16.4%) "non-anomalous" A-D or X. These proportions are quite consistent with Phase I. In the project to date overall (n=119) there have been 101 anomalous types (85%) and 18 (15%) A-D or X. The CBC mitochondrial data (n=135) show 97% anomalous (H, I, J, K, L, T, U, W, no N or V) versus 3% non-anomalous (C, X, no A, B or D).

In Phase II as in Phase I, the largest haplogroup represented was T. This was the haplogroup of 13 individuals, or 19.4%, in Phase II (n=67). In

CHEROKEE DNA STUDIES

Phase I (n=52), there were 14 T's (26.9%). Project-wide (n=119), the T's number 27 and account for 22.7% of participants.

Haplogroup U made the second highest appearance. Phase II had 10 individuals (14.9%). There were rather more U's (13, or 25.0%) in Phase I, bringing the total for both phases to date to 23, or 19.3%.

H was represented by 11 subjects in Phase II (16.4%) and 4 (7.7%) in Phase II. The total number of H's in the project is 15 (12.6%). In the CBC data, H is the largest haplogroup, accounting for 40.0% of individuals. The top three haplogroups (T, U and H) thus covered about half of participants across the two phases of the project.

Second tier anomalous types in Phase II were J (6, or 9.0%), L (6, or 9.0%) and K (4, or 6%). These moderately well represented haplogroups (J, K, L) accounted for about 21.8% of all participants and about 25% of anomalous types. The leading haplogroups T, U and H made up an average 45% of the anomalous samples.

At the bottom frequencies, anomalous haplogroups with 2 or fewer individuals were I (3.0%), W (3.0%), N (1.5%) and V (1.5%). These minor types accounted for 7.6% of the anomalous results in Phase I. They did not appear in Phase I. Project-wide, they represent 5% of results, and combining with CBC, which had 1 I and 2 W's, the minor anomalous types amount to 3.5% of haplogroup assignments. In addition, there have been four unknown haplogroups, all in Phase I, totaling 1.6% of the greater sample (n=254).

| Haplogroup | n= | freq. |
|---|---|---|
| A-D, X | 11 | .164 |
| H | 11 | .164 |
| I | 2 | .030 |
| J | 6 | .090 |
| K | 4 | .060 |
| L | 6 | .090 |
| N | 1 | .015 |
| T | 13 | .194 |
| U | 10 | .149 |
| V | 1 | .015 |
| W | 2 | .030 |
| Total | 67 | 100% |

*Unique Single Nucleotide Polymorphisms*

In Phase II, comparisons in all readily available worldwide databases (chiefly the Cambridge Mitochondrial DNA Concordance, Monson et al. and Mitosearch) produced 55 rare, unreported or unique SNPs on HVR1 and HVR2. A list of these mitochondrial DNA mutations of interest along with the haplogroups in which they occurred is provided in the figure opposite. A number of these yield matches within the project, or by comparison with CBC tested individuals, but there remain many individuals with such rare mutations that they do not match anyone in the world or at best only partially match others in the three samples (n=254).

The results of our analysis seem to implicate a specific, coherent and diverse gene pool of ancient structure and origin among present-day Cherokee descendants. Such a characterization is supported by the distribution of female haplotypes; invariable pattern of matches leading to mitochondrial linkage in North America, often to persons identified as Native American, and sometimes even as Cherokee; occurrence of very old mutations; and presence of unique SNPs that match with others in the sample, if with anyone.

The role of admixture depends on what population one "privileges." From the perspective of entrenched models and theories of genetics, the finding of H or any of the other anomalous haplogroups in the Cherokee, no matter how many or in what proportions, should naturally be explained as the result of post-1492 European intermarriage or "random mating" with Native Americans. In the scheme "A-D and sometimes X," the presence of T, U, J or any other anomalous type in the Cherokee *must* be attributed to recent admixture.

## Unique and Rare SNPs

| np | Hg | Phase II | Phase I |
|---|---|---|---|
| 16086C | C, L | 20, 51 | |
| 16124C | H, L | 52 | |
| 16129C | U | 55 | 11, 12, 13, 14, 16 |
| 16147A | N | 2 | |
| 16153A | T | 22 | 34 |
| 16154C | N | 2 | |
| 16163G | T, L | 5, 6, 16 | 24, 25, 26, 32, 50 |
| 16166C | W | 30 | |

| | | | |
|---|---|---|---|
| 16182C | U, T, B | 23, 56, 58 | 2, 11, 16, 51, 52 |
| 16183C | U, T, B | 23, 56, 58 | 2, 11, 16, 51, 52 |
| 16187T | H, K, L, T | 34 | 31 |
| 16188G | H, L | 45 | |
| 16188T | T | 21, 59 | |
| 16189D | T, L | 51 | 24, 25, 26, 32, 36, 50 |
| 16192.1T | L | 51 | |
| 16193.1C | U, H, T | 14, 42, 44 | 6, 41 |
| 16193.2C | U, H, T | 14, 42, 44 | 6, 41 |
| 16209C | L, A, J | 47, 61 | |
| 16218T | T | 37 | |
| 16222T | J | 8, 63 | |
| 16231C | J, K | 35 | 17 |
| 16248T | N | 2 | |
| 16257T | T, H | 21, 32, 59 | |
| 16258G | T, U | 40 | |
| 16261T | J | 8, 63, unknown | 37 |
| 16265R | L | 52 | |
| 16295T | L | 47 | |
| 16309A | U, L | 36, 64 | 21 |
| 16316G | L, H | 51 | |
| 16324C | T | 1 | 50 |
| 16327T | L | 50 | |
| 16343G | A, H, U | 33, 36 | 21 |
| 16355T | N, L | 2, 51 | |
| 16357C | H | 43 | |
| 16391A | U, B, I | 4, 46, 48, 54, 60 | 18 |
| 16482G | H | 24 | |
| 16526A | U | 65 | |
| 143A | C, L | 20 | |
| 149.1C | L | 50 | |
| 150T | T, U, L | 22, 36, 40, 44 | 15, 16, 18, 34, 43 |
| 152D | J, L, Unknown | 35, 52 | 33 |

| | J, U, | | |
|---|---|---|---|
| 185A | Unknown | 3, 32, 41 | 4, 8, 15, 16, 36, 45 |
| 189G | H, W, L, J | 12, 30, 31, 47, 63 | 43 |
| 194T | D, H, W | 25, 30, 31, 62 | |
| 199C | N, I, L, U | 2, 48, 51, 52, 54 | 20 |
| 207A | J, W, L | 8, 30, 31, 54 | |
| 214R | H | 24 | |
| 234R | J | 32 | |
| 236C | I, T, L | 48 | 41 |
| 242T | J | 8 | |
| 244G | L | 51 | |
| 249D | C | 20, 66 | |
| 250C | I | 48, 54 | |
| 290D | C | 20, 66 | |
| 291D | C | 20, 66 | |
| 310.1T | J, K | 35, 53 | |

We have seen, however, that cracks and whole chasms have developed in the formerly tidy, tied-up-with-ribbons "peopling of the Americas" hypothesis. Even if anomalous population components are ascribed to admixture, though, we still want to determine what time or times in the past, and from what source or sources, did that admixture enter into the picture. The condition that mitochondrial-line admixture is female-mediated, not male-mediated or autosomal, demands that we have a source population with a great number of women. Moreover, the female genetic founders must approximate the distribution, age and diversity of haplogroups in the study population (Cherokee descendants in the strict female line).

Gene flow into Native American populations historically has been almost exclusively the result of privileged European men taking lesser status American Indian female partners. Very few European women in colonial times bore the babies of Native American men. In the conquest of North America, Indian male lines were preferentially reduced and extinguished, while Indian women often became the prizes of war or simply an inevitable choice in a world overflowing with single males. If Native American women had children with European men, their daughters and maternal granddaughters perpetuated Native American mitochondrial DNA.

It bears repeating that only women can pass down trans-generational mitochondrial markers. The corollary is also true: men cannot be responsible for mitochondrial ancestry. All present-day mitochondrial haplotypes must trace back to a woman, usually to a mother who had at least two daughters.

Can our admixture be explained as coming from other time frames and possibly non-European origins? If it is ancient and deep seated rather than recent, does it even make sense to regard it as admixture?

Of the eleven cases of classic Native American haplotypes, none knew beforehand they had an "approved" type. None belonged to a Federal tribe or lived on a reservation, although two (Michael Joseph Little Bear, Sr., participant 17, A, and Tino De la Luz Thundereagle, participant 10, D) had Native American names. The majority joined the project just like the others to confirm genealogical rumors or traditions of having an Indian ancestor somewhere in the family tree (usually a distant unknown grandmother). Their primary motive for testing, in other words, was to find the truth, not to qualify for tribal enrollment or benefits. Many came from Latino or Hispanic backgrounds. Among American Hispanic people, at least, Indian ancestry or identifying as *indio* has historically not been seen as a socially desirable family trait, though a nationwide trend in recent years has witnessed Hispanics using "American Indian" to identify themselves on census forms (Roth 2012; Decker 2011).

The results of the test, according to Jesse Montes, a third generation American (20, C), were both surprising and galvanizing. "I always had a gut feeling that I was Native American, and it was such a relief to find out I have a strong line of it from my mother. I am usually a very quiet person, but I am so excited about this that I want to be recognized. This is me!" His mitochondrial type had five unique SNPs and fully matched four Puerto Rican matrilines, and no other type in the world. His mother's maternal grandmother was born in the southern part of Puerto Rico near Ponce. Family traditions mentioned Taino in both his mother's and father's lines. "I am hoping to now be able to connect with some of my ancestors online on my mom's side to discover even more from the Native American DNA test," said Montes. "It has given me a golden key." (See interview by Teresa Panther-Yates, September 23, 2014, on DNA Consultants Blog, "Jesse Montes: Where Do I Come From.")

Leroy James (25, D) had a rare mitochondrial type that matched the descent of just three people worldwide (HVR1 only), Kitty Prince of Bear River Athabaskans (Mattole), an anonymous Caucasian American (Twygdam 69) and an unknown line in Mitosearch (7MP7K). Katherine Frances-Prince was the wife of James Prince of the Mattole and a member of the Bear River Band of Rohnerville Rancheria located south of Eureka, in Loleta, California.

*Kitty Prince in 1921. Native American Indian - Old Photos Facebook Page (public domain photos). Kitty Prince's DNA (haplotype D) matched that of participant 25.*

*Nancy Ward Statue. See Yates (2012) 107. Nancy Ward's DNA matched that of Patricia Gurule of Denver, Colorado. © D. Ray Smith. Used with permission.*

Patricia Gurule (66) was a walk-in client at Denver DNA Center, an affiliate of DNA Consultants. She knew "absolutely nothing" about her heritage before taking an autosomal ancestry test from us and then joining the Cherokee DNA project. Her type of C matched, among several New Mexican, Sonora, Zacateca and Chihuahua lines, the DNA of Nancy Ward, the Cherokee Beloved Woman and Tribal Mother (ca. 1738–1822 or 1824; Mitosearch record 8U6AP and CBC 115669, Allene Gay Kearney; see Yates [2012], Chapter 8, pp. 106-117 on Ward). It also matched Gayl A. Gibson Wilson, an enrolled member of the Cherokee Nation of Oklahoma and participant in our pilot project, Southern U.S. Native American DNA. Wilson, who is Wolf Clan, has traced her descent to Sarah Consene, a daughter of Dragging Canoe, born about 1800 in the Cherokee Nation East (see Yates [2012] 48-49, 158). This is evidently an ancient and widespread haplotype in Mexico and the United States, linked in Cherokee genealogies with the Wolf Clan, the traditional clan of war chiefs and most prevalent affiliation of Cherokees since the nineteenth century (Panther-Yates [2013] 4-10). In "Nancy Ward DNA" we have a clear example of exact correspondence between genetic matriline and a historically documented, genealogically proven, tribally specific clan.

*Haplogroup H: Thorn in the Side of Theory*

Before our studies, haplogroup H had been reported in small frequencies in surveys of the Cherokee but routinely explained as post-Columbian European admixture (Schurr 2000). As noted in "Anomalous Mitochondrial DNA Lineages" (2009), it is the quintessential European haplogroup, responsible for about 40% of European populations today (Sykes 2001). If our sample reflected non-native women settling among the Cherokee and not the genetic trace of pre-Columbian founder types, one would expect the H to dominate the scene. Instead, we found H in only 16% of the samples in Phase II and 8% in Phase I. In the CBC data, on the other hand, it occupied the top position with 40%—exactly as we would expect from a cross-section of European Americans.

There were 11 subjects with H in Phase II. These were about equally divided between haplotypes that were unmatched or rare, judged to be possibly ancient Native American on the strength of the matches (5), and haplotypes of very probable recent European origin, several of them in fact corresponding to the CRS (6). All of the latter failed to submit convincing genealogies linking their form of H with descent from a Native American woman. The former (9, 11, 12, 27, 33), on the other hand, invariably had unique, unmatched SNPs combined with compelling genealogies. For instance, Joel Kenneth Harris, Sr. (11) had several unique mutations, including the rare 16319A, also occurring in haplogroups D, A and J*. Add these 5 to 3 similar cases of H from Phase I and the true percentage of likely Native American H matrilines project-wide appears to be 6.7%.

James Eric Walker (9) was one of the strong cases. He started family research only in 2010. Born in North Carolina, the 57-year-old, 6-foot-five-inch-tall Walker lives in Mobile, Alabama. "There was a lot of so-called dark stories, as in my Jewish-Cherokee Walker and James lines," he said. "So my inner drive sent me into the world of paper trail ancestry . . . I found so much sadness with my mother's side, but the stories were true . . . DNA did in fact put my mother's line to bed." In autosomal testing he matched a Native American forensic population labeled Brazilian Belem Amazonians (n=325). His documented and published family tree verifies direct descent from Nancy Beacham, born about 1845 in Virginia, the wife of an emigrant born 1837 in Russia (both died in Mobile).

Mary England (12) had the reference series on sector 1 but a rare mutation in sector 2 that caused her to match only four users in Mitosearch, all of whom reported unknown origins for the type. She traces her maternal line securely to Sally Bingham, born 1833 in Knox County, Kentucky (and tentatively beyond). An intertwined line in her family tree goes back to Hatchet Grey Letty Durham, a reported full blood Cherokee, born in Wilkes County, Georgia, who died September 1, 1843 in Floyd County, Kentucky. Another Cherokee line she has assiduously traced zigzags back to Aaron Brock (Chief Red Bird, born 1727, died February 10, 1787, Clay County, Kentucky.

*Great-grandmother Beulah David Cane (married name deFleron) was born March 16, 1876, the daughter of Nancy Beacham, born about 1845 in Virginia.*

*Grandmother Beulah Alexandra deFleron (married name Soderquist) was born November 7, 1905 in Mobile, Alabama.*

*Participant 9, James Eric Walker, has H ancestry that may be Native American. His grandmother and great-grandmother were known as Seminole-Cherokee.*

A third H is Sharon Rebecca Chatterton (nee Toms). Her unique configuration of mutations brings up no one in the Cambridge Mitochondrial Concordance and produces only a very few exact matches in Mitosearch, all from North America (4U6K5, GECV7, Y9UQC). One of her maternal ancestors was a Frazier.

*Sharon Chatterton's grandmother Peramelia Vaughn was born September 22, 1901, in Coffee County, Tennessee. Her mother was Mary Eveline Frazier. After marriage she went by Amelia Vaughn Street. "She could unwind her long hair to the floor," says Chatterton. She died October 7, 1987.*

*68-year-old Sharon R. Chatterton, participant 27, of Lady Lake, Florida, is an H who traces her line to 3rd-great-grandmother Lucinda Gilley, born 1801 in Franklin County, Ga. Lucinda's mother was named Dorcas. She married Zachariah Bush in Rutherford County, Tennessee.*

The earliest female ancestor's identity in all these cases support the phenomenon I have described elsewhere of an Indian trader, typically Jewish or crypto-Jewish, marrying the daughter of a Cherokee chief or headman (Yates 2012:46ff.). The mitochondrial evidence tells us that H was part of the pre-contact Cherokee population. H did *not* enter the Native American haplogroup array with a colonial English woman marrying an Indian ("admixture"). While it is fashionable, and even politically ordained, to dismiss the Cherokee grandmother "myth," which can be traced to a single, suspect source in the literature, and which grew legs on the Internet so that it now seems unassailable, the uncomfortable truth seems to be that a goodly number of families who do not deserve to be called "Indian wannabes" have a bona-fide Cherokee matriarch corresponding approximately to that description in their family tree (Martin 1996).

## T Haplotype Diversity and Sephardic Motifs

Our initial report remarked on the high incidence of haplotype T and compared its frequency to that of Egypt (23.4%). Phase II produced T's amounting to 19.4% of haplogroups in the sample, bringing its overall presence project-wide (n=117) to 23.1%, near the proportion reported in Iraqi and Iranian Jews, 24.4% (n=217, see Bedford, Table 4). Compare the high level in our study, Egypt and Iraqi and Iranian Jews to the much lower frequencies of T in Northwest Spain (6.9%), Portugal (9.2), Ashkenazi Jews (4.8), Sephardic Jews (11-14%), Great Britain and Ireland (9.1), North Central Italy (13.7), Western Saudi Arabia (12.5), Mitosearch (mostly U.S., 9.1) and National Geographic (8.7), and the T-intensive populations can be seen to surpass all the others by a factor of 2 to 5. On the basis of this comparison, we can safely call the T an aggregate among the anomalous Cherokees Middle Eastern in scale and importance.

In 2012, attention focused on T5, renamed T2e, and Felice Bedford of the University of Arizona published her article, "Sephardic Signature in Haplogroup T Mitochondrial DNA" (2012). "It was found that the rare motif [in subhaplotype T2e] belonged only to Sephardic descendents (Turkey, Bulgaria), to inhabitants of North American regions known for secret Spanish–Jewish colonization, or were consistent with Sephardic ancestry [sic]," Bedford wrote of the new Sephardic signature, T2e5. She dated the founder of the signature back to "one woman from Iberia who lived between 500 and likely 2000 years ago." So were there any instances of the new Sephardic signature, defined by mutations 16114T and 16192T, in our anomalous Cherokees? No, unsurprisingly, since Bedford found only 12 in an exhaustive search of world databases, but there were two cases of the parent sub-subhaplotype T2e, defined by mutations 16153A and 150T. They are Cheryl Green (Phase I participant 34) and Evie Nagy (Phase II participant 22). And as Bedford reminds us, "Suspicion of a signature in a minority ethnic group can be initiated with as little as a haplotype match in two unrelated individuals from that group."

The sheer diversity of T types in Cherokee descendants, just like their high ratio, would seem to point to a source in the Middle East, not Europe.

Although the phylogeny of T subclades and nomenclature is still somewhat unsettled (Pike et al. 2010), the prevalence and absence of subhaplogroups across different studies show strong similarities between the Cherokee sample and Iraqi and Irani Jews. Thus, T2b, which occurs at an almost non-existent level in Iraq, and reaches a high of 4.2% in Great Britain, is completely lacking in the Cherokee sample. T2e (6.9%) has a relatively high presence, as in the Ottoman Sephardim, Western Saudi Arabia and Italy. T1 (5.8%) is about the same as in Iraqi and Irani Jews (5.1%). Finally, there is a large amount, one-third of T subclades, categorized as T*. Their prevalence could be read as a sign of the antiquity of the Cherokee sample, with many T types which are common in the source population, but which have died out, not survived or have escaped being studied in standard contemporary genetic surveys. This inference is strengthened by the numerous unmatched T mutations, although a caveat should be added that the branches and sub-branches of T, as already noted, have not been completely dissected. Some of the T* haplotypes may be falsely assigned or need re-assigning.

Let it be noted here additionally that many of the T's in Phase II volunteered information they were Jewish by faith and/or descent.

## Tara in the New World

Kathleen Rogalla of Panama City, Fla. (49) joined the project in July 2010, after learning family secrets from her 92-year-old mother) and receiving "disappointing" results from other companies. Of one, she wrote, " My test results came in a few days ago and I was shocked and dismayed by the results. They have me as 100% European with no chance of being Native at all. That also means that there is little chance of being matched with others who have Native blood." Subsequent testing revealed "a trace" of Asian ancestry. Her maternal line traces to Elizabeth Hensley of Stafford County, Va. But her genealogy on file with the project also identifies Deborah Cook(e), wife of William Chisholm (born 1720 in Amelia County, Va.) as her remote ancestor in an unbroken female line. Amy or Annie, no last name, was Deborah's mother. Both Deborah and her husband were associated with the Cherokee in historical documents. Rogalla descends from their daughter Sarah, who married Thomas Tinsley. Another daughter, Margaret, married her first cousin John Chisholm, and their daughter, Annie, married John Walling of the well-known long hunter family in Tennessee. A son of William and Deborah Chisholm, John D., was a friend and advisor to Doublehead.

According to Rogalla's research, "A descendant's wife, Mary Ann Roberts filed an application to the Dawes Commission on behalf of her children. They were rejected. She said 'My children have Indian blood that comes from their father Eli Roberts who gets his Indian blood from his mother Joanna Tinsley (daughter of Thomas Tinsley and Sarah Chisholm) and her from her mother(Sarah Chisholm). Her mother was the sister of Absolom and William Chisholm whose names should appear on the Old Settler's Rolls west of the Mississippi River.'"

Another excellent witness for Cherokee enrollment, B.W. Alberty, testified: "I am a resident of Tahlequah, Cherokee Nation. I met Dave and William Chisholm near Belview Texas and they lived there on the [illegible] and I was introduced to them as living Cherokee's by George Harnage and also by William Harnage that is I know about them said they were kin of old Tom Chisholm of the Cherokee Nation (Thomas Chisholm was the interim 3rd Chief of the Western Cherokee Nation in Arkansas). Hornage told me they were relatives of old Tom Chisholm. That was the year of 1852 or 53. I would judge Dave Chisholm to be about 45 years old and William I think was the younger of the two."

John Ratling Gourd testified: "I am a resident of Tahlequah District, Cherokee Nation and am about 65 years old. I was acquainted with Absolom and William Chisholm when they lived low down in Georgia. This was about the time the Cherokee came to this country. They were among the first who left country and came west. They were Cherokees by blood in at least what was looked upon as such. I first saw Absolom and William Chisholm at a council on the fork called by John Ross in regard to the division of some money. These parties voted to not divide the money. They looked like Cherokee's and appeared to be half or three-fourths. I saw William Tinsley several times. I understand he married into the Chisholm family."

These historical accounts are given here in detail to document the early Cherokee affiliation of the line. More could be added. Suffice it to say that the Chisholms and all their marriage partners were well known to Cherokee leaders from the 1760s on, first in the East and later, continuously in the West. The famous Chisholm Trail was named for the family. All the names are well documented in Cherokee and Melungeon genealogies, as well as U.S. Indian treaties, chiefs-lists and agency records. If we estimate the earliest named Cherokee's birthdate to be around 1700, we are in a period when the first intermarriages between English settlers and Indian women took place. It is unlikely that Amy or Annie was the daughter of an English woman, and the line she founded was "admixture." There is every reason on genealogical grounds to regard her T* haplotype as Cherokee, not Eurasian.

Amy-Annie apparently produced many direct descendants in the United States and Canada and had distant genetic cousins in Europe. Her prolific form of T* (16126C  16294T 16296T  16519C 73G 263G 315.1C) exactly matched individuals with origins in England, Cornwall, Quebec, France, Mississippi, California, North Carolina, Russia, Texas and Florida. Many of the haplotype assignments and origins were "unknown." As it turned out, they also matched Timothy Joseph Benjamin (18), an adoptee residing in Alva, Florida, who subsequently was able to have the Catholic  charity unseal his adoption records, and who learned that he was born in Burlington, Vermont, his given name at birth Joseph David Ward.

The verdict in Rogalla's report stated:

> Although not one of the classic Native American lineages (A, B, C, D, and X ˗ Schurr), T has been discovered in the Cherokee, Choctaw and other East Coast Indians (data on file; see DNA Consultants Blog, "Anomalous Mitochondrial DNA Lineages in the Cherokee"). Most investigators attribute this to recent European admixture. But T haplotypes without exact Old World matches (we exclude T2 matches from consideration) could just as well be considered Native American if as prevalent as the subject's is in North America. The majority of the T* matches in Mitosearch are possibly Native American in our estimation. In the presence of a genealogical tradition of the female line being Native American the haplotype should therefore be pronounced Native American. The matches in Mitosearch to Tennessee, North Carolina and surrounding states point to the Cherokees, although matches in Canada suggest a Canadian indigenous woman (where T has also been identified). The T* matches that are truly European (such as V2DER, Russia) may represent a remnant of the original Middle Eastern lineage that survived in Europe, but the largest expansion of the lineage was clearly in North America.

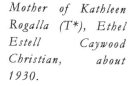

*Mother of Kathleen Rogalla (T\*), Ethel Estell Caywood Christian, about 1930.*

*Karen Worstell's grandmother Odessa Shields Cox (shown with her husband William M. Cox and Karen's mother Ethel as a baby about 1922) was born about 1904 in Indian Territory. She was known as Dessie. "My mother cut off all connection with her own mother sometime before I was born," says Worstell. "My grandmother has strikingly Indian features and I do wonder if perhaps she was an adopted Indian child."*

*Karen Worstell (56) tested as having a rather widely distributed T2c that matched Cherokees on official rolls, even though T is universally considered a non-Indian type. "There was tremendous secrecy about anything related to my Indian background," says Worstell. My grandfather used to call me 'squaw,' which would infuriate my mother."*

Ward is a common Cherokee surname. A T2 who also happened to have the birth name of Timothy Benjamin (18) was Deann Ward of Vincennes, Indiana (19). Ward traced her unbroken female descent to a 3rd-great-grandmother, Olive Thompson, born about 1800, died 1850 in Lincoln County, Tenn. Her parents are unknown. Olive Thompson married Garrett Merrill of Rowan County, North Carolina, a locale bordering on the Cherokee. Ward's great-grandmother, Emily Roper (a surname common on Cherokee rolls), was born in Tennessee, February 19, 1848, the daughter of Joseph Roper.

Karen Freeman Worstell (57) is a risk management professional in Gig Harbor, Washington, who wrote on April 24, 2010, "I just learned of the potential link between Cherokee and Eastern European Jews this morning. I was told I am Cherokee by my mother, and Scottish/Irish on my father's side. I am also deeply involved in the Messianic Jewish movement." Her rather widely distributed T2c haplotype exactly matched two participants in Phase I of the DNA Cherokee Project. Patrick Pynes, a professor of indigenous studies in Arizona, was a descendant on Mitosearch, traced the line to Mildred Gentry (1792-1852) and Nancy Gentry Little (b. 1801). "According to oral tradition, Nancy Gentry was of Cherokee descent," he wrote for the record. "She moved with her family from Tennessee to Clark County, Arkansas, in 1817. During the 1830s she lived with her husband James Little and children in Washington County, Arkansas. Several of her neighbors were of documented Cherokee descent or had family connections with documented Cherokees. Nancy's mother's name was possibly 'Delilah Clark.' Her father was likely Tyre Gentry of South Carolina."

Worstell says her mother passed away after a lengthy illness at the age of 90 and kept her family origins a secret. "Once when I asked her why, she said, 'I want you to have friends to play with.'" Worstell never met her maternal grandparents but always heard stories of Cherokee relatives. One of her ancestors was on the Trail of Tears. She has published an elaborate family tree on Ancestry.com but continues, like Patrick Pynes, to find the earliest link. Her maternal line research comes to an end with direct maternal ancestor Catherine Reed, born in 1776 in Loudoun County, Va. She married John Carlin on November 13, 1799, in Harrison County, (West) Virginia and died in Barbour County. Several of the figures she has identified in her research were labeled as mulatto in local records. Her mother's paternal grandmother was Choctaw. Says Worstell, " I don't know if I am chasing a myth or not."

### Haplogroups U, U2, U5 and K

Haplogroup U is very old and deep seated in Eurasian populations. Its top-level subclades can all be seen as haplogroups in their own right. Those uncovered in this phase of our study consist of U, U2, U3, U5 and K (formerly U8). There were no examples of U4, characteristic especially of Balto-Slavic countries and Finland; U6, associated with Berbers; U7 primarily from the East Mediterranean to India; or U9, spread from Ethiopia and the Arabian Peninsula to Pakistan.

The complex mega-haplogroup was born on the edge of Northeast Africa and Arabia some 60,000 or more years ago, when the first Homo Sapiens exited the African continent. Complex human societies began with U. In Europe, where U types today (11%) are the second most common after H (40+%), U was the first lineage to encounter and interbreed with the declining Neanderthals. U was identified as a minor haplotype in surveys of Cherokee and other Southeastern Indians (Schurr, Bolnick), although its presence was attributed to "admixture." It has also reported in Mexican Indians (Green). U2 was the mitochondrial signature of a link between archaic Europeans and modern-day Native Americans discovered in the 24,000 year-old Ma'lta skeleton whose DNA was recently sequenced from near Lake Baikal (Raghavan et al. 2014).

Vivian A. Santos-Montanez (14), a Hebrew School teacher in DeLand, Fla., took a combination of Jewish and Native American DNA tests for herself and several family members. Her mitochondrial mutation set produced only one exact match in the world: Mercedes Rivera-Rivera, born about 1915 in Utuado, Puerto Rico. Based on family traditions, Santos believes her maternal line could have come from Cherokees sold into slavery during the Spanish colonial period who joined Taino Indians living in the remote mountainous region of her native Puerto Rico.

U5, U5a and U5b samples include 5 participants from Phase II and 6 from Phase I, totaling 11 for the project, the bulk of all U's. U5 is of interest because of its important role in the peopling of Europe (Malyarchuk et al 2010). It is the oldest mtDNA lineage in Europe which is human, with an estimated age estimated at 50,000 years ago, greatly predating the expansion of agriculture. In the new three-fold scheme of

European ancestry, U5 is the largest contributor to the component known as WHG or Western European Hunter Gatherers (Lazaridis et al. 2014). U5 is also found in significant levels, however, in the Middle East, Northern Africa and Central Asia.

Elizabeth DeLand (67), who tested her mother Juanita L. Sims, a U5a1, had an unreported set of mutations in the Cambridge Concordance, but matched five persons in Mitosearch, all three different haplogroup assignments, U5 (Ireland), U5a1* (Alabama, Ireland) and Unknown (Ireland). DeLand reported that her grandmother and great-grandmother spoke Cherokee. The mother of Pamela Bowman, Juanita Wilson (65), was another U5a1, with no exact matches on both sectors. Her rare/unique 16526A was reported in a single case by Van Oven and has been discussed sporadically on Internet boards. Bowman is a member of the CBC. She shares her rare SNP with William Zachary Dylan Sizemore (179989), who traces his line to Lucinda Lusk, born January 31, 1823. The SNP also appears in the U5a1a* mutations of Dr. Bruce Dean (Phase I, no. 19), whose genealogy goes back to Jane Rose, a member of the Eastern Band of Cherokee Indians, and who matched Marie Eastman, born 1901, Indian Territory.

Turning now to U2, we have an interesting U2e haplotype in Carol Myers Rymes, a genealogist, Melungeon descendant (her uncle is a Sizemore) and CBC member who has pursued her mitochondrial line for several years. In Mitosearch, her single match was a descendant claiming descent from Bridget Garrity, born about 1816 in Ireland. Rymes also matched her own record in CBC data, plus Brian Voncannon, a Williams descendant. Rymes has been active in restoring the Occoquan Burying Ground in Prince William County, Va., and wrote a book on the descendants of Samuel Rymes. There were six U2e's in Phase I.

With Charlotte Walker (36), U3, we have an exotic haplotype that seems to match only Native American lines. U3 is a minor haplogroup centered around the Black Sea, with a strong presence today in the northeastern part (Colchis, Scythia, Transcaucasus, the Steppes). It could be related to ancient Indo-Europeans. There were two exact matches in Mitosearch, one from Alvina (or Elwina), born about 1820 in South Carolina and thought to be Native American, and another from Sarah Elizabeth Snyder, born 1828, origin unknown. The information from all three congeners is incomplete and uncertain. And as textual transmission experts say, "One witness, no witness." Participant 36 is the only instance of U3 to date. There are two examples in CBC data.

K (formerly H8) is an important Jewish haplogroup, and it has a small, but significant presence across all datasets. There were 2 (3.0%) in Phase I and 4 (nos. 13, 29, 34, 53, 7.7%) in Phase II. The CBC data shows 11 K's (8.1%). Haplogroup K is represented by 17 samples in a grand total of 252 participants (6.7%), a lower incidence compared both to European populations (10%) and Ashkenazi Jews (32-50%).

Three of our K's (Ashley Nielsen 29, Earl Dulaney 34, Ann Pyle 53) had such rare haplotypes, all with unique, partly overlapping mutations, that no exact matches could be found in the databases. It was felt that this specificity spoke for types that died out and were no longer reported in the rest of the world but survived in an exotic North American population, where they had been implanted in the remote past. By comparison, the chances of a large number of unmatched modern types dating to European admixture in the Colonial window of history were estimated to be slim.

## Major Jewish Haplogroup J

Haplogroup J, termed Jasmine in the scheme of Oxford Ancestors, is believed to have originated in the Old Near East and to have moved north and west into Europe, especially after the spread of agriculture beginning 5000-3000 BCE. It is found throughout Europe with particularly high concentrations around the eastern Baltic Sea and Russia, as well as in Bedouins and Yemeni, where it reaches frequencies of 25% or higher. J is a major Jewish female lineage (Thomas 2002), being a strong maternal contributor to Jewish, Arab, Greek and Italian populations. J is also the apparent carrier of congenital longevity and a host of "Jewish" diseases that are just beginning to be understood by medical science.

There were 6 J's in Phase II (nos. 3, 8, 32, 35, 41 and 63, composing 9%), 4 in Phase I and 17 in the CBC data, making for an aggregate of 10.7%, somewhat less than the level for the Middle East and Europe (12%).

There were multiple matches between participants. An example is James Richard Stritzel (8), whose form of J1b1 matched No. 63 on HVS1 with several mismatches on HVS2. Stritzel's grandmother, Eunice Mable, was adopted out of the Mohawk tribe and given the last name Ahern abt. 1900. His rare haplotype is similar to five J's reported in Phase I. Of these, Nadine Rosebush's type is not matched anywhere in the world. In other words, these J types seem to be specific to the micro-population in which they are found today and are not widespread. One might make an argument of inferred ancestry as follows, although other interpretations are also possible. The germ line and enclosing population may have originated in classical antiquity. Instances survived to the present in North America only because they were part of the discrete and continuous existence of a "people." This "people" had spread intact by discontinuous, long-distance migration from its point of origin, where in the course of centuries its presence became extinct.

## Rarest of the Rare: I, N, V and W

Turning now to the four haplogroups that first cropped up in Phase II, we have one or two individuals each with I (54 Swinney, 48 Francisco), N (2 Kellam), V (39 Ponder) and W (30 Carpenter, 31 Sponenburgh). Percentages, phylogeny and phylogeographic patterns are probably not meaningful. Let us note, however, that one of the I's (54) had no matches anywhere, while the other (48) matched Dicie Gray, born 1828 in North Carolina. The sole example, Norma Kellam, N1A, traces her mitochondrial line to Roanoke, Virginia. She had several unique SNPs and matched only a handful of other people. In medieval times, N gave birth to one of the four major Ashkenazi Jewish founder lineages, probably in the Rhine Basin.

*James Stritzel (8) was told by the first labs he went to that in "no way" could his DNA be Native American. His mother's line, however, was confirmed as Cherokee (or Mohawk) despite being an unusual type. Here the Manchester, Wash. resident carves a Deer Pipe after spending part of last summer training under a sixth-generation Lakota Nation Pipe Maker.*

*Norma Kellam (2) of Westminster, Calif. has maternal line ancestry in Virginia and matched only five Mitosearch users, two of whom also traced to Virginia. The other three pointed to Tennessee, Mississippi and unknown origins. Her maternal grandmother was Daisy Brooks (b. 1894, m. Cronk) and great-grandmother, Nancy Ann Tingery (m. John Sellars Brooks).*

## African L Haplotypes

Surprisingly, there were 6 L haplotypes in Phase II (9.0%). In Phase I, there were 3 (5.8%), and the CBC data include 7 (5.2%), bringing the total across all datasets to 16, or 6.3%. The most common haplogroup was L3, the oldest African lineage, associated with and most common today in East Africa. If the African DNA were the simple effect of gene flow into the Cherokee from historical-era slaves and freemen, one would expect West African centered L2 to dominate the results, as this is far and away the most prevalent type carried by African Americans (as much as 50%). L3, on the other hand, is characterized by a relatively greater presence in circum-Mediterranean and European populations. According to one authority, "L3 is more related to Eurasian haplogroups than to the most divergent African clusters L1 and L2" (Maca-Meyer et al. 2001). Sub-Saharan African L lineages account for 10% of the population in Saudi Arabia, and L3 occupies a prominent position (72% of them; Abu-Amero et al. 2008). It has also been observed in Slavic or East European populations, especially among Ukrainian Jews, possibly vestigial admixture from ancient slaves in the Roman Empire and Islam. L3 accounts for only one-third of L lineages within Africa.

We will highlight three L3's. Shelia Maria Wilson (52), who lives in New

Mexico, has 20 mutations on mitochondrial control regions 1 and 2, the highest number we have ever studied. Generally, the more mutations, the more ancient the type. There was, however, not even a remote match in databases, making hers a unique type reported only in North America. Wilson knows her genealogy only as far back as her great grandmother, Mrs. Julia Adams. The surname came from the Georgia slave master of her father Harry Adams. Harry, who called himself "Mali blasta," was kidnapped in Mali as a pre-teen shortly before the Civil War. Shelia's mother Willie Mae Adams, born in 1927, remembered seeing the whelps on her grandfather's back where he was whipped. "I had been informed by some relatives," writes Wilson, "that my great-grandmother was at least part Native American and White." Another L3 (47, Lovancia Francisco) matched a historical Native woman, A Te Anu, Muscogee.

*Willie Mae Adams was born June 2, 1904 in Butler County, Ga. She was the youngest girl of seven children. Her mother was a mix of black, Caucasian and Native American.*

*Shelia Maria Wilson (participant 52) carries an old and rare form of L3 that apparently left no descendants except for her and her family.*

Gregory Damon Haynes (no. 16) has another unique and otherwise unreported L3 haplotype, with a SNP found in no other person (16163G). His father had a rare American Indian Q haplotype with relatives on two Indian census rolls. His maternal grandmother was Lily Marie Benjamin (Blythe), born October 15, 1922 in North Carolina. Could his maternal line have been Cherokee? The question remains open, as it is extremely difficult to investigate the lines of ex-slaves.

## Haplogroup Distribution versus Europe and Other Populations, Based on Richards et al. 2000.

| Hg | N= | % | Europe | Egypt | Middle East | Eastern Med. |
|---|---|---|---|---|---|---|
| T | 27 | 23.1 | 8.4 | 23.4 | 11.9 | 6.0 |
| U | 23 | 19.7 | 22.2 | 7.8 | 26.3 | 16.4 |
| H | 15 | 12.0 | 53.5 | 14.0 | 36.8 | 47.9 |
| J | 11 | 9.4 | 9.5 | 6.3 | 11.4 | 12.7 |
| L | 9 | 7.7 | | 15.6 | | |
| K | 6 | 5.1 | 5.8 | 3.1 | 6.2 | 3.6 |
| I | 2 | 1.5 | | 4.7 | | |
| N | 1 | 0.8 | | 6.3 | | |
| Tot. | n=117 | ~80% | n=1021 | n=64 | n=2736 | n=165 |

## Conclusions

If we are to accept our sample as valid, several salient parameters of the study population labeled "Anomalous Cherokees" seem to leap out from the table of haplogroup frequency comparisons.

1) The first striking feature is the high amount of T lineages evident in Cherokee descendants. T is the leading haplogroup (23.1%), with a frequency on a par with modern-day Egyptians (23.4%) and Arabs (24.4%). That is more by a factor of 4 than the East Mediterranean, three times that of Europe and the United States and twice that of the Middle East. T is thus a defining mark of Cherokee ancestry. Where did it come from? We can safely rule out recent European admixture. As we have discussed again and again, there was no available source for a huge, sudden influx of female-mediated Middle Eastern DNA on the American frontier. Even Sephardic Jews (11-14%), many of whom were also Indian traders, could hardly have accounted for such admixture. Moreover, had it occurred in the colonial period or more recently the diversity, age and unique characteristics of the T haplotypes would not have yielded the patterns noticed in this paper. Most T's would have matched people in the Old World and we would simply be looking at an effect of migration. Instead, we have a North American branch of T with peculiar SNPs which is evidently a cross-section of a very old population originating in the Old World. The thesis of Donald

Yates' study of Cherokee history is that an expedition of Ptolemaic Egyptians and others in the 3rd century BCE served as the nucleus of settlers that became the Eshelokee (Cherokee). If this historical model is applicable, there was a severe bottleneck of DNA accompanying the establishment of the Cherokee, with many founder effects—something suggested by the frequent cross-matches, high degree of interrelatedness and clustering of types in our data.

2) The second glaring statistic is the relatively low amount of H (12%), which is the leading haplogroup in Europeans (~50%). If the admixture were attributable to European women in the colonial period we would expect it to be much higher. Again, the level is about the same as Egypt.

3) The third observation we can make is the similarity of haplogroups strongly associated with Jews (J, K at 14.5%) to European levels (15.3%). At whatever time period admixture occurred, whether in ancient or modern times, Jewish women likely formed part of it. Men cannot pass mitochondrial DNA. Like other contributions to the gene pool, J and K came from a feeder population or sub-population that had families on board. In other words, they could not have been the result of shipwrecked Portuguese sailors, Arab or Jewish merchants, soldiers or any of the other suspects often trotted forth. Judging also from the uniqueness of JK types and their diversity, we are looking at a Jewish signal deeply embedded in the structure of Cherokee populations.

4) L haplogroup frequency (7.7%) is about half that of Egypt (15.6%). East African-centered L3 predominates, not West and Central African-oriented L1 and L2 haplogroups, which are twice as abundant, and which define the majority of slaves and their descendants in the New World. We are unsure how to read this. It may be that in the nature of things, African American lines were under-sampled. Federal regulations and the controversy embroiling the Cherokee Nation of Oklahoma in their on-again-off-again rejection of freedmen as citizens might have served as a disincentive to blacks' testing their DNA. Blacks are also hampered in tracing genealogies, unlike whites or Hispanics.

Certainly, however, our data suggests there has always been a constant African component in Cherokee DNA, one that resembles North and East African populations rather than West and Central Africans. Beginning around the start of the Common Era, the Bantu expansion swamped all Africa with L1 and L2 genes. A high proportion of L3 could mean that admixture with the Cherokee predates that event. We have records of Phoenician colonization efforts as massive as the "30,000 desert-dwelling Moors from the hinterland of Carthage" in about 500 BCE (Yates 2012, p. 32). Mining operations then and now used a large number of women slaves, who were prized for their agility in negotiating small openings as well as their becoming inured to cruel conditions (this is still the norm in Egypt, India and Bolivia, though the workers are no longer legally considered slaves; see Del Mar 1902). The clan that specifically included black-skinned people among the Cherokee was called the Blue Paint or Panther (Ani-Sahoni; see Panther-Yates 2013, pp. 30-31). It was related to the original (Red) Paint Clan, named for the Paint People, or Phoenicians (Ani-Wodi).

5) Finally, we might remark on the minor (I, N, V, W), unknown (I 33, 36, 37, 40; II 33) and missing haplogroups (G, HV, pre-HV, M and other Asian types). I, N, V and W are minimally adduced in Egyptian, Palestinian, Arab and Turkish populations. They round out our picture of the original genetic inputs to the Cherokee, showing that the source of "admixture" was deep seated and diverse. The Cherokee population structure seems to be rather an effect of long-distance travel and conquest than of gradually developing encroachment, migration or genetic drift.

Admixture, just like the word "anomalous," is a relative term. Its use depends on one's perspective. Geneticists, as we have seen, tend to privilege a rather narrow body of recent U.S. and European scientific literature. It is time to de-colonize the human past and open our eyes to the diversity of American Indian peoples. The personal genealogies of over one hundred Cherokee descendants contradict popular and professional received wisdom about Indian nations.

## Addendum: Begging the Question

For science to be separated from pseudoscience, its findings must obey the rule of falsifiability. This term has often been misunderstood, but what it means according to philosophers of science is that empirical statements such as "All swans are white" must be "such that to verify them and to falsify them must both be logically possible" (Popper 2005). Otherwise, as Wolfgang Pauli famously remarked, an argument "is not only not right, it is not even wrong."

In plain language, we could say that so far from barking up the wrong tree, that dog don't hunt.

"All swans are white" is a falsifiable statement. It can be tested by observation and shown to be generally true (though false in cases of black swans). But such statements as "All American Indians descend from haplogroups A-D and sometimes X" is not falsifiable. Neither this generalization nor its converse is testable in any experiential way. No amount of corollaries, exceptions to the rule or qualifications will fix it.

"A woman of haplogroup A (or B, or X, or T, or W) founded a Cherokee matriline," on the other hand, is falsifiable. It is scientifically true in certain individual cases and datasets, as claimed in the present study ("experiment"), just as it is scientifically false in other instances.

Much of the surmises of science about the peopling of the Americas can be said to be on the wrong track. It can neither be proved true nor decided false that ancestors of American Indians crossed a hypothetical Bering land bridge at some time in the unknown past. Let us hope that the growing demand for truth from amateur roots-seekers and test takers will force professionals to predicate their research agendas and phrase their findings more carefully in the future. If they do not, they will be failing the public trust. There is also a need for science reporters and writers to frame their stories more responsibly. We have always said, "There are Indians and Indians."

# 7 A CASE STUDY IN GENETIC GENEALOGY

Franz Kafka wrote fiction acknowledged to be among the masterpieces of world literature. One of the more memorable works of the Jewish Austro-Hungarian insurance clerk is "The Metamorphosis." It tells the story of a man who wakes one morning to find he has been transformed into a cockroach. His mother and sister come after him with a broom.

When I first learned that both my mother and father's people were of Jewish ancestry—and what is more, Jewish-Cherokee descent—I felt I had entered a Kafkaesque fable. The cosmos had played an enormous joke that I was finally "getting" at the age of fifty. I was mad at my parents, aunts, uncles and grandparents for not cueing me in before. I confronted my mother, whose only response was, "So, what of it?" This I took as a tacit admission of complicity in the cover-up. My older sister and others, however, were ready to sweep the hyphenated monstrosity I had become back under the carpet.

When I first awoke to this peculiar heritage, I wrote a genealogy article for an e-mail discussion group on Rootsweb called "Indian Tribes Southeast." The title of the piece was "Seven Generations of Cherokee Blood." One of my conclusions after studying my personal family history was that part-Cherokee consistently married part-Cherokee. Even when the marriage partner came from far away and outside the other's locale, they seemed to pair with others of similar admixture, effectively conserving the bloodline. Rather than being thinned down by out-marriage, Cherokee heritage on both my mother's side and my father's—the Coopers and the Yateses—remained fairly constant at about one-quarter from generation to generation. A quarter-blood Cooper would marry a quarter-blood Blevins and their children would all be quarter-bloods. I postulated that the effect was not accidental or random.

Before the advent of DNA testing I computed a variable degree of Cherokee ancestry in my ancestors. I saw that many of my Jewish forefathers and foremothers exaggerated or discounted their admixture with the Indians, depending on the local historical circumstances. Nearly all of them hid their Jewishness under the smokescreen of crypto-Judaism.

How far I had come since that day in 1993 when an older cousin of mine told me the story of how my Cherokee great-great-grandmother Elisabeth Yates stole the cattle back from Gen. Sherman! That was my father's line. Lawden Yates died in 1978. He seemed to be a minimum of a quarter blood, mixed Cherokee and Creek. But he never advertised the fact. My mother was supposed to have all the Indian blood. She put it all on her maternal grandmother Goble. I subsequently found out that there was just as much Cherokee in Mother's paternal line, the Coopers. My grandfather J. W. Cooper and my grandmother Palestine (yes) Goble were double first cousins four times removed, doubly descended from Chief Black Fox. Descendants were still gathered around Creek Path, Black Fox's capital, and Coffeetown (Langston), where the Gobles lived.

Wherever I looked, I found Cherokee, generation after generation. My investigations suggested I was the sixth or seventh generation since the last of the full bloods lived.

In a crude way of reckoning, I believed four out of thirty-two of my ggg-grandparents were full blood Cherokee, making me one-eighth. I found only one ancestor proven to be non-Indian: Louis Graben, from Germany. He was at least Jewish. Besides Cherokee, the overwhelming element, there was a slight mixing with Creek, Cheraw, Saponi, Mattaponi, Choctaw, Chickahominy and various Algonquian tribes.

An obvious questions was if there was a pattern of Cherokee or part-Cherokee marrying another Cherokee, how to account for it—particularly when spouses might have concealed or even been unaware of their Indian blood? All lived in a predominantly white society in Georgia, Alabama and Tennessee. The chances of consistently selecting another Cherokee in the area were fairly slim. Most children in neighboring families married non-

Indians and Indian identification quickly disappeared.

A generalization many make is that when the blood degree drops below one-quarter there is a tendency no longer to identify as Indian, marry another Indian or raise your children with knowledge of the culture. One reason for the magic figure of one-fourth is that most of us do not interact with family members older than grandparents. In a simple metric, a mixed blood with one Indian grandparent is thus considered to be 1/4 Indian.

During Generation One (pre-1820) when the official U.S., state and local government policy was to extinguish Indian claims and bodily remove anyone as much as one-eighth degree native blood west of the Mississippi, the only Indians who managed to remain in the East kept a very low profile. Today, in Generation Six (Self-Determination), Indians are legally and openly asserting their own identity and culture. As long as the Indian Wars lasted, until 1889, it was dangerous to be an Indian. My Coopers survived because they lived in a backwoods area on Sand Mountain straddling county lines and state lines. Still, the government managed to repossess my great-grandfather's land in 1892 and innumerable cousins drifted to Indian Territory.

The Cooper tradition of being descended from chiefs was passed from Isaac Cooper to his son Isaac, to Isaac's son William, to grandson Peter Cooper, who testified to this effect on his Eastern Cherokee Application naming a Cherokee judge as a character witness. Peter's wife, Lindy Sizemore, was the carrier of the Sizemore secrets. She was a medicine woman and midwife, present at the birth of my mother October 22, 1918 on Sand Mountain in north Alabama.

*My Thirty-Two Great-Great-Great-Grandparents*
James B. Yates, part-Indian (Saponi-Cheraw?)
Unknown wife of James B. Yates, full blood Creek Indian
William O. Mitchell
Anna Thomas, half blood Cherokee
Yearby Denney
Lucy Storer
Thomas Ellard, probably part Cherokee Indian
Mary, wife of Thomas Ellard, probably part Cherokee Indian
Samuel McDonald, probably part Cherokee Indian
Mary Goodson, half blood Cherokee Indian
John W. Littleton Hooten, probably part Indian
Martha Jane Johnson, probably part Indian

Louis Graben
Mary (Polly) Kimbrell, half blood Cherokee Indian
Edward Elbert Kitchens
Ethel Melinda Jane Mason
Isaac Cooper, half blood Cherokee Indian, son of Nancy Blackfox, and one-eighth
Choctaw
Mahala Jane Blevins, part Indian, reportedly Cherokee
Richard Sizemore, part Indian
Elizabeth Forrester, part Chickahominy
Claibourne Bondurant, part Powhatan Indian
Mary, wife of Claibourne Bondurant, probably part or full Indian
Wiley Redwine, half blood Cherokee Indian
Avis Morely, part or full blood Indian
Corben Goble
Susanna Grant
William J. Wooten
Naomi
John Shankle, part Indian
Clarissa Proctor, quarter-blood Cherokee Indian (mother was Virginia Davis,
grandmother Mary Ann Black, daughter of Chief Black Fox, uncle was Dr. William
Alexander Davis, Chief of Sand Mountain Cherokees)
John Lackey, quarter blood Indian, including Cherokee
Patsy Weaver, half blood Cherokee Indian

*My Sixteen Great-Great-Grandparents*
James C. Yates, quarter blood Indian
Elisabeth Mitchell, quarter-blood Cherokee Indian
John C. Denney
Mary J. (Nancy) Ellard
Newton McDonald, quarter-blood Cherokee Indian
Susannah Emily Hooten
Joseph Graben, quarter-blood Cherokee Indian
Martha Kitchens
Jackson Cooper, Cherokee and Choctaw, grandson of Nancy Blackfox
Mary Ann Sizemore, part Indian, including Cherokee
James Bundren, part Indian
Sarah Redwine, three-quarters blood Indian
Cornelius Goble
Ellen Wooten
Samuel Shankles, part Cherokee
Dovie Lackey, three-quarters Cherokee Indian

*My Eight Great-Grandparents*
Henry Yates, one-quarter Cherokee, part Creek Indian
Mary Etta Graben, part Indian
John Henry McDonald
Sarah Denney
John Cooper, about one-half Indian
Nancy Bundren, about one-quarter Indian
James Lafayette Goble, part Cherokee
Lucinda Shankle, three-quarters blood Cherokee Indian

*My Four Grandparents*
George Yates, quarter-blood Cherokee Indian, part Creek
Era Pirl McDonald, part Cherokee Indian
J. W. (Dolph) Cooper, one-fourth Cherokee
Dovie Goble, half-blood Cherokee Indian

*My Parents*
Lawden Yates, part Cherokee-Creek Indian
Bessie Cooper, between one-fourth and one-half Cherokee Indian

Such was the raw balance sheet of my Indian heritage in 2000. Although there were no blank spots in my *stammtafel*, estimates of Indian admixture were sketchy. One of the firm traditions told to my mother and grandmother was that Grandmother Lucinda Shankles Goble was "three-quarters Cherokee Indian." As both her mother and father had a high quotient of Cherokee ancestry, this seemed fairly reasonable. Another clue was that my great-great grandmother Elisabeth Mitchell, whose mother's maiden name was Thomas, was "a "full blooded" Cherokee Indian from North Carolina. In the event she was probably only one-fourth, or less, her mother being half. Anytime the Cherokee blood was in the maternal line, it seemed to be emphasized and exaggerated by contemporaries.

Families attributed their differentness to being Black Dutch, Black Irish, Indian or Portuguese—anything but what was the underlying Jewish heritage. In my own case, the exotic looks were explained as coming from a Grandmother Goble's Indian blood. She didn't even have a first name. She was supposedly three-quarters Cherokee Indian.

Sometimes the stories became overtly illogical, as when the children of Nancy Cooper were said to be "two-thirds" Choctaw in one of the family

Bibles. Everything was pegged to the distaff side. My mother's father said all the Indian blood was on his wife's side. I later found out they both had about the same amount of Indian genetics and were in fact fourth cousins. I kept trying to push my lines back to reach the full bloods but never quite succeeded.

Has anyone ever noticed how many people point to having only one Indian in the family tree? I don't believe Indians come that way. Each must have two Indian parents. I also reject the notion that Indian genes penetrated a white bloodline by some sort of aberration, a rape or an adoption or a kidnapping. Our mixed race couples formed successful marriages of mutual love and respect, often producing ten or eleven children.

Sometimes, I found, there was better information about the ethnicity of more remote ancestors than recent ones. I wrote the family history book *The Bear Went over the Mountain* in 1995 largely ignorant of my Cooper line. Only with the wonders of the Internet did I learn about William Cooper, my 6th-great grandfather, an important figure in the settlement of Tennessee, and his half-Choctaw, half-Jewish wife Malea Labon. Their children were known in records as mulatto, "half-breed Portuguese" and "quarteroon," depending on times and locality. William must also have had an Indian mother, as the survey and exploration companies that hired him as a scout referred to him simply as Indian or half-breed. His father, James Cooper, was a planter on the James River who came originally from the Tower district of London and had several wives. Which one was James' mother is not known.

Were any of my direct ancestors enrolled in an Indian tribe? The earliest Cherokee rolls were begun in 1817 with the Reservation and Emigration Rolls. My 3rd-great-grandfather, Isaac Cooper, the son of Nancy Black Fox and grandson of Chief Black Fox (died 1811), was living in Cherokee territory during that time, but there is no indication he was enrolled. Rather, he was a career railroader, working for various far-flung railway companies. He died and was buried in Santa Cruz, Mexico. He would have been a half-blood Cherokee and one-eighth Choctaw.

Isaac's first cousin twice removed Benjamin Cooper (1772-1852) chose differently. One-eighth Choctaw from his grandmother Malea Cooper, plus having other Indian strains, he was classified as a Free Person of Color or Taxed Indian in Granville, N.C. But when he moved to Georgia and became a widower, he married Uwoduageyutsa or Pretty Woman, a Cherokee tribal member. Cornelius and Uwoduageyutsa Cooper with their children Sally, Nancy and Cornelius Cooper III were listed on the rolls in the East and emigrated during the high tide of Indian removal. They arrived in Indian Territory, May 30, 1834, with seven slaves. Nancy Cooper died soon after their arrival, and Sally remained unmarried. Cornelius Cooper III (whose mother was Benjamin's white wife) became a member of the Treaty Party and moved his family to Texas to escape the bitter infighting in Indian Territory. So there were no Cooper descendants on later Cherokee rolls from Cornelius and Pretty Woman.

What about my great-great-grandfather Cooper? According to the deposition of great-aunt Lily Wigley, nee Cooper, Eastern Cherokee Application 42035, in 1907, "Grandfather Jack Cooper was enrolled, so I am informed. He, it is said, was of Cherokee blood." But there is no record of Jackson Cooper having been enrolled. So apparently it was another case of "damned if you do, damned if you don't."

Peter Cooper's testimony on the family's Cherokee heritage is worth quoting at length:

> I claim Cherokee Indian blood through my father and his father. Father died in 1845-6; I was about or between 20 and 30 years old when he died; he was born in Kentucky. Don't know where grandfather was born but he came to this county from Kentucky. They, father and grandfather, were recognized as white folks when they lived; they lived with the white people; never heard of them living with the Indian tribe except that they were in this state (Ala.) when the Indians left. They did not leave when the Indians left; I don't know why the Indians left; I never heard of my father or grandfather getting money or land from the government on account of their Indian blood. I never heard of their being enrolled with the Cherokees; I don't why I was not enrolled in 1851; I was living with my grandmother at that time; my father and grandfather are both dead. I never heard of my grandfather living with the Cherokee tribe. I have heard grandmother say that we had the blood in us and have heard all people say so; Indians talked to me about it; they said I looked like I had the blood in me. In 1882 I was living in Jackson Co., Ala..; I was not enrolled at that time because I did not know anything about it; there was no agent through here. I never heard of a

treaty with the Cherokees in 1835—I heard about the Indians being sent away from here; I suppose my grandfather did not go because he did not want to. Signed Peter I. Cooper, Scottsboro, Ala., July 1, 1908. Eastern Cherokee Application (Miller Roll) 19589.

None of Isaac and Nancy (Blackfox) Cooper's children ended up enrolled. One granddaughter, Susan (Sukie) E. Cooper, who was at least one-quarter blood, married William E. Adkins, and the family moved to Arkansas, with some descendants living on the Cherokee Nation in Indian Territory but not enrolled.

Black Fox himself was presumably a full blood (although his name Enola is Choctaw). He was Supreme Chief of the Cherokee between 1801 and 1810 and was known in Washington as "the Cherokee King." He had four children by his Paint Clan wife, the daughter of the daughter of Peace Chief (or President, as he preferred to call himself) Attakullakulla and Nionee, Paint Clan. Black Fox, the only son, married Lucy Bolin, who died on the Trail of Tears. Their daughter Lucinda Lucretia Blackfox (1830-1880) is the sole known enrollee from the entire family. She was enrolled in Tahlequah as Lucinda Tadpole, roll no. 6125.

Chief Black Fox's daughters, who were full bloods, all married non-Cherokees. Mary Ann Black (born 1765) at first married a man named Pogue or Polk, then William Davis, a Scottish crypto-Jew. Most of their children were officially recognized as Cherokees, east and west. Their son, called Dr. Chief William Alexander Davis (born 1790), was entered for a reservation on the roll of 1817 after signing the treaty of July 8 of that year. He was also known as Young Davis and Day Noon. A daughter by his first wife, a white woman, is said to have disavowed her father because he married an Indian woman (Mary Burns, the daughter of Chief Arthur Burns). After the death of his new father-in-law, William Alexander Davis became chief of the Cherokee in Jackson County, inheriting the North Sauty reservation near Blowing Cave, comprising 640 acres. He sold this just before the Cherokee removal. It was supposed to have been the land set aside by law for an educational institution or college. In 1838, the family went over the Trail of Tears to Indian Territory. Most appear on the Henderson, Hester and Drennan Rolls.

A second daughter of Chief Black Fox was Nancy Blackfox (born 1775). She married Isaac Cooper, a soldier, gunsmith and ironworker and they had nine children, including my 3rd great-grandfather Isaac (Zack) Cooper, living at various times in different locations in Kentucky, Tennessee, West Virginia and Ohio. The children married into old Tennessee families and none went onto any rolls. A third daughter of the chief, Rachael, married a trader named Michael Cline. There is no further information on her.

As DNA testing became available, I traced my Yates and Cooper male lines (Y chromosome) with partially satisfying results. The Cooper pedigree proved to match a living Choctaw Cooper and Canary Islander of evident Sephardic Jewish descent. But I was most interested in my mother Bessie Cooper's mitochondrial lineage, allegedly Cherokee. Her presumed unbroken female descent from a north Georgia or North Carolina Indian woman who became the frontier wife of a Scottish-Lithuanian Jewish Indian trader, Enoch Jordan, is displayed here with all known descendants and offshoots. The names in boldface indicate female-linked descendants carrying, presumably, copies of her mitochondrial DNA type, as do I, being the son of Bessie Cooper.

## Generation No. 1

**1. CHEROKEE¹ WOMAN** was born Abt. 1775. She married ENOCH JORDAN.

Child of **CHEROKEE WOMAN** and ENOCH JORDAN is:

2.　　i.　**MARTHA² JORDAN**, b. Abt. 1795.

## Generation No. 2

**2. MARTHA² JORDAN** *(CHEROKEE¹ WOMAN)* was born Abt. 1795. She married ------- WEAVER.

Children of **MARTHA JORDAN** and ------- WEAVER are:

　　i.　**MATILDA C.³ WEAVER**, b. 1815, S.C.; m. (1) MOSES FENDLEY; m. (2) SILVA WEAVER.

3.　　ii.　**LUCINDA MARTHA (PATSY) WEAVER (?)**, b. February 14, 1815, North Carolina; d. Mississippi River (?).

　　iii.　**HENRY WEAVER,** b. 1818, S.C.; d. February 13, 1867, Gilmer Co., Ga.; m. MARY PRATHER; b. 1818, S.C.; d. December 05, 1896.

　　iv.　**JAMES LITTLETON WEAVER**, b. 1820, S.C.; m. MATILDA EMALINE RACKLEY, December 19, 1841, Gilmer Co., Ga.; b. 1819; d. June 22, 1901.

　　v.　**FRANCES ANN WEAVER**, b. August 07, 1824; d. January 1865, Nashville, Tenn.; m. WILLIAM JACKSON BALILES; b. 1821, Patrick Co., Va..

　　vi.　**NANCY WEAVER**, b. 1826; m. (1) WILLIAM B. VANDIGRIFF,

February 10, 1846, Gilmer Co., Ga.; b. August 21, 1822; d. April 24, 1877; m. (2) JOSIAH ELROD, May 03, 1884, Lumpkin Co., Ga..

### Generation No. 3

**3. LUCINDA MARTHA (PATSY) WEAVER³ (?)** *(MARTHA² JORDAN, CHEROKEE¹ WOMAN)* was born February 14, 1815 in North Carolina, and died in Mississippi River (?). She married JOHN S./L. LACKEY in Haversham Co., Ga., son of JOHN LACKEY and MARY. He was born March 04, 1814 in North Carolina.

Children of LUCINDA (?) and JOHN LACKEY are:

| 4. | i. | **MELMETH C.⁴ LACKEY**, b. November 21, 1839, Lincoln Co., N.C.; d. October 15, 1905. |
| 5. | ii. | **FRANCIS L. LACKEY**, b. August 09, 1842, N.C.; d. Abt. 1863. |
| 6. | iii. | **LOVINA (DOVEY) ADELINE LACKEY**, b. March 14, 1845, Gilmer Co., Georgia; d. June 05, 1888, DeKalb Co., Alabama. |
| | iv. | **LETITIA E. LACKEY**, b. May 01, 1848. |
| | v. | **LAFAYETTE W. LACKEY**, b. February 08, 1854; m. MARY -------; b. August 08, 1847; d. March 04, 1882. |
| | vi. | **ELIZABETH M. LACKEY**, b. April 03, 1857; d. August 22, 1933; m. JOHN CUNINGHAM. |
| | vii. | **ROBERT LACKEY**, b. January 22, 1863. |

### Generation No. 4

**4. MELMETH C.⁴ LACKEY** *(LUCINDA MARTHA (PATSY) WEAVER³ (?), MARTHA² JORDAN, CHEROKEE¹ WOMAN)* was born November 21, 1839 in Lincoln Co., N.C., and died October 15, 1905. He married MELISSA A. E. MITCHELL March 23, 1862 in DeKalb Co., Ala.. She was born Abt. 1840.

Children of MELMETH LACKEY and MELISSA MITCHELL are:

- i. JAMES G.⁵ LACKEY.
- ii. LUCINDA FLORENCE LACKEY, m. JOHN GIBSON.
- iii. ROSE LACKEY, m. PHILL GREEN POE.
- iv. JOHN G. LACKEY.
- v. WALTER L. LACKEY.
- vi. THOMAS NAPOLEON LACKEY, b. September 02, 1866; d. April 14, 1941.
- vii. LILIAN (LILLY) LACKEY, b. 1868; m. ------ HALL.

**5. FRANCIS L.⁴ LACKEY** *(LUCINDA MARTHA (PATSY) WEAVER³ (?), MARTHA² JORDAN, CHEROKEE¹ WOMAN)* was born August 09, 1842 in N.C., and died Abt. 1863. He married SAMARAH J. STEWART September 22, 1860 in DeKalb Co., Ala., daughter of ROBERT STEWART and CHEROKEE (?). She was born January 11, 1837 in Alabama.

Children of FRANCIS LACKEY and SAMARAH STEWART are:

i.   LUCINDA[5] LACKEY, b. September 17, 1861; d. July 21, 1900; m. GEORGE WESLEY SHANKLES; b. Abt. 1861.
ii.  ROBERT LACKEY, b. January 11, 1863.

**6. LOVINA (DOVEY) ADELINE[4] LACKEY** *(LUCINDA MARTHA (PATSY) WEAVER[3] (?), MARTHA[2] JORDAN, CHEROKEE[1] WOMAN)* was born March 14, 1845 in Gilmer Co., Georgia, and died June 05, 1888 in DeKalb Co., Alabama. She married (1) MILLIGIN FOSSETT March 12, 1860 in DeKalb County, Ala.. He was born Abt. 1840, and died Bef. 1866. She married (2) SAMUEL G. SHANKLES September 04, 1866 in DeKalb Co., Ala., son of JOHN SHANKLES and CLARISSA PROCTOR. He was born Abt. 1846 in Alabama, and died January 05, 1902 in DeKalb Co., Ala..

Child of **LOVINA LACKEY** and MILLIGIN FOSSETT is:

i.   **SEABORN[5] FOSSETT**, b. January 02, 1861, Alabama; m. (1) SUSANNA N. GOBLE, March 04, 1879, Jackson Co., Ala.; b. 1859, Ala.; m. (2) ADDIE LONG, November 02, 1902.

Children of **LOVINA LACKEY** and SAMUEL SHANKLES are:

ii.  **ELIJAH[5] SHANKLES**, b. Abt. 1865.
7.   iii. **GEORGE W. SHANKLES**, b. Abt. 1866.
iv.  **MELVINA SHANKLES**, b. Abt. 1868; d. Buried atop Sand Mountain.
v.   **JOHN H. SHANKLES**, b. Abt. 1869.
8.   vi. **LUCINDA C. SHANKLES**, b. Abt. 1872, Alabama; d. Abt. 1898, Alabama.
vii. **BARBARA A. SHANKLES**, b. Abt. 1874.
viii. **SOPHRONIA (FRAUNIE) PALESTINIA SHANKLES**, b. Abt. 1876; m. JEPTHA THOMAS WOOTEN, Abt. 1893; b. 1875.
ix.  **THOMAS G. SHANKLES**, b. October 15, 1878, DeKalb Co., Ala.; d. December 13, 1893, DeKalb Co., Ala..
9.   x. **REUBEN SIDNEY SHANKLES**, b. September 30, 1886.

**Generation No. 5**

**7.** GEORGE W.[5] SHANKLES *(LOVINA (DOVEY) ADELINE[4] LACKEY, LUCINDA MARTHA (PATSY) WEAVER[3] (?), MARTHA[2] JORDAN, CHEROKEE[1] WOMAN)* was born Abt. 1866. He married TEXAS A. DENNIS September 25, 1898 in DeKalb Co., Ala..

Child of GEORGE SHANKLES and TEXAS DENNIS is:
10.  i. JOEL THOMAS[6] SHANKLES.

**8. LUCINDA C.[5] SHANKLES** *(LOVINA (DOVEY) ADELINE[4] LACKEY, LUCINDA MARTHA (PATSY) WEAVER[3] (?), MARTHA[2] JORDAN, CHEROKEE[1] WOMAN)* was born Abt. 1872 in Alabama, and died Abt. 1898 in Alabama. She married JAMES LAFAYETTE "FATE" GOBLE September 30, 1886 in Jackson Co., son of CORNELIUS

GOBLE and ELLEN WOOTEN. He was born July 1864 in Georgia, and died January 22, 1918 in Hog Jaw, Jackson Co., Ala.

Children of **LUCINDA SHANKLES** and JAMES GOBLE are:

> i. **SEABORN E.⁶ GOBLE**, b. December 1888, Alabama.

11.    ii. **DOVIE PALESTINE GOBLE**, b. March 02, 1890, Kirby's Mill, Jackson Co., Alabama (?); d. March 19, 1920, Langston, Jackson Co., Alabama.

> iii. **MATTIE A. GOBLE**, b. August 1892.

12.    iv. **GEORGIA "GEORGIE" L. GOBLE,** b. March 1894; d. Abt. 1920.

**9. REUBEN SIDNEY⁵ SHANKLES** *(LOVINA (DOVEY) ADELINE⁴ LACKEY, LUCINDA MARTHA (PATSY) WEAVER³ (?), MARTHA² JORDAN, CHEROKEE¹ WOMAN)* was born September 30, 1886. He married SADIE FRANCIS MORRIS March 04, 1902 in DeKalb Co., Ala.. She was born December 03, 1886.

Children of REUBEN SHANKLES and SADIE MORRIS are:

> i. CALVIN⁶ SHANKLES.
> ii. LILLY BEATRICE SHANKLES, d. August 15, 1993.
> iii. SAM SHANKLES, b. January 19, 1903.
> iv. OLER SHANKLES, b. May 24, 1905.
> v. WALTER SHANKLES, b. May 30, 1910.
> vi. DOVIE SHANKLES, b. October 12, 1913.
> vii. GRANVILLE ISAAC SHANKLES, b. May 03, 1918.

13.    viii. M. A. HARDING SHANKLES, b. May 20, 1920; d. May 08, 2000.

14.    ix. MOLLIE SHANKLES, b. February 22, 1923.

### Generation No. 6

**10.** JOEL THOMAS⁶ SHANKLES *(GEORGE W.⁵, LOVINA (DOVEY) ADELINE⁴ LACKEY, LUCINDA MARTHA (PATSY) WEAVER³ (?), MARTHA² JORDAN, CHEROKEE¹ WOMAN)* He married CELIA PAULINE WRIGHT.

Children of JOEL SHANKLES and CELIA WRIGHT are:

> i. GARY⁷ SHANKLES.
> ii. ELWIN SHANKLES.
> iii. HOBERT LEE SHANKLES.
> iv. ALFRED SHANKLES.
> v. FERIBY C. SHANKLES.

**11. DOVIE PALESTINE⁶ GOBLE** *(LUCINDA C.⁵ SHANKLES, LOVINA (DOVEY) ADELINE⁴ LACKEY, LUCINDA MARTHA (PATSY) WEAVER³ (?), MARTHA² JORDAN, CHEROKEE¹ WOMAN)* was born March 02, 1890 in Kirby's Mill, Jackson Co., Alabama (?), and died March 19, 1920 in Langston, Jackson Co., Alabama. She married JOHN

WESLEY MONROE DOLPHUS "DOLPHY" COOPER January 31, 1912 in Jackson Co., son of JOHN COOPER and NANCY BUNDREN. He was born December 05, 1881 on Sand Mountain, Ala., and died May 29, 1960 in Ft. Payne, Alabama.

Children of **DOVIE GOBLE** and JOHN COOPER are:

     i.  **GRANVILLE LEE[7] COOPER**, b. November 26, 1914, Langston, Ala.; d. March 23, 1988, Rossville, Walker Co., Ga.; m. OLA FAYE JAMES, August 28, 1949, Rossville, Ga.; b. April 23, 1924, Fort Payne, Ala..

    ii.  **BESSIE LOUISE COOPER,** b. October 22, 1917, Langston, Jackson County, Alabama; died January 7, 2006, Ft. Walton Beach, Okaloosa Co., Fla.; m. (1) LAWDEN HENRY YATES, January 18, 1942, Muscogee, Oklahoma; b. September 25, 1916, Lineville, Clay Co., Ala.; d. August 28, 1978, Lineville, Clay Co., Ala.; m. (2) RAY STEPHENS, Abt. 1979; b. Abt. 1915, Georgia; d. 1993.

**12. GEORGIA "GEORGIE" L.[6] GOBLE** *(LUCINDA C.[5] SHANKLES, LOVINA (DOVEY) ADELINE[4] LACKEY, LUCINDA MARTHA (PATSY) WEAVER[3] (?), MARTHA[2] JORDAN, CHEROKEE[1] WOMAN)* was born March 1894, and died Abt. 1920. She married THOMAS "TOM" DAVIS.

Child of GEORGIA GOBLE and THOMAS DAVIS is:

    i.  **MARTIN LUTHER "LUKE"[7] DAVIS**, m. ------ WILBURN.

**13.** M. A. HARDING[6] SHANKLES *(REUBEN SIDNEY[5], LOVINA (DOVEY) ADELINE[4] LACKEY, LUCINDA MARTHA (PATSY) WEAVER[3] (?), MARTHA[2] JORDAN, CHEROKEE[1] WOMAN)* was born May 20, 1920, and died May 08, 2000. He married JEWELL C. -------.

Child of M. SHANKLES and JEWELL ------- is:

    i.  GLENN H.[7] SHANKLES.

**14.** MOLLIE[6] SHANKLES *(REUBEN SIDNEY[5], LOVINA (DOVEY) ADELINE[4] LACKEY, LUCINDA MARTHA (PATSY) WEAVER[3] (?), MARTHA[2] JORDAN, CHEROKEE[1] WOMAN)* was born February 22, 1923. She married WILLIS WARREN MOUNTAIN. He was born December 29, 1921.

Child of MOLLIE SHANKLES and WILLIS MOUNTAIN is:

    i.  BARBARA[7] MOUNTAIN, b. November 15, 1952; m. RONALD O. BURNS; b. September 13, 1953.

When I received my report from the testing service, I was shocked. My haplogroup was H, a common European lineage. I went to three other labs to prove these results wrong. They all agreed. But for three years I thought I was, in effect, somebody else. As it turned out, the sample had been switched at the Houston-based lab. I had received somebody else's mitochondrial mutations in my report. After all that effort, friends told me I may as well act as my own company and offer full services. So I did. DNA Consultants started with a mistake.

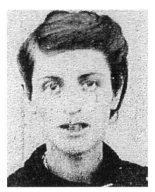

*Five generations of mitochondrial haplogroup U2. Top, from left: Mary Nell Anderson, author's sister; our mother Bessie C. Yates; her mother Dovie Palestine Cooper. Bottom, from left: the latter's maternal aunt Mary Lackey Haston; Mary's uncle, son of Lucinda Lackey, Melmuth Lackey.*

My haplogroup from the Cherokee woman was verified as a unique form of U2e, at that time still considered impossibly Indian. After inaugurating Phase I of the company's Cherokee DNA Project, I became Participant No. 11, matching no one in the world, but coming close with an HVR2 match to Participant 13, who traced her matriline back to Susanna Owens,

Cherokee, b. 1760, Granville Co., N.C. Phyllis Starnes of Harriman, Tennessee (#13) had strong Melungeon ancestry just like my mother. She also had a Middle Eastern-seeming type of Cherokee mitochondrial DNA with a similar history to my own, with genealogy leading back to Granville County, where both my famous Jewish Indian trader ancestors originated.

### Miller Roll Testimonies

Of all the surnames in my family tree one in particular seems to consistently raise official hackles and sound the alarms. My 2nd-great-grandmother was a Sizemore. The very mention was enough to make genealogists erupt in high dudgeon and sane people scramble for cover. Why? Because it is one of the few cases of Indian descent being claimed through the male line, by surname. The merit of almost all claimants with the Bureau of Indian Affairs has traditionally been judged on female descent. Even if surnames are involved, it is the female link of that is critical.

The Guion Miller Roll is a list of Eastern Cherokees who applied for money awarded in 1905 because of a 1902 lawsuit in which the Eastern Cherokee tribe sued the United States for funds due them under the treaties of 1835, 1836 and 1845. Claimants were asked to prove they were members of the Eastern Cherokee tribe at the time of the treaties, or descended from members who had not been affiliated with any other tribe. Guion Miller, an agent of the Interior Department, was appointed as a commissioner of the Court of Claims to compile a list of claimants. He made an extensive enrollment of the Cherokees in 1907 and 1908.

When the Miller Court of Claims was in session, only grandfather J. W. Cooper in my direct ancestry was alive and eligible. He was in his twenties. His father John Cooper was dead, as were his grandparents, Jack and Mary Ann Cooper. His wife-to-be, Pally Goble, was a teenager. Her mother Lucinda Shankles was dead. On June 22, 1907, he filed an application to become enrolled as a member of the Eastern Band of Cherokee Indians (Guion-Miller Roll No. 42018). He gave his age as 26 and usual place of residence as Henegar, Alabama, at present, Long Island, Alabama. He appears to have based his claim on the blood of his grandmother, Mary A. Sizemore Cooper, among others. That apparently was the kiss of death. His brother James Cooper and five sisters also gave detailed affidavits. All the Coopers' applications were summarily rejected. They were docketed with the six volumes of Sizemore testimony in the court's final papers.

Peter Cooper, my cousin three times removed, gave additional testimony naming Black Fox. He attempted to have a member of the influential Keys family confirm the Coopers' right to receive Indian monies. But the damage was done. The Coopers had been condemned with the Sizemores. Peter's wife was a Sizemore, while Jackson Cooper, the pivotal figure in a generation of claims, was also married to a Sizemore. Even though Peter was a great-grandson, and Jackson a grandson, of full blood Nancy Cooper, they were out of luck.

It is doubtful the Keyses would have helped the situation anyway. Like the Coopers and Sizemores they were Sephardic Jewish in origin, Many were noted as "bright mulattoes," or "other free" in Virginia and North Carolina records before they settled in what became north Alabama. In 1817, when a choice was given to the Cherokee to settle on a reservation in the east for life or emigrate west, Samuel Keys and his three sons Isaac, William and Samuel applied for and obtained reservations on Sand Mountain. Isaac Keys was married to Elizabeth Riley, William, to Sally Riley, and Samuel, to Mary Riley. The Riley sisters were all granddaughters of Chief Doublehead (Chuqualatague) through the two sisters Ni-go-di-ge-yu and Gu-lu-sti-yu Doublehead.

During Indian Removal, some Keyses managed to stay in Alabama, while others went on the Trail of Tears. Richard Keys (Chapman Roll 1686) lived for a time in Fabius on Sand Mountain before moving to Indian Territory with his large family. He died February 6, 1892, and was buried in Paw Paw Bottoms, Muldrow, Sequoyah, Indian Terrirtory. He was the Dick Keys named as a character witness on Peter Cooper's ECA. Richard Riley Keys (1813-1884), a brother of Letitia Keys who was married to Minerva Nave, served as Judge on the Cherokee Nation Supreme Court. Samuel Riley Keys, born 1819, Fabius, married Mary Hannah Easter, a Choctaw.

Did the Sizemores have a meritorious case? According to the website of a non-federally-recognized tribe in Clay County, Kentucky, where Sizemore is one of the most frequent surnames on the rolls, "Our family stories and trees trace back to a 2,000 member Whitetop Laurel Band of Cherokees, which existed for at least a decade. The band was founded sixty years after the Trail of Tears, and nine years before the Eastern Band of Cherokees in 1905. The tribe was located in the tri-state Virginia, North Carolina and Tennessee borders." Furthermore:

GENERAL INDEX.

| NUMBER | NAME | STATE | NUMBER | NAME | STATE |
|---|---|---|---|---|---|
| 15167 | Sizemore, George B. | W.Va | 39096 | Sizemore,- Mina L. | N.C. |
| 22714 | " George W. | Va | 12234 | " Mirtie A. | Ala |
| 38842 | " George T. | Ga | 30514 | " Morgan D. | N.C. |
| 37629 | " Grady | Ky | 39007 | " N. Zokourse | N.C. |
| 7440 | " H. H. | W.Va | 35848 | " Nancy E. | Ga |
| 17317 | " H. H | Ala | 12138 | " Nancy L. | W.Vn |
| 18656 | " Harden | W.Va | 17097 | " Naomi | W.Va |
| 9589 | " Harvy L. | W.Va | 18655 | " Ned | W.Va |
| 32616 | " Hayes | N.Va | 18739 | " Ned | W.Va |
| 33917 | " Henry | Ala | 2569 | " Odey C. | Ala |
| 34420 | " Henry | W.Va | 20916 | " Ora F. | Ala |
| 32616 | " Henry B. | W.Va | 21666 | " Otto | Ala |
| 31947 | " Hiram | Ky | 8049 | " Owen | Va |
| 9590 | " Hiram | W.Va | 10131 | " Owen | W.Va |
| 10122 | " Hiram | W.Va | 34423 | " Owen | W.Va |
| 12684 | " Hiram | Va | 12329 | " Owen J. | W.Va |
| 34431 | " Hiram | W.Va | 14799 | " Owen M. | W.Va |
| 37630 | " Hiram | Ky | 34407 | " Owen M. | Tenn |
| 12117 | " Hiram M. | W.Va | 10142 | " Philip | W.Va |
| 32517 | " Hiram J. | W.Va | 18651 | " Phillip | W.Va |
| 33916 | " Howard | Ala | 9591 | " Philip S. | W.Va |
| 10120 | " Isaac | W.Va | 17452 | " Polly | W.Va |
| 6344 | " Isaac L. | Ala | 38270 | " Rachabl | Tenn |
| 35301 | " James (Gdn) | N.C. | 12105 | " Richard | W.Va |
| 33837 | " James " | N.C. | 21655 | " Richard G. | Kans |
| 34430 | " James | Tenn | 4916 | " Robert C. | Tex |
| 39009 | " James R. | N.C. | 12944 | " Robert F. | W.Va |
| 14661 | " James F. | W.Vn | 28202 | " Robert Lee | W.Va |
| 29254 | " Jas. R. (Gdn) | N.C. | 14461 | " Robert M. | Ala |
| 29255 | " Jas. H. | N.C. | 12934 | " Rosa J. | W.Va |
| 34452 | " James O. | W.Va | 6337 | " Rosa L. | Ala |
| 18650 | " James Owen | W.Va | 33339 | " Rosella | N.C. |
| 33307 | " James R. | N.C. | 21426 | " Roxie C. | Ala |
| 29978 | " Jennie | W.Va | 14467 | " Rozetta | Ala |
| 10115 | " Jessie | W.Va | 14479 | " Rufus E. | Ala |
| 20913 | " Joel A. | Okla | 17320 | " S. K. | Ala |
| 9516 | " Joel H. | Ala | 18740 | " Samson | W.Va |
| 9512 | " Joel R. | Ala | 12528 | " Samuel | Va |
| 17305 | " Joel T. | Okla | 34232 | " Samuel B. | Tenn |
| 16469 | " Joel W. | Ala | 34366 | " Sarah | W.Va |
| 31949 | " John, Jr. | Ky | 18659 | " Sean | W.Va |
| 9086 | " John | W.Va | 8052 | " Seanie | W.Va |
| 29652 | " John | Ky | 27194 | " Shade | W.Va |
| 39931 | " John B. | Tenn | 20917 | " Shirley B. | Ala |
| 9809 | " John F. | Ala | 38430 | " Sidney | N.C. |
| b2562 | " John H. | Ala | 12943 | " Stella M. | W.Va |
| 38630 | " John H. | N.C. | 33308 | " Stella May | N.C. |
| 43194 | " John Henry | N.C. | 38906 | " Stephen | Ky |
| 14457 | " John M. | Ala | 12485 | " T. F. | Ala |
| 38415 | " John Marion | W.Va | 9104 | " Theodore | W.Va |
| 12104 | " John R. | W.Va | 14477 | " Thomas | Ala |
| 13005 | " John T. | W.Va | 41775 | " Thomas | Tenn |
| 34408 | " Joseph I. | Tenn | 17293 | " Thomas B. | Ala |
| 12934 | " Julia A. (Gdn) | W.Va | 39934 | " Thomas H. | Tenn |
| 30771 | " Laura C. | N.C. | 39269 | " Thomas Patton | Tenn |
| 15162 | " Lewis A. | W.Va | 43543 | " Thomas S. | S.C. |
| 35566 | " Lizzie | W.Va | 30516 | " Tilden V. | N.C. |
| 19741 | " Lorence | W.Va | 35860 | " Virginia F. | Tenn |
| 2564 | " Luther S. | Ala | 17319 | " W. C. | Ala |
| 12235 | " Margaret C. | Ala | 18164 | " W. L. J. | W.Va |
| 6336 | " Margaret J. | Ala | 12940 | " W. T. | W.Va |
| 38414 | " Marryann | W.Va | 2563 | " Wade H. | Ala |
| 14455 | " Martha L. | Ala | 38773 | " Washington I. | W.Va |
| 14468 | " Marthie J. | Ala | 14630 | " Wiley | W.Va |
| 9094 | " Mary | W.Va | 39933 | " Wiley | Tenn |
| 14466 | " Mary C. | Ala | 40091 | " Wiley | W.C. |
| 35915 | " Mary M. | Ga | 40728 | " Wiley (Gdn) | W.Va |
| 39008 | " Manda J. | N.C. | 41776 | " Will A. | Tenn |
| 15165 | " Miles | W.Va | 32924 | " William | Ky |

*Page of Sizemores from the Miller Roll.*

Over 2,000 of this same group of Sizemores applied for the Eastern Cherokee for membership and all 2,000 were rejected. The Eastern Band of Cherokee admitted they were Indian but they were denied for various reasons. Those who made the decision to reject the Sizemore claims were clear in their statement that Sizemores were Indians, but since none of their ancestors had willingly registered in any Cherokee census, they were not accepted.

Documentation and DNA proves beyond any doubt that this Family is Native American. This Sizemore project also states the Native bloodline blood could have gone back as far as 300 years.

The multi-volume book series *Cherokee By Blood* documents this story. Vol. 1, page 171 bears the testimony of Whitetop Chief William H. Blevins:

The word 'Chief' in my application, means that I am chief of the White Top Band of Cherokee Indians, an organization of the principal Cherokee Indians living about White Top, and was perfected about ten years ago. We organized so as to demand our rights in a body. We thought we had not been getting them before. In 1896, we wanted to go to the Indian Territory, and organized for that purpose. They were all Sizemore descendants. No one else was allowed to become a member if it was known. I have read the Decree of the Supreme Court of the United States referred to in my application, and have it at home. My father, Armstrong Blevins, I do not think, was a party to the treaty of 1836 and 1846. I am putting my own interpretation on the decree."

Such a position turned the tables on federal Indian policy by focusing on patrilineal rather than matrilineal rights.

When I started my DNA studies (chapter 3), only one of the male lines I investigated proved to be an Indian type. This was the Sizemore sample, which turned out to be Q. The specific form of Q (haplotype) widely matched American Indian DNA from Panama and other places in the Americas. Paradoxically, though, some Sizemore lines showed R1b (Western European). Exhaustive research by Alan Lerwick of Salt Lake City suggested all Sizemores in this country could be traced to the London merchant Michael Sizemore, buried in the Flemish cemetery of St. Katharine by the Tower in 1684. That was the same parish as the Coopers. It was known as a district filled with Jews and crypto-Jews near the financial heart of London.

A son of Michael, William Sizemore or Sismore, husband of Margery came to America. His male haplotype appears to have been R1b. The

Indian haplogroup Q3 begins showing up in the descendants of his grandson Edward (the Tory) and great-great-grandson George (of All) Sizemore. The likely suspect is Henry Sizemore, b. abt. 1698. The only descendants of this Indian male who developed a distinguishing mutation were the Barnwell District, S.C. Ephraim cluster, which has a value of 18 in DYS 464d. This is my line, from Richard Sizemore, whose daughter Mary Ann married my great-great-grandfather Jackson Cooper. Henry's brother, Ephraim (b. abt. 1696) continued the R1b line, though he married a part-Indian named Mary and their child Ephraim was recorded as a Mulatto, a contemporary term for taxed Indian, that is an Indian living with the whites not Indians. Ephraim was mixed from the mother, not the father; his Y-chromosome haplotype continued to be R1b. His brother William (m. Winifred Greene, who was Jewish) passed the R1b gene to John H. Sizemore who married Mollie Gregory (who was Jewish). These Gregorys migrated with the Yateses, Coopers, Sheldons and Rameys through Pittsylvania Co., and Mordecai Gregory was part of a *minyan* in Wayne Co., Ky. with Isaac Cooper, John Adair and others. There is no male-only Indian genetics in any of Ephraim's descendants.

So Edward (Tory Ned) and James (father of George All) must both have come from the same father. If Henry himself was not the carrier of Q3 he was cuckolded twice by the same Indian male and raised Edward and James as his own. George All's mother (Henry Sizemore's wife, Elizabeth Rhodes, told him he was "all" Indian. She herself may have been another Mulatto; her name was probably the origin of the many of the Rhodas in the family. But it is more likely James' unknown wife was as Indian or part-Indian as he was. The legends tell how the Indians tried to take him back. Edward also married a Mulatto woman, Elizabeth Jackson, whose father William Jackson (married to Dorcas Greene) had the Cherokee chief's name of Bear Hart. So we see a definite pattern in this line from Henry, who is otherwise only a shadowy figure.

Sizemore descendants tracing back to Henry Sizemore, son "Old Ned" Sizemore (hanged by Col. Ben Cleveland on the Tory Oak in Wilkesboro at the end of the American Revolution), grandson George Edward Sizemore (who married Annie Elizabeth Aruna Hart), grandson George "Chief Of All" Sizemore (who married Agnes Shepherd) and grandson Ephraim Sizemore, the author's 4th great-grandfather (who came to Sand Mountain from South Carolina), tend to be comfortable with accepting their Indian heritage. But not always so with descendants of John Sizemore of Pittsylvania County, Virginia, who preserved the original R1b lineage of Sizemore males and had no claim to consider themselves Indian on that basis alone. Many debate the Sizemore Indian heritage without realizing it can travel down female lines as well as male. Moreover, male Sizemores, whether they had R1b or Q, were crypto-Jews in the mold of the Coopers, Harts, Gregorys, Bollings, Greenes, Jacksons, Parkers, Bagleys and Brocks with whom they married, generation after generation. Surnames of Sizemore marriage partners read like a Who's Who of crypto-Jewish genealogy: Adams, Asher, Bailey, Belcher, Blevins, Bondurant, Callicut, Canady, Chese, Colbert, Crownover, Dougherty, Emanuel, Ford, Gold, Harris, Minor, Moniac, Osborne, Pinte, Siler, Palmore, Shankles, Wade, Weir, West, Weston. Once again, Jewish and Indian identities were conflated in the eyes of contemporaries and posterity.

We will see the upshot of the Sizemore matter at the conclusion of this chapter. It has a genealogical solution. But first let us return to DNA. With the Jewish and Indian skeletons continuing to chatter incoherently, I conceived it might be possible to induce the original skeleton in the Sizemore closet confess his story. When "percentage tests" first appeared, I was eager to find out what they might reveal about my odd mixture of ethnicities. My admixture test in Jan. 31, 2007 from DNAPrint/Sorenson Genomics exposed a common flaw in genetic tests. It showed that I have 8% Native American, the rest "European" (as the makers misleadingly term Caucasian, including Middle Eastern and South Asian). Since my mitochondrial haplotype is a form of U2* similar to others in the study "Anomalous Mitochondrial Lineages in the Cherokee," it was apparently interpreted by ABD 2.5 as a non-Native American type. Much of my Cherokee heritage appeared to be glossed over by the test since the genetics community does not recognize Old World contributions to Native American tribal populations, dismissing U, T, X and other haplogroups as non-Native American.

## Percentage Testing

When 23andme came along, I signed up and walked the gauntlet. My mitochondrial haplogroup was unchanged, U2e, though it still matched no one on the planet. From the admixture profile, I learned that I was only 0.4% Asian or Native American and 92.2% European (46.7% British and

Irish). Less than 0.1% was unassigned to an origin.

I also availed myself of the EURO-DNA test from AncestryByDNA, based on a new set of AIMs. The "European" part of my ancestry was analyzed by DNAPrint in January of 2007. It was reported to consist of 19% Middle Eastern and 18% Southeast European. (I didn't know before that Europe embraced the Middle East.) The Greek, Egyptian and other Eastern Mediterranean ancestors I thought were Cherokee failed to appear in the Native American admixture test indicating only 8% but evidently made a covert showing in the EURO-DNA results. If a third of the "Middle Eastern" and "Southeast European" ancestry is in reality Cherokee owing to their East Mediterranean roots, and if it is placed in the Native American column instead, that would bring my true Native American quantum to 19%, a figure more in line with genealogical estimates.

None of the tests on the market seemed to have a good grip on European DNA, despite the fact that Europe was known to divide neatly into genetic populations corresponding to linguistic and national borders. As soon as DNA Consultants released its own EURO DNA I quickly scanned the nationalities fingered by autosomal population analysis—not AIMS, but aggregate forensic comparisons. I had come to recognize the usual suspects, compiled from the 24 populations available from ENFSI (European Network of Forensic Science Institutes). But the field now represented 71 populations and far surpassed ENFSI or any other database in commercial use. It had, for instance, the first data for countries like Hungary, Lithuania, Malta and Iceland. So how would my familiar genetic genealogy predictions—Scotland, Ireland, England, Belgium and the rest—shake out in the new oracle?

Some of the top matches—ranking even above British Isles or Northern European ancestry—were Central European, which surprised me.

Slovakia? Romania? Hungary? To be sure, I had always had a fascination with these countries. In my youth I studied in Europe and traveled to Budapest and Bratislava. I had also been to Romania in the days of its Communist regime, when my longhaired travel companion and I were welcomed like long lost relatives or conquering pop heroes.

Admittedly, the results of an autosomal ancestry test are cumulative and combinatory. While they *do* reflect all your ancestry, as no other test can, you are cautioned not to use the matches to try to pinpoint lines in your family genealogy. There is always a temptation to over-interpret.

Recall that my European percentages from AncestryByDNA had yielded suspiciously confirmatory results: 20% Southeast Europe. That struck me at the time as odd, as I had no known ancestors coming from that direction. Yet Hungarian was now one of my top metapopulation results. The Scottish (my grandmother was a McDonald) made sense, as did all the other matches from what I knew. But I was unaware of any strong Central or Southeast European lines.

### Sizemore Quagmire

Then I recalled the Sizemores. My great-great-grandmother was a Sizemore. The Sizemores were multiply connected with my Coopers (my mother's maiden name). In Colonial times, the two London merchant families lived on adjoining tracts of land on the west bank of the James River. Their fortunes were made on the Occaneechi Indian trading path that started on the other side of the river from Jamestown and eventually debouched in Cherokee country. Could the Central European effect in my EURO result be from those redoubtable Sizemores?

Much ink has been spilt—and many a keyboard abused—over the Sizemores. There are pitched battles in cyberspace on the question of their ethnicity. One camp has them down as Melungeons and admixed Cherokees with crypto-Jewish strains. Another maintains the Sizemores were a lily-white old Virginia British family. According to "Sizemore History and the Origin of the Surname, by Joy King," on a Family Tree DNA sponsored site, Sizemore is an English surname signifying "Descendant of Sigmar (victory, great) dweller on the Saxon's wasteland." She cites Elsdon C. Smith's *Dictionary of American Family Names*, a curious little non-scholarly book first published in 1956 and out of print since 1973. Apparently this was the best she could do. Think Götterdämmerung and the Wasteland!

As mentioned, Alan Lerwick upset the apple cart by deriving America's entire clan of Sizemores from Michael Sismore (note spelling), who lived in the most Jewish section of London. Daniel Defoe, of crypto-Jewish ancestry, a descendant of the illustrious Foa family, was a neighbor.

Sizemore is not a British surname. If it were it would be spread throughout the careful records of the kingdom such as Domesday Book or the Pipe Rolls and be mentioned in the many handbooks that have mined England's ample archives for surnames and genealogies, not in a single, doubtful, evanescent compilation of American surnames by one Elsdon C. Smith. It was clear to me long ago that neither my Sizemores nor my Coopers were Mama Bear, Papa Bear families. Like Gomez and Morticia of the Addams they possessed a strong ethnicity. One could just not say what it was exactly. Spurred by my EURO DNA test results, I dug into my subscription at Ancestry.com and learned that Michael Sismore was born Michael Seasmer in Ashwell, an important village in north Hertfordshire, November 1, 1620. His parents were Edward Seasmer and Betterissa (a form of Beatrice). New information! Alert the list moderators and genealogy guardians! Sigmar was a red herring!

Seasmer is the same as Zizmer, an old Central European Jewish surname adduced in multiple families in Israel, Romania, Czechoslovakia, Germany, Austria, Russia, Moldavia and the United States. Edward and Michael are favored given (I would not say Christian) names in the U.S. branches. The Hebrew letters, which can be viewed on numerous burials in Israel, are (reading right to left) RMZZ. Cooper is a similar Jewish surname, common in Russia and Lithuania and Israel as well as the British Isles and the U.S. In fact, my father's surname, Yates, is a Hebrew anagram common in the same countries, meaning "Righteous Convert."

"Soltan's" user comment on the original post brought out more electrifying information for me: "About Sizemore. If it really relates to Zizmer, Cismar etc. then it is a pure Hungarian surname: Csizmár, with the meaning of boot maker (Csizma=boot from the old Turkish word of *cizme*). Please note that the referenced areas of Slovakia and Transylvania are former Hungarian territories, so the connection is clear and matches with your DNA."

Hertfordshire was an important center for British Jewry, mentioned in the works of Hyamson, Jacobs and others. A good hypothesis to explain the transformation of Michael's name from Seasmer to Sismore and thence to Sizemore is this. His grandfather, a Zizmer, came to England in the time of Elizabeth, perhaps via the Low Lands, possibly as a soldier or cloth merchant. This could account for Michael Sizemore's burial in the Flemish cemetery of St Katharine's by the Tower, usually reserved for foreigners. It also explains the predilection in descendants for such names as Ephraim, Michael, Edward, William, John, Richard, James, George, Hiram, Isaac, Samuel, Solomon and Henry. And why girls were named Lillie, Lydia, Louisa, Naomi, Pharaba, Rebecca, Sarah and Vitula. The last name (also found in my wife's grandmother's name) was a Jewish amulet name. It meant "old woman" in Latin and was given to a child to augur a long life.

Zismer took the form of Cismar, Cismarik, Zhesmer, Zizmor, Ziesmer, Zausmer, Cismaru and Tzismaro—all amply attested in the records of European Jewry, including Jewish Gen's Holocaust Database, with records of over two million victims of Nazi genocide.

So our bizarre genetic genealogy journey ends where it started. Was it for nothing that Kafka died saying he wanted to be reborn as "a Red Indian"?

*Sequoyah in the only surviving contemporary oil portrait, attributed to Henry Inman (1801-1846). Private Collection. ©Tony Holman. Used with permission.*

# 8 THE SHAPE OF THINGS TO COME

The DNA Consultants Blog made a definite splash with its first post in August of 2009, when "Anomalous Mitochondrial DNA Lineages among the Cherokee" reported on the results of Phase I of the Cherokee DNA Project. We reproduce here some of the related posts over the next few years. Whether they are about genetics, history, archeology, rock art or world religion, we think you will agree they capture fresh, emerging topics in the public eye and serve as harbingers of the exciting revelations of genetic genealogy.

## Acadian Anomalies
*Anomalous Native American Lineages Now Identified Also among Micmac Indians*

After posting "Anomalous Mitochondrial DNA Lineages in the Cherokee," and after being interviewed on the subject by an Internet radio show host, I was contacted by participants in the Amerindian Ancestry out of Acadia Project who were struck by similarities in results for the two groups. Established in 2006, the Amerindian Ancestry Out of Acadia DNA Project mission is to research and publish the mtDNA and Y chromosome genetic test results of site participants who descend from persons living in Nova Scotia and surrounding environs in the 17th and 18th centuries, focusing specifically upon the early population of l'Acadie.

As part of its mission, the Project develops a database of published mtDNA and Y Chromosome test results and encourages the sharing of this information among other similarly focused studies for the purposes of comparison and the advancement of science and research.

According to Project Administrator Marie A. Rundquist, "We descend from both Amerindians (mostly Mi'kmaq) and the early French settlers who arrived in Port Royal in the 1600s, many of them single French men who married Amerindian wives, whose families would become pioneers of the New World. Our family lines have extended well-beyond the original boundaries of what was known to the French as Acadia, but to our AmerIndian ancestors as Mi'kma'ki, as our ancestors settled the outer-reaches of Nova Scotia, including Cape Breton, Newfoundland, New Brunswick, Prince Edward Island and Quebec. Our family lines continue to extend, traversing the entire North American continent and beyond."

Rundquist adds, "Many who live in the United States trace their genealogies back to the first Acadian AmerIndian immigrants who arrived in Louisiana after being deported from Nova Scotia by the British in 1755 (in the "Grand Deportation')—and belong to a 'Cajun' community known worldwide for its food, flair, fun, and love of all things French.

Several members of the group, as it turns out, have rare haplogroups X, U, and other "anomalous types," as compiled by DNA Consultants and reported in the previous blog post. Some highlights from the study of Cherokee descendants are:

- H, the most common European type today, is virtually absent, demonstrating lack of inflow from recent Europeans
- J present in lines explicitly recognized to be Cherokee
- X the signature of a Canaanite people whose center of diffusion was the Hills of Galilee, hypothetically correlating with Jews and Phoenicians
- U suggesting Eastern Mediterranean, specifically Greek
- K also suggesting Eastern Mediterranean or Middle Eastern, hypothetically correlating with Jews and Phoenicians
- T reflecting Egyptian high frequencies found almost nowhere else

According to Elizabeth Caldwell Hirschman, the Cumberland Gap mtDNA Project with overlapping territory with the Cherokee and Melungeon homelands in the Southern Appalachian Mountains also shows elevated frequencies of T. Project administrator Roberta Estes recently published the results of a large study of Native American Eastern Seaboard mixed populations "in relation to Sir Walter Raleigh's Lost Colony of Roanoke" in the online *Journal of Genetic Genealogy* 5(2):96-130, 2009.

It was titled "Where Have All the Indians Gone?" To which, several people replied, "We're all still here, thank you very much."

Harvard University professor Barry Fell in *Saga America* (1980) presented historical, epigraphic, archeological and linguistic evidence suggesting links between Greeks and Egyptians and the Algonquian Indians of Nova Scotia, Acadia and surrounding regions around the mouth of the St. Lawrence Seaway, particularly the Abnaki ("White") and Micmac Indians. He noted in his previous study *America B.C.* (1976) that the second century CE Greek historian Plutarch recorded that "Greeks had settled among the barbarian peoples of the Western Epeiros (continent)." Fell inferred from Plutarch's passage that "these Greeks had intermarried with the barbarians, had adopted their language, but had blended their own Greek language with it."

In an appendix, Fell assembled extensive word-lists comparing Abenaki and Micmac vocabulary in the areas of navigation, fishing, astronomy, meteorology, justice and administration, medicine, anatomy, and economy with virtually identical terms in Ptolemaic Greek. One example is Greek *ap'aktes* Abenaki/Micmac *ab'akt* English "a distant shore."

Fell's work was continued by John H. Cooper, "Ancient Greek Cultural and Linguistic Influences in Atlantic North America," *NEARA Journal* 35/2.

## Archeology Venturing into Uncharted Waters, Or At least Starting to Get Its Feet Wet

*American Schools of Oriental Research Annual Meeting: Tracking the Med's Stone Age Sailors*
Andrew Lawler

According to Andrew Lawler in *Science* magazine, genetic studies are beginning to fill in the missing pieces in the history and prehistory of seafaring. "By carefully sorting genetic data from living people, a researcher at this recent meeting covered in *Science* reported that around 6000 BCE, early seafarers indeed spread their seed—both agricultural and genetic— from their homeland in the Near East as far west across the Mediterranean as Marseilles, but no farther," writes Lawler.

No farther? Could that be because they have looked no farther?

Gunnar Thompson's new study, whose first print runs have already been exhausted, *Ancient Egyptian Maize*, builds a well-documented and persuasive case that "Indian corn blossomed with equal vigor along the shores of the Nile River *and* Gulf of Mexico at the very dawn of history."

You may say that Gunnar Thompson is not a "real" researcher, but we would counter that 400 corncobs on ancient tombs and papyrus scrolls of Egypt and corncobs depicted with copper weapons on ancient ships are real enough.

"Male regents in the Middle East and India sent mariners overseas in search of the world's purest copper deposits. These were located in the Mediterranean Sea on the Island of Cyprus, in the Persian Gulf on Megan Island, and on Isle Royale in the Upper Great Lakes Region of North America. This worldwide exploration took place in approximately 6000 BCE...all the way to the shores of North and South America" (p.2).

## Book of Dead Brought to Life
*Exhibit at British Museum Underlines Our Debt to Egypt*

Andrew Robinson reviews the British Museum's new exhibition "Journey through the Afterlife" in this week's *Nature* (468:632f.). London has the largest collection of these guidebooks customarily placed beside mummified corpses in the graves and tombs of the dead. It is not likely the large exhibit will travel, however, because of the fragility of the paints and papyrus scrolls.

The ancient Egyptians called these compilations the "book of coming forth by day," because they conceived that the soul (*ba*) of the deceased flew about during the daylight hours and continued to enjoy life. It was Egyptian excavators who coined the term "book of the dead."

According to the catalogue, it was Egyptian religion, despite its pantheon of animal-headed deities and plethora of magic spells, that was the foundation of Western systems of morality. The expression "light-hearted" reminds us of this. The Egyptians believed—thousands of years before Hammurabi or Moses—that you were answerable for your lies and sins upon death, and that your heart would be weighed by the god Anubis against the feather of truth.

## On the Trail of Spider Woman

*Thoughts about the origin of mitochondrial haplogroup B and Mother Earth symbolism among the Hopi, Zuni, Hohokam, Fremont Indians and others*

I got a holiday present from my wife, an unusual little book titled *On the Trail of Spider Woman. Petroglyphs, Pictographs, and Myths of the Southwest,* by Carol Patterson-Rudolph (Santa Fe: Ancient City Press, 1997). Putting this intriguing study together with a travel book by David Hatcher Childress, my son and I took a four-day road trip into the homeland of the Indians credited with having the first civilization in the Southwest, a settled town life marked by desert agriculture, canals, pottery, baskets, ballcourts, plazas and adobe pueblos, pithouses and kivas. Previous occupants of the area were non-sedentary hunter-gatherers considered to be "paleo-Indians."

We visited Painted Rock Petroglyph Site outside Gila Bend, in the middle of nowhere, and ended the trip in the barren sands outside Phoenix, where we began it, visiting the Hohokam Pima National Archeological Monument, also known as Snaketown. The former is little seen, and the latter cannot be seen. The Pima (now Gila River Indians) had Snaketown's ballcourt and other ruins reburied by backhoes in the 1970s. The caretakers of this declared national treasure decided not to open it to anyone to view or visit because of its "sensitive" nature. There are no signs, no roads, nothing left above ground.

*View of pecked records and markings of Hohokam, 200 B.C.- A.D. 1300, on granite outcropping called Painted Rock.*

At Painted Rock, the first paradox we pondered was why it was called "painted" rock when there is no paint. Petroglyphs are the result of pecking away the dark desert varnish to make a negative image on the underlying lighter rock. We wondered if it had anything to do with the Paint People, or Phoenicians, Kanawah Indians of the East Coast or Cherokee and Saponi Paint Clans.

The second mystery was the abundance of snake imagery. Famously, snakes in Indian tradition stand for boats and water. We noticed a Corn Cross, the symbol of the Feathered Serpent or Quetzalcoatl religion, multiply introduced into Mexico from both the East and the West by white, bearded strangers in ships, who brought rule by laws and numerous arts of civilization and banned human sacrifice.

The third thing we remarked upon were the many Great Goddess, Earth Mother or birthing/fertility symbols. Such places were undoubtedly shrines where women came to be blessed and get married and give birth. Sun Park in Hopiland has numerous hemispherical carvings about two inches wide where people ground out minerals to eat. These cupmarks or cupoles at petroglyph sites puzzled most archeologists until an important scholarly journal article clarified their meaning as part of a worldwide phenomenon known as pica (pronounced "PIE-ka"), "the desire to ingest nonfood substances such as rock powder, clay, chalk, dirt, and other material by some humans, especially pregnant women" (Kevin L. Callahan, "Pica, Geophagy, and Rock-Art in the Eastern United States," in *The Rock-Art of Eastern North America,* ed. Carol Diaz-Granados and James R. Duncan, Tuscaloosa: U of Alabama P, 2004, p. 65.)

In general, it may not be going too far to say that petroglyphs are ignored both by archeology and anthropology. Their study is a no man's land. Sun Park has a birthing cave and birthing stone. Canyon de Chelly has the most photographed Mother Earth rock formation in the world, Spider Rock, a chthonic monument discussed on page 83 of the Spider Woman book by Patterson-Rudolph.

*Who Were the Hohokam?*

There were also clear images of horses, riders, people praying, spirals, axis mundi (center of the earth) symbols like the iron butterfly and cross, labyrinths, bilobed axes, irrigation plans, horned beasts, felines, palaces or villages and warriors with spears and shields. We searched in vain for anomalous depictions of whales, elephants and deep-water fish, found at other similar sites, but the sun was sinking. We did not have time to make a thorough inspection of the motifs. There is a famous petroglyph of a whale at Old Oraibi.

The name Ho-ho-kam is usually explained as meaning "Those Who Are Departed," but such an etymology is more a gloss than a literal translation reflecting its meaning and origin. Like many words in the Hopi, Zuni, Pima and Azteco-Utan languages it is composed of South Semitic elements. In Egyptian, it literally means "Sea Peoples" or "Foreigners." The historic Sea Peoples came from Asia Minor and once threatened to overwhelm the Egyptian empire. The Philistines and Phoenicians are related to them. They were remarkable for their feather bonnets. Like their relatives the Cretans, they practiced a long-protracted continuance of the Stone Age's Mother Goddess worship down into the Bronze Age.

Haplogroup B is the signature lineage of certain Indians in North America. Its ultimate source is Southeast Asia (not Mongolia, as has been suggested for the other three classic Native American haplogroups A, C and D). From an epicenter in Taiwan and Sundaland it took multiple migratory routes to the Americas (Eschleman et al. 2004). It has high frequencies in Polynesia, which was settled from Southeast Asia. B attains majority status among the Western Indians of the U.S. such as the Hopi, Zuni (77%), Anasazi (78%), Yuman, and Jemez Pueblo (89%), and it is found in levels approaching 70% in the Cherokee and Chickasaw.

We believe Spider Woman is simply an aspect of Great Goddess worship brought by those who came from Southeast Asia through Polynesia and helped colonized the American Southwest. She is the same as the Earth Mother. In most cultures, she gives way to sky and sun deities and male hierarchies. But her religion seems to have persisted in the Hohokam, Cherokee and Hopi tribes in a similar fashion to cults surviving in the Cretans, Phoenicians and Sea Peoples.

According to Hopi and other traditions, at the end of the last age the Mother Goddess ceased to be the leader of the people in their wanderings and went back "under the sea" *to the east and west* whence she and they had emerged. We can only infer from this that Spider Woman, as she was called in Asia and the Pacific, and the Great Goddess, as she was known in the Old World of the Middle East, relinquished her role as supreme deity to the new male pantheons and withdrew across the Pacific and Atlantic Oceans to the distant origins of civilization outside the Americas. Ironically, her memory survived better among the Indian nations than in the war-torn empires and materialistic cultures that came to dominate world history elsewhere. American Indian societies today offer rare vestiges of matriarchy as opposed to patriarchy.

## Haplogroup B and the Water Clan
*Native Hawaiians and Native Americans*

In a previous post, "On the Trail of Spider Woman," we suggested that petroglyphs in Arizona and Utah with female goddess symbolism and birthing ceremonies were connected with the Hohokam ("Sea Peoples") and other Indians who followed in their wake, corresponding approximately to archeology and anthropology's Basketmaker Culture. In this and a series of posts over the next few months, we will show pictures of "emergence" petroglyphs from Hawaii, New Guinea, California, Hopi, Zuni, Pima, Papago, Fremont, Zuni, Mimbres, Palavayu and Eastern Woodlands cultural sites that support this thesis. We believe them to be the stepping stones of female haplogroup B and associated lineages.

Mitochondrial Haplogroup B does not have as its dissemination center Mongolia or Siberia or Central Asia but Southeast Asia, specifically Taiwan and Indonesia, and is characteristic, in contrast with Indian groups emphasizing A, C and D, of the Pueblo Indians and some Southeastern Indians such as the Cherokee and Chickasaw and Choctaw. It entered the Americas in successive waves, some of them seaborne, over many millennia.

## Haplogroup N in Europe and the Middle East
*And Now in the Cherokee...*

Haplogroup N1a became prominent in genetics literature when the studies of Wolfgang Haak et al. on 7500 year old skeletons in Central Europe revealed that 25% of the Neolithic European population might have belonged to this lineage. The skeletons were found to be members of the Linear Pottery Culture (LBK ware) credited with being the first farming culture in Central Europe.

The study was a major development in the debate on the origin of

European populations, since Brandt et al. argued that "The discovery of mitochondrial type N1a in Central European Neolithic skeletons at a high frequency enabled us to answer the question of whether the modern population is maternally descended from the early farmers instead of addressing the traditional question of the origin of early European farmers."

*7,000 Year-Old Linear-bandkeramik (LBK ware) from Stone Age Germany.*

## Neolithic Revolution

Two competing scenarios exist for the spread of the Neolithic from the Near East to Europe:

- Demic diffusion (in which farming is brought by farmers), for example Renfrew's NDT - Anatolian hypothesis
- Cultural diffusion (in which farming is spread by the passage of ideas), which is the assumption in Alinei's Paleolithic Continuity Theory.

The study's authors concluded: "Our finding lends weight to a proposed Paleolithic ancestry for modern Europeans."

N currently appears in only .18%-.2% of regional populations. It is widely distributed throughout Eurasia and Northern Africa and is divided into the European, Central Asian, and African/South Asian branches based on specific genetic markers. Exact origins and migration patterns of this haplogroup are still unknown and a subject of some debate.

Although not one of the classic Native American lineages (A, B, C, D, and X), N has been identified in the ancient Southwest in the Fremont

Culture centered in Utah. It is one of the Middle Eastern lineages that appear in the Cherokee and other Indians (see DNA Consultants Blog, "Anomalous Mitochondrial DNA Lineages in the Cherokee"). Most investigators attribute this phenomenon to recent European admixture. But such haplotypes if only instanced in North America without exact Old World matches could just as well be considered Native American.

It has been suggested that N is also characteristic of the Sea Peoples, who may have traveled to the American Southwest in antiquity.

*Hawaiian altar with water-clan icon.*

The first picture (above) comes from the western coast of the island of Hawaii. It is considered one of the oldest religious shrines in the Hawaiian Islands. It shows a stick figure carved into a rock set in the ground. As we will see, this is a typical "emergence" figure marking the arrival of a people in a new phase of existence. The symbolism is of a female mother figure giving birth, her progeny here depicted by the tail-like extension coming from between her legs. There are thousands of variations of this tribal or clan mother iconography scattered over Asia and the Americas (but not apparently found in Europe or Africa).

The Hawaiians considered the western coast of the Big Island their place of emergence. According to their legends, their people came from the sea from the southwest and were noted for their ability to twist plants and fibers into ropes. Their capital was hence called Hilo (twisted, plaited). On account of their subtlety in these arts they adopted the hula (twist) dance as their national dance. Its original purpose was as a fertility ritual to increase population. (Johannes C. Andersen, *Myths and Legends of the Polynesians*, Tokyo: Tuttle, 1969.) The main song sung during the enactment of the *hula* was called *The Water of Kane, or Waters of Life*.

The Hawaiian Mother symbol illustrated on the opposite page seems to be connected with a certain clan. As is often the case, the head of the female figure is differentiated to show which clan. This one has horns and could represent a dragonfly. This insect recurs in American Indian petroglyphs where it is associated with the Water Clan and fertility rites. To read the Hawaiian petroglyph properly we might say, "Here is the spot where the Head Mother of the Water Clan emerged and gave birth to her people." It is likely (although no legends are preserved regarding its use) that women made offerings here to become fertile, attract husbands and be delivered of healthy children. In similar ceremonial sites, such figures mark an actual birthing stone where women squatted to give birth, attended by midwives and clan mothers.

*Native American Parallels*

To show the physical resemblance of the Hawaiian design to American Indian symbols we will reproduce thumbprints below from different traditions. They will be linked together and explicated in subsequent posts in this series.

*"Lizard Woman" petroglyphs from Arizona/Utah.*

*"Lizard figure" at "ceremonial" Burnt Ridge Petroglyph Site, Madison County, Kentucky.*

*Water Clan symbols from petroglyph handbook, Springerville (Zuni) cultural territory in Arizona. From left: meander, snake, chevrons in triline, emergence.*

## Emergence Petroglyphs Pacific-wide

Emergence petroglyphs as featured on previous blog posts about the Hopi, Sea Peoples, Hohokam, Fremont Indians and Cherokee ("Haplogroup B and Water Clan Symbols") have also turned up now in Patagonia in southern Chile, on the tip of the South American continent's Pacific Coast.

They were identified in Hawaii previously. These findings suggest the stick figure of a woman giving birth, or emergence petroglyph, is Pacific-wide and confined to that hemisphere, not instanced in Europe, the Middle East or Africa.

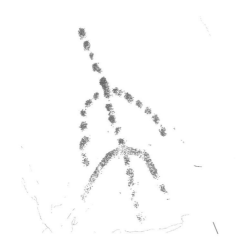

*Patagonian emergence petroglyph is reproduced from the International Newsletter on Rock Art (INORA), no. 58 (2010), where it was reported discovered in a cave of the Madre De Dios Archipelago 2000-2008. The researchers attributed it to the Kaweskar Indians, "a nomadic sea people now vanished." Its style matches similar petroglyphs from Hawaii and the American Southwest. It was grouped with sun disks, dancing figures and a horned anthropomorph, all painted in red ochre. The name Kaweskar means simply "Mankind." INORA.*

## Autosomal Testing for Native Americans

If you think haplogroup testing for Native American DNA is in sad shape, you should look at autosomal testing. It has been practically nonexistent. Even a major 2007 study by Wang et al. has glaring gaps and methodological quandaries. Wang, S. et al. (2007). "Genetic Variation and Population Structure in Native Americans." *PLoS Genetics* 3/11.

DNA Consultants' newest autosomal product is the Native American DNA Fingerprint Plus, based on 21 published studies of Native American population groups, as well as customer data on file. Results for many individuals were validated with older haplotyping methodology.

There were data for 3,583 Native Americans available in development of the product. These test results came from articles published between 1997 and 2009. Samples included individuals identifying with tribes or nations as follows:

Apache
Athabaskan
Huichol
Inupiat
Kichwa
Lumbee
Navajo
Salishan
Yupik

The following geographical areas were represented:

Alaska
Arizona
Brazil
British Columbia
Colombia
Ecuador
Florida
Guatemala
Mexico
Michigan
Minnesota
North Carolina
Oklahoma
Ontario
Saskatchewan

Nothing labeled as Cherokee—the largest Native group in the U.S., with more than 400,000 representatives—has ever been tested. Anecdotally, people of Cherokee descent often receive matches to North Carolina or

Michigan Native Americans. The reason for the latter matchup is obscure. North Carolina as the Cherokee's original homeland makes a lot more sense.

## Rigged Genetics
*If the facts don't fit the evidence change the facts . . .*

We always suspected the genetics community of clinging to stale dogmas and being slow to acknowledge emerging new evidence about American Indians. But we did not dream that their officiousness extended to changing the information given by test subjects to bring it into conformity with preconceived conclusions.

Not until we heard Marcy's story.

"Over the years, I've heard complaints that [a DNA testing company] is not really responsive when you have questions about unexpected results," Marcy said. "They usually suggest further testing, which of course, means more revenue to them.

"I've had some major disagreements with [a DNA testing company] over how they list results for mitochondrial haplogroup ancestral origins . . . . I found out they were taking dozens of T2's who had listed their earliest known female ancestor as being from America or the United States, changing this and placing them in the 'unknown' category. They claimed that because our haplogroup was designated European, our ancestors couldn't be from the United States!

"Now this was nonsense, because at the same time, they allowed people to claim other similarly-colonized western countries, like Cuba. It's my opinion that if participants list a country of origin for their earliest known female relative, that should be what is on the web page, not something assigned by [a DNA testing company] because as they told me, it may 'confuse people,' or contradict current scientific data.

"As a consequence [the DNA testing company's] publicly reported ancestral origins has nothing to do with our haplogroup's ancient Cherokee clan mother. The chips should fall where they may."

Now this is not professional behavior on the part of a DNA testing company. It prevents new findings from coming to light.

In a study of 52 individuals claiming direct maternal descent from an

American Indian woman, mostly Cherokee, we found that they were unmatched anywhere else except among other participants. Haplogroup T emerged as the largest lineage, followed by U, X, J and H. Similar proportions of these haplogroups were noted in the populations of Egypt, Israel and other parts of the East Mediterranean.

DNA testing companies do a disservice to their customers and to science by failing to call results as they appear without doctoring them. It is time geneticists stopped bringing all American Indians over the Bering Straits and forcing test subjects into the Procrustean bed of outmoded theory.

## Gene Surfing

Gene surfing is a process in population expansion whereby certain variations become prominent and dominant in a short time, appearing to skip the slow, steady, uniform accumulation of variegation and diversification. According to a study of the population structure and genealogies of Saguenay Lac-Saint-Jean in Quebec, this type of drastic change accompanied the immigrant wave front that spread over the area in the 17th century. "Deep Human Genealogies Reveal a Selective Advantage to Be on an Expanding Wave Front" in *Science* magazine describes the resulting demographics.

*Abstract*

Since their origin, human populations have colonized the whole planet, but the demographic processes governing range expansions are mostly unknown. We analyzed the genealogy of more than one million individuals resulting from a range expansion in Quebec between 1686 and 1960 and reconstructed the spatial dynamics of the expansion. We find that a majority of the present Saguenay Lac-Saint-Jean population can be traced back to ancestors having lived directly on or close to the wave front. Ancestors located on the front contributed significantly more to the current gene pool than those from the range core, likely due to a 20% larger effective fertility of women on the wave front. This fitness component is heritable on the wave front and not in the core, implying that this life-history trait evolves during range expansions.

So gene surfing in an expanding colonization phase can produce a genetic revolution whose effects will be felt for hundreds or thousands of years downstream in history.

We wonder if the same wave front demographics might explain some of the following population phenomena:

- Large-scale triumph of Norman male lineages following the conquest of England in 1066.
- Selective expansion of Middle Eastern genes in Tennessee (including Cherokee families, Jewish male and female lines and Melungeons)
- Relatedness among Jews and "Jewish diseases"
- Diversity-within-uniformity of Polynesians
- Population replacement of Old European (U, N) by Middle Eastern genes (T, J) in Europe as a result of the Neolithic Agricultural Revolution

Many students of history are puzzled why old populations have the allele frequencies and heterozygosity clines they have. Genetic drift is only part of the answer. Gene surfing and selection in deep history are the rest of it.


## New Study Confirms Radical Drop in Native Populations

Recent genetic studies have tended to throw cold water on the size and decimation of American Indian populations on European contact after 1492. A new study shows the falsehood of this thinking, and perhaps we are back to using the word "conquest" instead of the euphemistic term "contact." The conqueror of the Americas was not Europeans, though, but the diseases they unleashed on Indians.

According to *Science* magazine, "a study published this week in the *Proceedings of the National Academy of Sciences* pushes the pendulum back toward dramatic population declines. Using both modern and ancient mitochondrial DNA (mtDNA) from Native Americans, an international team concludes that about 500 years ago, the number of reproductively active Native American women quickly plunged by half, indicating a 'widespread and severe' contraction in population size."

The study summarized is: Brendan O'Fallon and Lars Fehren-Schmitz, "Native Americans Experienced a Strong Population Bottleneck Coincident with European Contact," *Proceedings of the National Academy of Science* (Dec. 5, 2011), doi: 10.1073/pnas.1112563108.

Critics of the study say that the conclusions may be illusory since we do not have a lot of ancient Native American DNA. But we will never have a lot of Native American DNA. That objection seems lame, and we applaud the new study as at least a step in the right direction of rectifying the true story of the Americas and escaping the apologist blinkers of colonial "Smithsonian-styled" methodologies and mindsets.

*Southeastern Indian diorama.*

## Ruins of Possible Maya Settlement in North Georgia

In what a December 22 report in *RawStory* describes as possibly "the most important archeological discovery in recent times," the ruins of a stone city believed to be at least 1,100 years old have come to light in the mountains of North Georgia. Interest in the Kenimer Mound, a large, five-sided pyramid in the foothills of Georgia's tallest mountain, Brasstown Bald, near Blairsville in the Chattahoochee National Forest go back to a 1999 University of Georgia dig led by archeologist Mark Williams.

At least 154 stone masonry walls for agricultural terraces were exposed, plus evidence of a sophisticated irrigation system, prompting Richard

Thornton to speculate that the site corresponds to Yupaha, a town explorer Hernando de Soto searched for unsuccessfully in 1540. Thornton relates the site to other Maya-like ruins in the Southeast and believes the people who build it were the Itza Maya, a word that carried over into the Cherokee language of the region.

Traditional oral histories such as those recorded by Constantine Rafinesque have always traced the origins of the Natchez and other pre-Muskoghean Native Americans in the Southeastern U.S. to Mexico. Rafinesque thus distinguishes between the Itzcans (or Aztec) and the Oguzhians (Algonquians).

The site is called Archaeological zone 9UN367 at Track Rock Gap and is a half-mile (800 m) square and rises 700 feet (213 m) in elevation up a steep mountainside.

## Reconstructing Your Parentage and Ancestry

*This exercise is included as an illustration for adopted persons or those whose parents are deceased or unavailable for autosomal DNA testing.*

Every year in the United States about half a million paternity cases are performed proving or disproving whether an alleged father is the true parent of a child. Sometimes there is a court order to do this; at other times, it is sheerly for personal information. The determination of parentage is made based on a simple comparison of a small rock-hard number of genetic markers in the DNA fingerprint of the child and alleged father. Samples are extracted from a 30-second cheek swab and processed at any of an estimated 2,000 forensic labs across the country. The standard in place since about 1997 has been a set of 30-32 biallelic or double values each person carries on loci spread across their chromosomes, making for a virtually unique identification signature that reflects the equal DNA input of mother and father (and in fact all grandparents and all ancestors).

Often termed CODIS markers (standing for Combined DNA Identification System), these alleles or variations are the magic numbers underlying the popularity of paternity tests as well as the national passion for jailing or exonerating crime suspects. If a value is found in the DNA profile of the child and is not present in the two observed values of the alleged father on the same locus, this constitutes what is known in the paternity business as an exclusion: the alleged father is almost certainly *not* the true father. Conversely, if *all* the alleged father's values can be detected in the child's on each location, one after another, that male is judged to be the child's biological father to a 99.999% certainty. Paternity tests are simple math.

A famous paternity test involved proving who was the true father of the baby born to Anna Nicole Smith in 2006. After her death in early 2007, several men came forward claiming to be the father, including a European prince, Anna Nicole's bodyguard and a convict who had been a former boyfriend. Larry Birkhead pressed his case. When the results came in, he was declared by Bahamian court to be the baby's biological father. The child's original birth certificate was amended to show this.

Can paternity testing be used in a reverse process to establish the identity of a father, given only the child's DNA profile? No, but with enough DNA profiles available for comparison the missing member of a family group can be reconstructed by comparing alleles they must share, called obligate. Doing so is a matter of logic and statistics, mostly just either-or, deductive logic.

I became interested in reconstructing a parent's profile after many of DNA Consultants' customers inquired if such a calculation or estimate was even possible. Some were adopted persons who had no recourse to testing their parents, some knew one parent but not the other, and some had no access to parents. They were either uninterested or unavailable. In a special category were females who were only-children with both parents deceased who wanted to know something about their father, but who could not take a Y-chromosome haplotyping test, as they did not carry a copy of their father's male DNA. In this respect, autosomal DNA testing is the great equalizer.

My father Lawden Henry Yates died in 1978. My mother Bessie Cooper Yates lived to the advent of DNA tests, but I failed to obtain any sample from her before her death in 2006. I had siblings and half-siblings still living, however, so in 2010, I constructed a family group autosomal DNA study with the help of Crystal Wagner at Chromosomal Laboratories/Bode Technology. The results were very satisfying.

*Step One*

I was fortunate to have the participation of three half-sisters by my father, along with his second wife, their mother. Comparing mother and daughters I was able to verify the obligate alleles each daughter *must* have received from the mother.

Autosomal alleles are fixed in our genealogy, have little or no mutations (unlike YSTRs, which mutate from generation to generation, as do mitochondrial nucleotide positions, though more gradually over time) and derive from both parents equally by recombination at the moment of conception. They are copied and preserved without change in every cell of our bodies. The mother is responsible for half of the equation. By a process of elimination the other number on each row of the lab report *must* represent the father's contributions. This method is completely logical and unequivocal. There can be no other answer to the problem. No studies suggest these pieces of our double helix DNA change significantly in transmission from one generation to the next or mutate over time in genealogies. Their values and patterns are strictly attributable to heredity.

*Step Two*
The father's alleles are confirmed by a comparison with three children by his first wife, my mother.

*Step Three*
By the same watertight process we can now proceed to the mother's reconstructed DNA profile. In it, we can expect to visualize the final piece of the puzzle, proceeding from the known to the unknown according to the immutable laws of autosomal DNA and genetic inheritance.

We have arrived at my mother Bessie Yates' DNA profile by a multi-step process of extrapolating it using three of her children and three children by her husband's second marriage, along with the test results of my half-sisters' mother. Seven tested profiles yielded two reconstructed ones. In the process we have also recovered my deceased father's DNA profile.

*Separating Mother and Father's Contributions to Ancestry*
Having overcome these hurdles, I was most interested in the utility of the results. I felt confident about the method. But what excited me most was to see how my own autosomal ancestry results might be respectively apportioned in my parents. For this, I ran a DNA Fingerprint Plus on them both. The findings were very satisfying to me personally, helping solve

many questions I had always had about what ancestry I got from my father, what from my mother and what from both.

Let's start with American Indian admixture. My own DNA Fingerprint Test, as well as percentage tests through another company, suggested a relatively large amount, perhaps one-quarter all told by various measures, but family tradition had placed Native American heritage solely on my mother's side. To be sure, my mother gave me a Native American mitochondrial haplotype, indicating a female line going back to a Cherokee woman in Georgia, traced as far back in records as 1790. Extensive genealogy research showed, however, that my father's great-grandmother was also a Cherokee with the surname Thomas from North Carolina. What did the new autosomal DNA profiles say?

On a rough measure, I have received a "double dose" of Native American II, a marker co-relating with 80% of 24 tested American Indian populations in the atDNA 4.0 database. (Two siblings and one half-sibling received only single doses.) This seemed to indicate that I had some degree Native American (not possible to say how much) from both parents. True enough apparently, judging from the top world matches for my mother and father.

Autosomal STR loci do have mutation rates, but they are not believed to be significant. John M. Butler, *Fundamentals of Forensic DNA Typing* (Amsterdam: Elsevier, 2010), pp. 402-3.According to these frequencies, my mother and father's Native American ancestry reinforced each other in me to make my top four matches Native American (or Siberian-Mongol-Turkic), so that I am about twice as likely to be graded into the Native American category by population statistics than the European. Similar conclusions emerged from my siblings' tests, and a diminished presence of Native American indicators was confirmed in my half-siblings, although their mother seemed to evince some Native American as well as my father, the shared parent. All participants in this study had grandparents born in North Alabama.

Further observations are possible. For instance, I was surprised to see a large indication of Jewish ancestry in my father's profile. Genealogy confirms as much, as the family surname is Hebrew (an anagram of Ger Tzedek similar to Katz, Kohen Tzedek). The emigrant Yates figure was reportedly an English Jew in seventeenth-century Virginia. My mother also showed Jewish ancestry. Both parents matched Melungeons, an

Appalachian ethnic type suspected to have Sephardic Jewish forebears. My father's family included uncles named Josephus, Manaen, Irbin, Azariah, Lazarus and Sherith—apparently his Middle Eastern matches were truthful to a partial Muslim background. My mother's mother was named Palestine, and the names Isaac and Jacob were ubiquitous in her family tree. But neither side of the family claimed any Jewish heritage. It was left to autosomal DNA to reveal that hidden inheritance.

Although never performed before to my knowledge, this method of reconstructing autosomal profiles can be useful to others seeking to recover unavailable relatives' genetic fingerprints and to separate parents' contributions to their children's ethnic and ancestral stories. Since it is based on immutable markers in DNA it rests on more solid ground than Y chromosome alleles or mitochondrial mutations. The challenge in exploiting the method is to have enough subjects in your family group study. In my case, I was fortunate to have a prolific father with six living children. I would like to conclude by thanking all my siblings, half-sisters and my father's widow. Their participation made it possible to present a true first in DNA genealogy.

## American Indians and Turkic People Share Deep Ancestry
*We've known or suspected as much for a long time*

American Indians and Turkic peoples of the Altai region of southern Siberia share common ancestors. American scientists Thomas Jefferson and Constantine Rafinesque were the first to demonstrate this genetic similarity, long before the days of DNA. Now an article in *American Journal of Human Genetics* has clenched the argument with mitochondrial and Y chromosomal DNA studies.

The groundbreaking citation is: Matthew C. Dulik et al., Mitochondrial DNA and Y Chromosome Variation Provides Evidence for a Recent Common Ancestry between Native Americans and Indigenous Altaians, *AJHG* 90/2, 229-246.

From *Old World Roots of the Cherokee*, a book appearing June 15 by Donald N. Yates:

—Thomas Jefferson thought American Indians were Turks and Tartars coming across the Bering Sea from Asia, while his contemporary John Filson believed them to be Phoenicians. (See Boorstin, Daniel J. *The Lost World of Thomas Jefferson*, Chicago: U of Chicago P, 1993.)

—"Many other empires having begun to rise in the vicinity of Aztlan, such as those of Bali [Indonesia, perhaps Oppenheimer's Eden in the East?], Scythia [Russian steppes], Thibet, Oghuz [Lake Baikal area], the Iztacan were driven eastwards, north of China; but some fragments of the nation are still found in the Caucasus, &c. such as the Abians or Abassans, Alticezecs [Altai Turks], Cushazibs, Chunsags, Modjors, &c. (Rafinesque)

—"The six Iztacan nations being still pressed upon by their neighbours the Oghuzians [Uigur Turks], Moguls [Mongols], &c. gradually retreated or sent colonies to Japan, and the islands of the Pacific ocean; having discovered America at the peninsula of Alasca [Alaska, a Chinese word], during their navigations, the bulk of the nation came over and spread from Alasca to Anahuac, establishing many states in the west of America, such as Tula [Toltec], Amaquemeca, Tehuajo [Tewa, Tiwa, Tawa], Nabajoa [Navajo], Teopantla, Huehue, and many others.

—"After crossing the mountains, they discovered and followed the Missouri and Arkanzas rivers, reaching thus the Mississippi and Kentucky (26-27)."

When will American history books catch up to this new proof? We predict: never. The jingoistic Smithsonian has its own versions of things and these are ingrained into anthropological dogma as deeply as Manifest Destiny. Interestingly, Turkish and Muslim historians have already entered it as a basic fact of history. They have long claimed American Indians as their genetic cousins.

## Were Solutreans in America Ancient Egyptians?

Yes, according to Bill Tiffee, whose article on Solutreans in America will appear in volume 29 of the series Epigraphic Society Occasional Papers. Titled "Were Ancient Egyptians the Solutreans Who First Settled America?" the new study, he says, "looks at the possibility that the Solutreans who first settled America were from Egypt, and that the genetic marker X is found in the highest concentrations among the Druze (who migrated from Egypt

1,000 years ago) and the descendants of the Moundbuilder Native groups including the Sioux and Algonquin and possibly the Cherokee." We have previously suggested that the Cherokee incorporate both Greek and Egyptian DNA. Chapter 3 of my new book *Old World Roots of the Cherokee* is devoted to the DNA story of the so-called "anomalous" Cherokee lines, including haplogroups T and X.

Several prominent scholars have argued that Europeans known to archeologists as the Solutreans of France and Spain around 18,000 years ago were the first to settle the Americas. Tiffee examines the similarities between Solutrean and Clovis or Paleo-Indian stone technology and reconstructs the Solutrean culture in Egypt beginning 24,000 years ago (p. 119). He links ancient Egyptians with genetic marker E-M78, mitochondrial haplogroup X, Tula and the Spiro Complex mounds in Oklahoma, among other North American sites. He also discusses the Great Flood of about 10,000 years ago, the legends surrounding Osiris and the rise of agriculture in southern Turkey (Göbekli Tepe).

"Perhaps," he concludes, "Egyptologists need to rethink their paradigms of ancient Egypt. And perhaps modern Native American descendants of the Moundbuilders, the Algonquin groups, Sioux, Cherokee, Chickasaw (and other Native cultures closely related to mound-building) need to reconsider where their most ancient ancestors came from (129)."

In DNA Consultants' Cherokee DNA study, "Anomalous Mitochondrial DNA Lineages in the Cherokee," as well as numerous blog posts since 2009, it was reported that haplogroups U, T, K, J, N, X and L are found in Cherokee descendants in frequencies mirroring those of Egypt.

## Bering Land-Bridge Theory Reasserted

The tripartite Asian Model of the peopling of the Americas through "Beringia" was re-asserted with "the most comprehensive survey of genetic diversity in Native Americans so far" in a study published in *Nature* this week, "Reconstructing Native American Population History," by Harvard's David Reich et al. If ever there was a blue chip study, this is it. Only it is more like junk bonds in which no one should put stock.

If you read the fine print of this new issue from the Ivy League establishment, you will discover that geneticists are still ignoring anything that does not support their preconceived conclusions:

• Although the authors claim to go beyond examining single loci on the mitochondrial genome or Y chromosome and to analyze instead 364,470 SNPs, they are still stuck on the same biased samples. In one of their feats of prestidigitation, they statistically filter out "West-Eurasian-related and sub-Saharan African related ancestry in many Native Americans" (p. 371). They ignore anything that does not support their preconceived conclusions.

• Anthropologists have always insisted on the Bering Land bridge. Geneticists start with anthropologists' assumptions and test their model. Guess what? After enough manipulations you can make it work!

• Whole genome sequencing was adopted because it has become most economical, but half the samples were just adopted into the new study after doctoring the preexisting data. These biased data (Pima, Inuit etc.) were not reliable when they were collected (as far back as the 1990s), and have only been improved through statistical voodoo. The new Indians' samples (heavily geared to Mexico, Central America and northern South America) were probably subjected to SNP investigation out of interest in biodiversity and possible medical applications anyway. The motives of investigators who mostly belong to medical faculties are tainted.

Here's the conclusion:

> Our analyses show that the great majority of Native American populations—from Canada to the southern tip of Chile—derive their ancestry from a homogeneous 'First American' ancestral population, presumably the one that crossed the Bering Strait more than 15,000 years ago. We also document at least two additional streams of Asian gene flow into America, allowing us to reject the view that all present-day Native Americans stem from a single migration wave, and supporting the more complex scenarios proposed by some other studies. In particular, the three distinct Asian lineages we detect—'First American', 'Eskimo–Aleut' and a separate one in the Na-Dene-speaking Chipewyan—are consistent with a three-wave model proposed mostly on the basis of dental morphology and a controversial interpretation of the linguistic data.

So we're back to Greenberg and other discredited purveyors of the linguistic explanation of human diversity, something they used to call racism. Maybe that's because culturally inferior American Indians make such great subjects for grant getting in the first place. Especially if they are safely dead, on a reservation, or far away and helpless and completely extraneous to our society.

## Out of Asia

"All the lights in the House of the High Priests of American Anthropology are out; all the doors and windows are shut and securely fastened (they do not sleep with their windows open for fear that a new idea might fly in); we have rung the bell of Reason, we have banged on the door with Logic, we have thrown the gravel of Evidence against their windows; but the only sign of life in the house is an occasional snore of Dogma. We are very much afraid that no one is going to come down and let us into the warm, musty halls where the venerable old ideas are nailed to the walls."

These biting words were penned by Harold Sterling Gladwin in *Men out of Asia*, the famous archeologist's most popular, non-technical work.

Published in 1947, Gladwin's book presented a maverick view of the peopling of the Americas identifying five migrations of diverse races including Negrittoes and Austronesians to the New World. Heretically, he placed the first migration as early as 25,000 years ago and argued that the earliest colonists were Australoid.

The reaction of his colleagues in the anthropological establishment was stony silence shading off into harrumphs and pshaws of injured pride, for Gladwin illustrated *Men out of Asia* with campy cartoons by Campbell Grant making fun of the sacred keepers of knowledge at the Peabody Museum at Harvard, Carnegie Foundation and Smithsonian Institution. In one, the dean of Southwest and Maya archeology Alfred V. Kidder is depicted as Dr. Phuddy Duddy sitting in academic robes atop a whistle sounding the alarm of illogical chronology. In another, a bespectacled Gladwin and his tweedy friend Professor Earnest Hooton of Harvard are shown in the academic doghouse "by request."

The Establishment is still uncomfortable about Gladwin, who died in 1983 after a distinguished career of more than 60 years. Although willing to praise his meticulous fieldwork on the Hohokam at Snaketown and exacting methodologies developed at the research center he founded at Gila Pueblo outside Globe, Arizona, they do not know quite what to say about his conclusions and hypotheses, which grew more adamant toward the end.

The destroying angel of unorthodox theories, Stephen Williams of the Peabody Museum, can only think that Gladwin succumbed to his "whimsies" and grew soft-headed in his old age. "I have always regarded *Men Out of Asia*," Williams writes in *Fantastic Archeology* (p. 229), "as a sort of 'hyper-diffusionist' spoof."

We wonder whether the honorable gentlemen in Harvard Yard and Castle on the Mall do not protest too much.

In a similar high-toned snipe, Williams dismisses the author of *Pale Ink* with its discussions of ancient records of Chinese explorations in America as "a sweet old lady (p. 185)." Louis Leakey, who believed on the basis of the Calico Early Man excavations he organized in California that humans occupied North America as long ago as 400,000 years, comes in for like treatment. Williams implies that Leakey was senile and hurried in his judgment (p. 303).

If a controversial interpretation of the archeological record cannot be debunked as lacking "soil truth" or the hard-won verities of the dig and thus being nothing but "armchair archeology," then one must resort to that time-honored device of the Ivy League sneer. For instance, Jeffrey Goodman's controversial *American Genesis* "mimics a scientific book very well" (p. 303), but it cannot possibly be taken seriously because, well, you know, no person in his right mind subscribes to a North American or Asian origin for humans! In addition to coming from a homely, unpatrician Western background, Goodman was also part Native American, which helped make him a pariah.

# 9 WHERE THERE'S SMOKE

*We continue our review of DNA Consultants Blog items with stories of breaking news about American Indian genetics and interviews with some of the participants in the Cherokee DNA Study.*

## Haplogroup T Among the Cherokee
### *A Surprising Middle Eastern Component*

Haplogroup T (named Tara by Bryan Sykes in *The Seven Daughters of Eve*) is usually not seen as a Native American lineage. But it is discussed as such in Donald Yates' *Old World Roots of the Cherokee*, where it takes its rightful place among other Middle Eastern haplogroups like U, J and X. Moreover, several geneticists have drawn attention to its prevalence in New World Jewish and Crypto-Jewish populations.

The following comes from Chapter 3, "DNA," pp. 55-57, and discusses some living examples of "Taras" who verified their Native American genealogies with a DNA test from DNA Consultants in 2007-2009, as reported in "Anomalous Mitochondrial DNA Lineages in the Cherokee."

Maternal lineage T arose in Mesopotamia approximately 10,000 to 12,000 years ago. It spread northward through the Caucasus and west from Anatolia into Europe. It shares a common source with haplogroup J in the parent haplogroup JT. Ancient people bearing haplogroup T and J are viewed by geneticists as some of the first farmers, introducing agriculture to Europe with the Neolithic Revolution. Europe's previous substrate emphasized older haplogroups U and N. The T lineage includes about 10%

of modern Europeans. The closer one goes to its origin in the Fertile Crescent the more prevalent it is.

All T's in the Cherokee project are unmatched in Old World populations. They do, however, in some cases, match each other. Such kinship indicates we are looking at members of the same definite group, with the same set of clan mothers as their ancestors. So let us briefly introduce some of these descendants of Middle Eastern-originating Cherokee lines.

Jonlyn L. Roberts, had a puzzling, but typical genealogy that led her to embark on a lifelong quest for answers. Her mother, Zella, was adopted by the George and Mary Hand family of Hand County, South Dakota in 1901. Little information was passed down, but piecing together clues from her childhood, Roberts believes that her mother's original family might have come from the Red Lake Ojibwe Indian Reservation or one of the North or South Dakota reservations. At any rate, her mtDNA haplotype is a unique form of T, one with certain distinctive variations in common with others in the study.

Another T in the study fully matched four people other people, all born in the United States. One of these noted their ancestor as being Birdie Burns, born 1889 in Arkansas, the daughter of Alice Cook, a Cherokee.

Gail Lynn Dean (T) is the wife of another participant, whose type belongs to anomalous U. Both she and her husband claim Cherokee ancestries.

T participant Linda Burckhalter is the great-great-granddaughter of Sully Firebush, the daughter of a Cherokee chief . Sully married Solomon Sutton, stowaway son of a London merchant, in what would seem to be another variation of "Jewish trader marries chief's daughter."

Two cases of T represent descent in separate lines from the historically documented Gentry sisters, Elizabeth and Nancy, daughters of Tyree Gentry, who moved to Arkansas in 1817. The tested descendants are aunts or cousins of Patrick Pynes, a non-registered Cherokee and professor of American Indian studies. Learning of the results of the study, Pynes commented, "The possible connections to Egyptian heritage among these Cherokee descendants are especially interesting. We have a photograph of one of the women in this T* line (a granddaughter of Nancy Gentry, I think), and she is wearing an Ankh necklace. We all thought that was kind of strange. As far as I know, the Gentrys were Methodist Episcopalians."

Three participants with T previously unknown to each other, and living in different parts of the country, turn out to be very close cousins descended from the same Cherokee ancestress. Their mitochondrial mutations exactly and fully match. Two claim Melungeon ancestry—a Yates male-linked cousin of the author and a relative of Phyllis Starnes (U, matching the author's). The third has adoption in the family, so the female ancestry is unknown.

A case of rare T5, Cheryl, took not only the mitochondrial test but also our CODIS-marker-based ethnic population test, DNA Fingerprint, to validate "Cherokee or Jewish ancestry" from her mother. The results of the DNA Fingerprint Test show Ashkenazi Jewish in the No. 1 position, followed by assorted American Indian matches. Cheryl says that she is exploring returning to Judaism, but that in the remote Texas town where her family lives there are few avenues or resources to pursue.

As tabulated in Appendix A, our small survey shows a great deal of diversity and relatedness. It includes more than a few participants who discovered they share the same Cherokee ancestry, maybe even the same clan. Unlike a random sample of the U.S. population, they exhibit a mix that turns the conventional numbers on their head. Haplogroup H, instead of an expected 50% dominant position, is one of the smallest, with only 7.7%. Haplogroup U, an older lineage representing the Stone Age colonization of Europe before the ascendency of H, contributes 25% of the total number. Haplogroup X, marked by an exiguous presence elsewhere, attains a frequency in the Cherokee more than tenfold that of Eurasia or rest of Native America.

Yet the most startling statistic concerns T haplotypes now verified in the Cherokee. At 27%, they constitute the leading anomalous haplogroup not corresponding to the types A, B, C, or D. Several of them evidently stem from the same Cherokee family or clan, although they have been scattered from their original home by historical circumstances. So much consistency in the findings reinforces the conclusion that this is an accurate cross-section of a population, not a random collection of DNA test subjects. No such mix could result from post-1492 European gene flow into the Cherokee Nation. To dismiss the evidence as admixture would mean that there was a large influx of Middle Eastern-born women selectively marrying Cherokee men in historical times, something not even suggested by historical records. Mitochondrial DNA can only come from mothers; it cannot be imported into a country by men.

If not from Siberia, Mongolia or Asia, where do our anomalous, non-Amerindian-appearing lineages come from? The level of haplogroup T in the Cherokee mirrors the percentage for Egypt, one of the only countries where T attains a major showing among the other types. In Egypt, T is three times what it is in Europe. Haplogroup U in our sample is about the same as the Middle East in general. Its frequency is similar to that of Turkey and Greece.

## Where Do I Come from: Monica Sanowar

*A Red-Hot Tale from the Nation's Capital*
By Monica R. Sanowar

I took my first test with Family Tree in 2006. This test showed my mtDNA as L3e2b2 and it went like this:

52% West African
39% European
9% EAST ASIAN
0% Native American

I could not believe the East Asian part, and I shrugged it off and thought—that has to be Native American.

So, fast forward—I took another test with Ancestry.com. This was autosomal and showed:

48% - West African
44% - European
8% - UNKNOWN

How can you be UNKNOWN?

Neither of these tests really breaks down what country your people may have originated from. So then I tried 23&me, their autosomal offering. The results:

49% - West African

48.3% European - Central - Northern - Non-specific

and the leftovers were .7 EAST ASIAN & NATIVE (although the NA box did not turn red)

and 1.4% UNSPECIFIED

I knew from family history that NA was on both sides of my fence. I also was aware that I had four of the traits Melungeon people have. I have the ridge in the back of my head that you can lay your finger in; I have ridges on the teeth and I can make the clicking sound on the shovel teeth; I have the Asian eyefold, and the very high arches. Can't get my foot inside of a boot and if I do, I can't get it off. I was amazed that I got my results in less than two weeks!

Finally, I tried DNA Consultants. Its test was the very first that didn't show "UNKNOWN" or non-specific. Everything was accounted for, although I did find a few shocks. No one told me about Sephardic Jews or the Portuguese. At last, a test verified my Native roots with valid matches to tribes or nations and confirmed Native American autosomal markers— from both parents, as I had been told.

I got into Native culture back in 1983 when I started to go to powwows. I finally felt at home. I enjoyed seeing people that looked like me, mixed. My great-great-great grandmother was listed on the FREE NEGRO LIST where it asked How Freed? And it was written BORN FREE. Then came a description— a light-skinned black, with long straight black hair and a small scar on her hand. Below is a picture of her daughter, Alethea Preston Pinn. Alethea's father was a white man named Allen Preston. Alethea had seven children with James E. Colvin, who was white, and all of their children were put on Walter Plecker's list of "mongrels" not allowed to vote or go to school. That was 1943. Not that long ago.

So, I got a second cousin to take the test with 23&me who comes directly from Sarah Pinn (the alleged light-skinned black woman). My cousin's haplogroup came in A2N – Native American.

I know that some things may show and some not, but DNA Consultants' test knocked the EAST ASIAN right off the page. I've learned a lot of different things with DNA testing, but DNA Consultants' is the best one I have seen and is well worth the money.

I love it when these geneticists and genealogists out there decide what you do or do not have in your family tree, especially the Indian part of the tree. As if this just could not have happened . . . . I am proud of all of it. I can just about hang up a flag from everywhere.

I can't praise the DNA Fingerprint Plus enough and wish I'd known about it years ago. I really appreciate all of the knowledge and insight Dr. Yates has about genealogy and history that I was totally unaware of. I actually spoke to him on the phone at length and he truly made my day. I highly recommend DNA Consultants' service to people who are looking for the truth about their genealogy.

And speaking of spicy mixtures, check out my hot sauces at Sun Pony. They've got secret, all-natural ingredients just like the family!

*Elizabeth Colvin, a granddaughter of Alethea Preston Pinn.* "Contrary to the belief and convictions of many people, long hair really does exist in my family," says Monica Sanowar. "It isn't a made-up fantasy and this was long before hairweaves. My cousin's hair was down to her calves."

*Alethea Preston Pinn, my great-great-grandmother on my paternal side.*

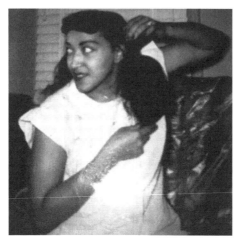

*My mother, Mary Wood.*

*Guest blog author Monica Sanowar is the founder of Sun Pony Distributors Inc., makers of a line of all-natural, wholesome condiments and energy supplements found in stores up and down the East Coast. Her first hot sauce was Yellow Thunder and her Native name is Sundancer. SunPony's D.C. Redbone Hot Sauce is the official hot sauce of the Anacostia Indians, D.C.'s little known indigenous people, who were first recorded by Capt. John Smith in 1608. Sanowar lives in Washington, D.C., not far from the Anacostia's village site, now a national historical landmark. Watch grassdancer Rusty Gillette in a video about D.C. Redbone.*

### Where Do I Come From: Teresa Panther-Yates

*I Found My Grandmother's People*
By Teresa Panther-Yates

I grew up thinking I was English on my father's side and French-Cherokee on my mother's. But I also knew there was a mystery in my Southern Gothic family. And no one was talking about it. It took me most of my life to document my

Melungeon and Jewish ancestry. I learned a lot on my journey through perseverance, but I learned the most from the DNA Fingerprint Plus. That journey has been a long one.

Our family reunions were bizarre. Grandmother, named Etalka Vetula, and my Aunt Elzina would arrive from an obscure town in Alabama looking just like two witches from Oz. At least that is what I thought when I was six. They wore clothes from another time and place. Sweeping black Victorian dresses with high collars, long sleeves and black lace-up boots in the heat of summer. It was the 1950's. No jewelry adorned their necks, and no smiles appeared on their faces.

It was especially discomfiting since my mother looked and acted like an early Cher, wearing flamboyant Spanish skirts and always tossing out witty and outrageous remarks. The witches and she did not get along. Whispers about "Black Dutch" circulated around the dinner table with slivers of pecan pie. Fried chicken was the main dish with tall, silver candles at the center lighted at dusk. We never ate ham. We never went to church.

If it was Christmas, it was spelled Xmas. There was no mention of the baby Jesus. Ornaments, songs, and holiday cards were generic and dissembling. My mother once shooed away carolers singing "Silent Night." Her favorite holiday tune was "Rockin Around the Xmas Tree." But we did not sing this around my severe aunts. The tree was decorated with redbirds and popcorn. My father would use the comics to wrap presents, not because we were poor. He was a doctor.

My maternal grandmother, Luta Mae, would have had taken me out of the Indian calico floral dress before my aunts arrived, putting on a black velvet one, to my dismay. I was the very picture of Wednesday from the Addams Family.

Of course, my family seemed normal to me. I did not know why most mothers I knew looked more like Doris Day or why they shunned my beautiful, dark-olive skinned mother at the country club, or why their children would not play with me. This was the South in the 50's before integration. Wasn't I white? I was confused.

When I married Don, we became very interested in our genealogy and would spend many weekends researching in archives and libraries and trying to not go blind looking at microfiche. On one of these weekends, we visited my Aunt Elzina. I have six Elzinas in my family. As amiable as ever, she jeered, "You will never discover the truth about my mother's people." She did let slip an interesting story about Great-grandmother Redema. When Redema was a young girl they "arrived on a rich man's farm to train his horses." Afterward they managed to buy the farm. Were they Gypsies? Aunt Elzina's arrogant challenge made me the more determined. There were several clues that I began to add up. I remembered that my mother took me aside when I was twelve (the age when a young girl is given a bat mitzvah in the Jewish faith). Did I know I was named after a little Sephardic Jewish girl "running around in the Arizona desert"? I thought it an odd remark, as I did not know any Jews.

We read Brent Kennedy's book and discovered many of our ancestors were Melungeon. Don looked up the name Etalka and determined it was Hungarian and Yiddish. My father gave me two paintings of my great-great-great-grandparents. I said, "Dad, these people are not English or French. They are too dark. What are they?" He said, "You ask too many questions. If you keep digging, you will find people you do not want to be related to."

A second cousin sent me a fragment of a letter she discovered a great-granduncle of mine had written. It was in Demotic Egyptian. After my Aunt Elzina died, I discovered from documents my father shipped on to me in cardboard boxes that before my line of Rameys were in France, they were in Egypt.

Before I got these records, we had just started the business DNA Consultants. Don ran my profile. Egyptian was at the top. I laughed, "This has got to be wrong!" But DNA doesn't lie.

I got expected information as well as some surprises. Melungeon was near the top. My grandfather had always told me he was part Cherokee. I got a Native American marker. But I also got things that threw me. My mother probably loved Spanish skirts for a reason. I have a lot of Iberian results. I did not know I had Turkish ancestry. This is a common match for anyone with Melungeon ancestry. And English? Near the bottom! It turns out I have more Mediterranean and Eastern European ancestry, as well as Jewish. I have two out of three Jewish markers, one a Sephardic Jewish marker, confirming my mother's talk to me, and proving one of the reasons that led to my open return to Judaism. I do have Hungarian matches as well as Romanian/Transylvanian matches (originally Hungarian territory), which confirmed Don's suspicion that Etalka was Hungarian. It turns out to be a diminutive of Adele, a Hebrew name.

So I found my grandmother's people, despite Aunt Elzina and other family members who said it couldn't be done.

## Native Americans Have Deep Ancestry in Europe
*Shocking, Long Overdue Revision to American Indian Genetics*

> The ecstatic waters . . .
> Through their ancestral patterns dance.
> —William Butler Yeats, "News for the Delphic Oracle"

We've been saying it all along but it looks as though geneticists may be forced by new findings in ancient DNA to finally admit that early Siberian people and present-day Native Americans both have strong roots in Europe, perhaps only secondarily in Asia. The nuclear genetic bomb was dropped by Danish geneticist Eske Willerslev at a conference on "First Americans Archeology," held October 16-19, 2013, at Santa Fe, N.M. The city that gave birth to the original atom bomb hosted a glittering roster of speakers in a venue better known for its turquoise jewelry, fry bread and avante garde art, including big draws Achilli, Adovasio, Dillehay, Gonzalez and Schurr.

The paradigm-shifting conference program will be commemorated with a book *Paleoamerican Odyssey* ($56) to be published by Texas A&M Press later this year.

Leaked reports in the news  media focused on Willerslev's paper, "Genetics as a Means for Understanding Early Peopling of the Americas," which concerned the genetic sequencing of two ancient Siberians' bones discovered in the 1920s and now in the Hermitage Museum in St Petersburg. Analysis of a bone in one of the arms of a boy found near the village of Mal'ta close to Lake Baikal yielded the oldest complete genome of a modern human sequenced to date.

Of the 24,000 year-old skeleton that was Exhibit A, Willerslev was quoted in *The Siberian Times*, as saying, "His DNA shows close ties to those of today's Native Americans. Yet he apparently descended not from East Asians, but from people who had lived in Europe or western Asia." He added, "The finding suggests that about a third of the ancestry of today's Native Americans can be traced to 'western Eurasia.'"

The 4-year-old boy, who died 24,000 years ago in a homeland previously assumed to account for all the Indians who crossed a theoretical Bering land-bridge and founded the First Americans, had a male Y-chromosomal haplogroup of R1b, the most common lineage in modern Europe, and a female mitochondrial lineage of U, the dominant prototype in pre-historic Europe. As it happens, I am the same combination, R1b for male and U for female, as are innumerable others in our in-house study on Cherokee DNA, published some five years ago.

Whereas previous "peopling of the Americas" stuff has clung to and recycled haplogroup studies (sex-lines), the new shock research relies on autosomal DNA, total genomic contributions from all ancestral lines, not just male-only, not just female-only descent. The title of a blog from Eurogenes rightly emphasizes this: "Surprising aDNA [autosomal] results from Paleolithic Siberia (including Y DNA R)."

When we introduced the 18-Marker Ethnic Panel as an enhancement for our main autosomal product, DNA Fingerprint Plus, five years ago and counting, we presented a map of prehistoric human migrations showing without any equivocation that "Native Americans," even as Cavalli-Sforza demonstrated two decades ago, were closer in genetic distance to Europeans than Asians. In fact, we claimed, on the basis of autosomal DNA, that having Native American I or Native American II was a result discrete and separate from East Asian, since Native Americans obtained frequencies of its occurrence as high as 80% and Asians were on the polar opposite of the scale, at the bottom for carrying it. Other methods frequently confused Native American and East Asian to the point of invalidity, particularly those products claiming to arrive at racial or ethnic percentages.

The moral is that autosomal DNA trumps Y chromosome and mitochondrial evidence, and only ancient autosomal DNA can truly explain modern DNA. Even one of the most antipathetic students of American Indian DNA, Theodore G. Schurr, seems to be rethinking the rigid definitions that have built careers and won tenure for geneticists and anthropologists for decades. For the fanatics who have been toeing the party line on haplogroup Q, as set down by Schurr's company, Family Tree DNA, and its followers, we note the following statement of recantation or at least qualification, taken from the Santa Fe program:

"Tracing Human Movements across Siberia and into the Americas: New Insights from Mitochondrial DNA and Y-Chromosome Data." In this paper, I present genetic data from native Siberian and indigenous populations of North America that help to address questions about the process and timing of the peopling of the Americas. These new genetic data indicate that Eskimoan- and Athapaskan-speaking populations are genetically distinct from one another, as well as each to Amerindian groups, and that the formation of these circumarctic populations was the result of two population expansions that occurred after the initial expansion of settlement of the Americas. Our high-resolution analysis of Y chromosome haplogroup Q has also reshaped the organization of this lineage, making connections between New World and Old World populations more apparent and demonstrating that southern Altaians and Native Americans share a recent common ancestor. The data also make clear that Y-chromosomal diversity among the first Native Americans was greater than previously recognized. Overall, these results greatly enhance our understanding of the peopling of Siberia and the Americas from both mtDNA and Y-chromosome perspectives.

"Genetic genealogy" has become a buzzword, but to my knowledge few research studies or blogs and hardly any commercial tests authentically combine the two concepts. According to genealogy, I am about one-quarter Choctaw-Cherokee and three-quarters European. But genetics says my mitochondrial line (U2e) is Eurasian, even though I have traced it to a Cherokee woman who married the Indian trader Enoch Jordan about 1790 in north Georgia. Estimates from other "genetic genealogy" companies for my Native American ancestry, and I've taken them all, range from 0% (23&me) to 8% (Family Tree DNA, AncestryByDNA).

DNA Consultants, which I founded in 2003, does not give percentages of ancestry by policy, but half my top matches in our autosomal analysis are Native American, and North Asian/Siberian is No. 1 in my mega-population result, followed by Central Asian and Native American (and only distantly by Northern European). On an autosomal approach, if not haplogroup basis, my genes are Native American, which is how I self-identify. If I were to be pulled over for being a brown person in the state of Arizona, where I currently reside, and Sheriff Joe ran my DNA profile numbers through the system he would find that I am 15 times more likely to be North Asian than Northern European, and twice as likely to be American Indian than East Asian, European American or Hispanic.

*Getting with the Program*

If and when geneticists get serious about identifying the European sources of the American Indian gene pool, and hopefully they will round up not just one suspect (Denmark?), I would like for those who get paid and promoted to study us to please consider the following points:

—"First New Cherokee Data Published in More Than Ten Years" (announcement, August 1, 2012) described numerous instances of U.

—Stephen C. Jett, who taught geography at the Ohio State University 1963-1964 and then at the University of California, Davis, serving thrice as Geography chair and becoming emeritus in 2000, current editor of Pre-Columbiana, has frequently pointed out that just because Native American haplogroups match Siberian haplogroups doesn't mean the population of either Native America or Siberia was the same in remote history as today. He considered this a big fallacy of Big Science.

—Constantine Rafinesque, whose *History of the American Indians* was the first and most comprehensive treatment of the subject, believed all the early settlers of the Americas came "through the Atlantic," and only beginning about 1000 BCE did the Iztacans and Oguzians (Central Asian Turkic peoples) arrive. See our blog: "American Indian and Turkic People Share Deep Ancestry" (June 6, 2012).

—Canadian environmentalist Farley Mowat, the author of thirty-seven books, has constantly challenged the conventional knowledge that Vikings were the first Europeans to reach North America. In *The Farfarers* he describes the Alban people of Old Europe as visitors and colonists from the time when walrus hunters discovered the sea routes to the West before the Bronze Age. America's original name of the White (or Beautiful) Land is mentioned by Rafinesque and in Hindu, Greek, Egyptian, Mesopotamian, Arabic, Algonquian Indian, Irish, Norse and Chinese accounts. See "An Interview with Farley Mowat" on YouTube.

—Cyclone Covey of Wake Forest University, among other historians, has noted that Clovis Culture appears fully formed without any antecedents in America, with the most perfect examples of Clovis points traced in a cline of occurence in archeological sites to the Atlantic Coast.

—The earliest Americans clearly practiced the same Mother Goddess religion elaborately documented in the east Mediterranean and Old

Europe by Marija Gimbutas. Their ideas of matriarchy or gylany (shared rule by men and women, a word coined by Riana Eisler) did not come from Asia.

—When customers of DNA Consultants with various degrees of Native American admixture have their European population matches analyzed, a frequent top result is Finland or Finno-Ugric or Uralic. This "false match" could be explained by shared ancestry between the present-day Finns (where U is the modal haplogroup) and ancestors of Native Americans coming from Europe. Consider taking the EURO DNA test ($99).

—John L. Sorenson and Carl L. Johannessen in *World Trade and Biological Exchanges before 1492* (2009) document several plants that originated in the Eastern Hemisphere (not Asia) and traveled early by human hand to the Americas. For instance, Cannabis sativa (marijuana) moved from Western Asia or Europe to Peru by 100 CE, and mugwort (Artemisia vulgaris) was brought to Mexico from across the Atlantic Ocean by 1500 BCE. Both grow in profusion in Europe and temperate parts of Central Asia. Goosefoot (an important Ohio Valley Moundbuilder staple), cotton, coconuts, bananas, turmeric and North American myrtle likely took the same route. In the opposite direction, Mexican agave spread to the Mediterranean world by 300 BCE.

We expect that when the definitive report on the Siberian boy's 24,000 year-old genome appears in the journal *Nature*, where it is at press, their hair may fall out. At any rate, the European origins of Indians is going to be a game changer not only in genetics, but anthropology, archeology, government and, perhaps most significantly, in the self-awareness of millions of Americans who count Native Americans among their ancestors.

## Spanish Documents Suggest Irish Arrived in America before Columbus

By Kerry O'Shea (@IrishCentral.com), May 13, 2014

While Christopher Columbus is generally credited with having discovered America in 1492, a 1521 Spanish report provides inklings of evidence that there were, in fact, Irish people settled in America prior to Columbus' journey.

"Researchers feel certain that there was a colony of Irish folk living in what is now South Carolina, when Christopher Columbus "thought" he had discovered the New World," writes Richard Thornton for  .

In 1520, Peter Martyr d'Anghiera, a historian and professor, was appointed by Carlos V to be chronicler for the new Council of the Indies.

Though Martyr died in 1526, his report, founded on several weeks of interviews, was published posthumously in a book named *De Orbe Novo* (About the New World). The book has been published and translated numerous times in the centuries since then. The passages concerning the land that would become Georgia and the Carolinas were always included, but generally ignored, says Thornton.

While interviewing Spanish colonists, Martyr took note of their vicious treatment of Chicora Indians. However, he also included in his report that the Spanish colonists had a very good relationship with another nearby colony, which Martyr reported to be named Duhare.

Physically, the people of Duhare appeared to be European according to the Spanish colonists in the area. The people of Duhare had red to brown hair, tan skin and gray eyes, and were noticeably taller than the Spanish. According to Spanish accounts, the people of Duhare were Caucasian, though their houses and pottery were similar to those of American Indians.

The king of Duhare was said to be named Datha and was described by the Spanish as being a giant, even when compared to his peers. He had five children and a wife as tall as him. Datha had brightly colored paint or tattoos on his skin that seemed to distinguish him from the commoners.

## China Wire Part One

*Did the Chinese Settle in Northern Mexico and the American Southwest?*

We had just finished a meal of delicious fish tacos at what was to become our favorite Mexican restaurant on the Southside of Phoenix. The cook and owner was a lady from Sinaloa. She asked what I did for a living, and when I told her DNA testing, she immediately said, "I imagine our DNA in Mexico is a combination of Spanish, Indian and Chinese, right?"

Her frankness took me aback. I have read all that Bancroft, Menzies, Thompson, Mertz, Stewart and others have to say on the pre-Columbian Chinese presence. Our favorite source is actually a book little read today but excellent and authoritative. *Fusang: The Chinese Who Built America* was published in 1979 by the impeccable American historian of multiculturalism, Stan Steiner. He covers the subject very thoroughly and definitively in *Book One: The Chinese Who Discovered America*, beginning with the Buddhist missions to America in 441 CE.

Recent contributions by Charlotte Harris Rees continuing the scholarly work of her father Hendon M. Harris, Jr., (*The Asiatic Fathers of America*) have literally put Chinese exploration and settlement on the map, if not in the textbooks.

What *will* it take to persuade people of the fact of Chinese visits and even colonization and influence? Evidently, more than a steady stream of respected bestsellers and blockbuster exhibitions at the nation's capital.

Yet as Steiner notes in his introduction (p. xi), "The mysteries of history are only mysterious to those who are ignorant of them." Perhaps DNA could help dress up an old topic and make even the willfully ignorant take notice?

Alu insertions are short stretches of DNA implicated in the study of disease. They provide useful markers for the study of inter-population affinities and historical processes. Data on these systems are not numerous in Native Americans and related Asiatic populations. What has been published is highly specialized and not for the faint of heart.

Haplotype studies have occasionally found Asian types in the New World, though these anomalies are usually brushed aside. That not more attention has been paid to them is surprising in the light of ancient "Amerindian" DNA. One of the oldest and perhaps most leading pieces of evidence came from a 5,000-year-old burial in China Lake, British Columbia (!). The two individuals were both mitochondrial haplogroup M, a type that is widely distributed and even dominant in parts of Asia today. But the discoverer, a genetics professor, despite the fact that he was of Asian ancestry himself, could not bring himself to regard the individuals as having Asian ancestry. He timorously concluded only that "the founding migrants of the Americas exhibited greater genetic diversity than previously recognized" (p. 642). See "Mitochondrial Haplogroup M Discovered in Prehistoric North Americans."

M is the single most common mtDNA haplogroup in Asia, according to Kivisild et al. ("The Emerging Limbs and Twigs of the East Asian mtDNA Tree"). It peaks in Japan and Tibet, where it represents about 70% of the maternal lineages and is pervasive in India, where it has approximately 60% frequency. Among the Chinese, haplogroup M accounts for approximately 50% of all people.

In our own studies of Sephardic haplotypes, we found a not-insignificant number of cases of O3, a pure Asian type, for instance, Burquez (Mexico) and Ronquillo (New Mexico); see chapter 3, "Sephardim in the New World," in *Jews and Muslims in British Colonial America* (2012). Unbroken Chinese descent from Native American males marrying Mexican women is a more natural explanation than far-wandered Chinese merchants among the Spanish settlers.

We look forward to investigating the female lineages among the colonial populations especially of New Mexico, Sonora, Sinaloa, Nayarit, Jalisco, Colima and Michoacán. In the meantime, it occurs to us that perhaps autosomal DNA may harbor some of the answers.

Stay tuned for our next post, which will report an investigation of three autosomal markers that could provide solid evidence for Chinese DNA buried in the genetic record of West Mexico and the American Southwest.

### China Wire Part Two
*Buddhist Priests in Arizona*

*Monument on northeast boundary of the Ironwood National Forest in the Samaniego Hills.*

By and large, the genetics literature on American Indians has been confined to small, scattered samples gleaned from modern groups. This morass of information is vast, growing, and inconclusive.

Attempting to present the "peopling of the Americas" from such a reductive approach is like playing a game of Solitaire with important cards missing.

One Brazilian geneticist completely despaired of any solution as long ago as 2002. Francisco Salzano wrote in an article titled "Molecular Variability in Amerindians: Widespread but Uneven Information, that "the present trend of favoring essentially applied research suggests that the situation will not basically improve in the future" (*Anais da Academia Brasileira de Ciências*, vol. 74, no. 2, p. 1). It hasn't, of course. We shall not attempt here anything like a synthesis of the subject, although a later installment in this series will tackle the autosomal DNA story. Only alternative approaches such as alu insertions, human lymphocyte antigens and autosomal DNA can possibly shed light.

## *Turning from DNA to Actual History*

In the meantime, let us continue the thread begun with "Did the Chinese Settle in Northwest Mexico and the American Southwest?" (blog post, July 30, 2014). In Part One, we saw that the Mexicans and Chinese retain memories of Chinese settlement in the New World if most Americans do not.

The classic historical reference is a Chinese text about the Land of Fusang, an account redacted in the 14th century describing events going back to the fifth century. It occurs in the 41st Book of Chüan (or Kuen 327) in the 230th volume of the Great Chinese Encyclopedia, a vast imperial compilation known simply as The Chinese Classics. Joseph de Guignes, a learned French Orientalist, sinologist and Turkologist, brought it to the attention of the Western world in 1761.

De Guignes identified the original narrator as Hwui Shen (or Hui Shen), a Buddhist priest from Kabul (Afghanistan, then part of India), who visited ancient Mexico with four or five other priests in 458 CE Hui Shen appeared before the Chinese emperor in 499 and gave an exact account of his travels, surviving in several versions (see the summary in Henriette Mertz, *Pale Ink*, pp. 21-22).

De Guignes' report on the Chinese in the Americas appeared in the papers of the French Academy of Inscriptions and Royal Society of London and confounded Europe. Savants over the next two hundred years—Julius Klaproth (1831), Dominique Alexandre Godron, Joseph Needham—confirmed Hui Shen's place in history. In 1885, Edward P. Vining published the provocatively but succinctly titled *Inglorious Columbus: or, Evidence that Hwui Shen and a Party of Buddhist Priests from Afghanistan Discovered America* (see extensive bibliog. in Stan Steiner, *Fusang*, p. 240-44).

If Buddhist priests were living in sixth century Arizona, skeptics may charge, they can't have left much proof of their existence. Their landfall in the Americas was no doubt accidental. They left no enduring mark. It's as if it never happened. In fact, it probably did not happen. Hui Shen's story is a charming Chinese fairy tale, right?

### Mesoamerican Religious Practices

To the contrary, there are numerous signs of a deep and lasting Asiatic imprint in Mexico. No less an authority than Hubert Howe Bancroft devotes many pages to the bewilderingly diverse forms of religion among ancient Mexican Indians. Of those in Sonora, Sinaloa and Durango, he writes: "They had innumerable private idols, penates of all possible and impossible figures, some being stone, shaped by nature only" (*Native Races,* vol. 3, *Myths and Languages*, San Francisco, 1882, p. 179).

*Lingams and cross at San Xavier.*

He notes that some Western Mexican tribes worshipped a black stone like the Kaaba in Mecca, and that Quetzalcoatl and other divinities were connected with stone-worship (p. 281). One Americanist "even explains the meaning of the name Quetzalcoatl despite the usual definition as 'twin of a precious stone.'"

If all this sounds like lingam worship, maybe it really is. In our rambles through the Ironwoods National Forest we were surprised to discover an altar we dubbed Bighead in a hidden cove When we questioned a Papago elder he recognized the place immediately and said it was one of his people's most sacred shrines.

The closest member of the Tohono O'odham Nation, as the Papagos are now known, lives in Tucson, thirty miles away, but certain religious leaders still know this now-empty territory like the back of their hand.

We were not completely shocked after this, when we visited the Mission of San Xavier del Bac, which serves as the parish church for the Papagos living around Tucson. There we photographed a collection of Shaivistic lingams placed beneath the giant Christian cross. The heirs of the Hohokam may have adopted the creed of the Jesuits and Franciscans but apparently they cling to some of their old forms of worship.

## Some Possible Echoes in Place-Names

Mertz proposes that the very word Sinaloa (in Nahuatl *Zineloque*) is derived from Chinelos, "foreigners." She draws attention to the Huichol Indians, who live around Colima, a possible origin point according to a consensus of archeologists for the early Hohokam. These carriers of Arizona's first advanced native culture arrived around 400 CE from the south with a fully formed society, featuring, among other things, distinctive pottery, copper bells, cremation practices and irrigation knowledge.

"The religious nature of the Huichol," writes Mertz, "and their attendant religious ceremonies, had strong Buddhist characteristics . . . Some Huicholes bore such striking resemblance to the Chinese that the Mexicans called them 'Chinos'" (p. 73).

Mertz speculates that certain place-names in the Sonoran Desert and West Mexico coast commemorate Asian colonies. The name of Picacho, the hat-shaped landmark that dominates the barren lands between Phoenix and Tucson, may derive from Pi-k'iu (compare Sanskrit Bhiksu "mendicant priest").

Sacaton, an important Hohokam town, seems to bear the name of the Buddha's clan—Saka or Sakya. Prince Siddhartha Shakya (5th century BCE) was the founder of Buddhism and came to be known as Gautama Buddha. Related, according to Mertz, are the names Zacatecas and Zacatlan.

Vague legends and twisted linguistic analogies. Where's the hard evidence?

*An Unusual Petroglyph*

Not far from Picacho Peak and Tucson are the Santa Catalina Mountains, and on the Golden Ranch north of the Catalina State Park are the San Ysidro Ruins. Here is located what we suggest is as hard a piece of evidence as you could hope to find. It is a petroglyph of the Buddha meditating in a lotus position. Unmistakable, the iconic figure appears on a rock panel over older, conventional fertility figures and hunting scenes and can be dated to about 1500 years ago (see photo).

If Buddhist priests came to the Hohokam heartland long ago, as recounted in the Chinese Classics, they were hardly idle travelers or adventurers. They were self-described missionaries with a serious purpose. They expected to find people they could communicate with and convert. That the Hohokam and their parent populations already included a sizable Asiatic element is a given.

Asian residents, not mere visitors, are frankly implied in a Chinese poem quoted by Steiner:

Where the sun rises
In the land of Fu Sang
There is my home.
Seeking fame and riches
I came to the land
Of the eternal flowers.

So the "Land of the Eternal Flowers," Fusang, is West Mexico, from Arizona, California and Sonora to Colima, Jalisco, Nayarit and Michoacán.

Hwui Chen went back to the Orient, but obviously other compatriots of his stayed and called America home.

In Nayarit, which appears to be the center of Chinese and Buddhist influence, Bancroft reports that the ancient inhabitants conceived of heaven or paradise as filled with ministering healers "with shaved heads." After death, he writes, the good Indians "went to a place . . . where they lived under the care of men with shaved heads" (p. 529). They also believed in transmigration of souls (p. 529).

Being for the most part celibate, the men with the shaved heads cannot have left progeny, so it would be fruitless to look for their legacy in the DNA record. But that is not the case for the Chinese merchant who emigrated to Fusang to seek fame and riches. Moreover, Chinese junks were capable of transporting an entire colony numbering in the thousands, including women.

Could there be an autosomal trace of gene flow from the East, if not a Y chromosome or mitochondrial trail? Our next post will examine this possibility.

## China Wire Part Three

*Rare Chinese Allele Found Among Navajo, Southwestern U.S. Hispanics and North Mexican Indians*

Like about 5 percent of North Americans, Francesca Serrano was adopted. She never knew her birth parents. Determined nonetheless to find out her ancestry, she took our DNA Fingerprint Plus, an autosomal test based on an analysis of STR frequencies that can suggest overall ancestry matches to world populations. The caseworker who prepared her report was amazed at all the apparent Chinese ancestry mixed with Hispanic and Native American.

After delivering the report recently, we nervously interviewed Serrano, who works in an East Coast DNA diagnostic center. She explained that the results made perfect sense. She grew up in Colima, Mexico, and people often asked her, "Do you have any Asian going on in you?"

Taking a closer look at her 16-locus STR profile, we noticed several unusual alleles. We will focus on one of them in this report, a value of 9 at D16S539. Admittedly, this is only one tiny ray of light into the genomic inheritance of a person, but geneticists have proved the utility of examining single STRs like this.

*Sioux Need Not Apply*

A rather sensational article—if genetics literature can ever be considered crowd-inciting—appeared in 2007, when Kari Schroeder and her team at the Department of Anthropology, University of California, Davis, showed that a value of 9 at D9S1120 cropped up in sample profiles of 35.4% of North and South American Indians as well as "West Beringians." This marker was later dubbed a "private allele" shared by the members of a small hunting party that crossed the Bering Land Bridge and spread through the Americas many, many moons ago (the "single entry" theory).

STRs mutate almost as slowly as mitochondrial DNA and can therefore be useful markers for deep ancestry (see our post, "Evolution and Ancestry: DNA Mutation Rates," October 23, 2012). One must be careful, however, not to make too much of them. For instance, the Sioux and Jemez reported 0.0% frequency of the touted allele (see Schroeder et al., "Haplotypic Background of a Private Allele at High Frequency in the Americas," *Mol. Biol. Evol.* 26/5 [2009] 1003), but that doesn't make them any less Indian than the others. Try telling any Lakota Sioux he is less Indian than the others.

In Hispanic people in the American Southwest, our allele (which we will call for the sake of convenience "the Serrano allele") occurs in only 8% percent of the population. It is not even among the most common possible numbers on that location; a repeat of 11 occurs in 31%.

*Analysis and Conclusion*

From these figures, we get a general picture of the Serrano allele running relatively high, though still a minority report, in Western Hispanics, Mexicans and Indians. It is highest in the Navajos (who are rumored to have migrated from Chinese Turkistan in historical times). It is about the same in Arizona Hispanics as Mexicans from Chihuahua. We have no data from Sonora or Sinaloa, unfortunately.

| Population | % D16=9 |
|---|---|
| Southwestern Hispanics | 7.9 |
| California Hispanics | 10.3 |
| Arizona Hispanics | 11.1 |

| Navajos | 16.8 |
| Apaches | 9.9 |
| Chihuahua | 11.2 |
| Huichol Indians Chiapas | 7.5 |
| El Salvador | 12.8 |

Although present at an average frequency of about 12% in American Indian populations, the Serrano allele reaches its highest level among the Salishan Indians of British Columbia, where it is 30%. In neighboring regions of Canada, indigenous people have only about 8% of it (Saskatchewan aboriginals).

Everything comes from somewhere, and the Serrano allele in terms of human history is no exception. Its frequency is low or entirely absent in European populations and extremely high in East Asian, where it is highest among the Atayal tribe of Taiwanese aborigines (52%). It is also elevated among the Evenks (one of Russia's native peoples), the Japanese, Pacific Islanders and Koreans. It is about the same level in Central, North, Chaozhou, Sichuan, Cantonese and Singapore Chinese populations, about 25%.

Like all alleles it is found in Africa, the ultimate source of all present-day humans, in modest amounts, but in even scarcer quantities in all the populations between there and North Asia. It enjoyed an enormous expansion in China.

It averages only 2.4% in all Native Americans, showing it is an extremely rare allele for American Indians to have overall. This being the case, is it found in any of our "anomalous" Cherokees? The answer is yes. Several participants who have their autosomal scores as well as the mitochondrial results report that D16=9 is one of their alleles. It is in fact found in my own profile (Donald Yates), along with some Chinese top matches.

On the face of it, then, D16=9 could come from either deep ancestry in China or Mongolia. Mongolia but not China is a shared deep ancestry with modern-day Native Americans. In the case of the Navajo it probably comes from both sources combined. Its great elevation in that population seems to suggest a historical infusion from Chinese, which matches Navajo migration legends. With Southwestern Hispanics it may also be the vestige of historical gene flow from Chinese, not just the sign of deep Mongolian-Siberian roots. Whether that is the story with Cherokee profiles must await an answer from further investigations.

Serrano's No. 1 match on the basis of her entire profile (13 loci) is Chinese Hui - Ningxia. In this homeland of the Tangut people which once formed part of the Xia Xian Empire, the value of 9 on this marker is modal, with a frequency of 30%.

What are we to make of a single allele that is relatively rare in Native Americans, even rarer in European, Middle Eastern and other populations, but modal in some Chinese populations, with an apparent ancient center of diffusion in Taiwan? We conclude that it just may be a vestige of Asian DNA from China's ancient and medieval periods of history, not deep history tracing back to Siberia.

In our next post we will see if any confirmatory evidence comes from other avenues of investigation.

### Nobody Can Tell Me Who I Am
*Postings from the Edge*

They called her Mother Qualla—a stately, bluish-gray skinned schoolteacher in New York with angular features, thin lips and quick, intelligent eyes. Brian Wilkes and I drove her to her motel room at a meeting of the Southwestern Cherokee Confederacy in Albany, Georgia.

That was twenty years ago but I shall never forget Mother Qualla's take on Indian recognition. She listened to our stories, looked at us sternly and said, "No one can tell *me* WHO I AM!"

Such words could well serve as the mantra of more than a hundred dedicated genealogy seekers in DNA Consultants' Cherokee DNA Project who are proving the geneticists wrong. Participants in Phase II received a thank-you email from the company September 20 that provided many with the confirmation they had long sought in vain from previous testing.

"I always had a gut feeling that I was Native American," said San Pablo, Calif. resident Jesse Montes, a California Latino who resembles nothing so much as Sir Joshua Reynolds' 1762 portrait of Ostenaco (see above). "It was a big surprise and relief to discover I am Indian in both my father's male and my mom's female line, just as family stories said we were." His mitochondrial sample turned out to be haplogroup C, the type that matches Cherokee Beloved Woman Nancy Ward and a whole line of chiefs from the Wolf Clan, including Dragging Canoe.

Although none of the participants previously knew each other, many found out they were related as descendants of the same Cherokee ancestor and evidently belonged to the same clan. Indeed, several were adoptees totally uninformed about their ancestry before joining the project.

Juanita Sims was one of the frustrated clients of previous testing, which can often be cut-and-dry, case-closed on the matter of who is Indian. Said niece Elizabeth DeLand, "She originally had the test done because her grandmother and great-grandmother spoke Cherokee and she is trying to find it in her DNA." Sims proved to have a rare form of U5a1 DNA, fully matching a woman born in Walker County, Alabama, in 1828. DeLand enrolled her aunt as Participant #67 in the study, one of the last to be accepted.

Under the rules of Family Tree DNA's Cherokee DNA Project, "Native American mtDNA Haplogroups are A, B, C, D and X," and any others are ineligible. The Federal Bureau of Indian Affairs, Cherokee Nation of Oklahoma, Eastern Band of Cherokee Indians and United Keetoowah Band adopt similar restrictions for what they consider "true" American Indian DNA types.

Of the 67 participants, eleven of them (16%) tested with other companies first, including Family Tree DNA, Ancestry.com and DNA Diagnostics Center. On the other hand, about half (47%) got first-time test results from DNA Consultants' service lab, Genex Diagnostics of Vancouver, British Columbia. About a third tested with Sorenson Genomics of Salt Lake City, Utah, a source used by the company in the first two years of the phase's existence. Two participants did not want to reveal the identity of their lab.

Despite not having to pay for benefits of being included in the study, all candidates had to purchase either a Native American Test or Report Only analysis. As a measure of their passion to find answers, they collectively spent an estimated $50,000 between one company or other, according to Holli Starnes, project administrator and assistant principal investigator.

In addition to cross-comparisons within the project, all participants will be now compared to 135 mitochondrial records from the Cherokee DNA project assembled in 2002-2011 under the aegis of the late Chief Joe White and longtime administrator Marcy Palmer of the Central Band of Cherokee.

According to Jan Ravenspirit Franz, webmaster for the CBC, this project was closed and reorganized by its sponsor Family Tree DNA, where it currently lists 51 members, but the wishes of the original participants are being respected and all data has been maintained for continuing analysis.

In a preliminary tabulation, 16% of participants proved to have direct female descent in "standard" American Indian haplogroups A, B, C, D and X. The majority (84%) had what are commonly recognized as "non-Indian" haplogroups.

With surnames like Allen, Harris and Wilson (four of these), and Little Bear, Thundereagle and Buitenhuis, they joined from Tennessee, Washington State, Oklahoma, Texas and Connecticut. Some verified ancestors they knew about from the paper trail; others met new figures on the trail blazed by modern genetics. One matched Kitty Prince of the Bear River Athabaskans; another, Cherokee Beloved Woman Nancy Ward (haplogroup C).

"My grandmother and her family always said we were Cherokee and I know that they were afraid of looking too brown and would always stay out of the sun," wrote one participant. "They didn't want to be connected to Native Americans at all. I feel like I have missed part of my heritage and would like to know if this story is true."

She happened to have haplogroup H, a controversial type for Indian ancestry, but matched three possible Cherokee descendants and no one else.

Another, who happened to bear the African haplogroup L3, matched several ancestors claimed by others in the records and reported to be Cherokee. A similar L3 turned up in a California man and was reported in A Te Anu, a Muscogee Creek woman.

One man, an adoptee, managed to get his adoption papers opened on the strength of his DNA testing. His mitochondrial DNA was a rare form of T* that coincidentally matched that of others in the project, and no one else in the world.

As in Phase I, rare T haplotypes accounted for about one-fifth of participants and was the leading anomalous Cherokee type. H and U, as well as K and J were also prominent. New additions came in the form of W (2), N (1), L (6), I (2) and V (1).

Two participants (B and U) had family stories they were Jewish.


## Where Do I Come From: Jesse Montes

I grew up in the Southwest in Richmond, California. My father was from Guayama, Puerto Rico, and my mother was from Maui, Hawaii. My paternal great grandparents kept a diary and worked in the sugarcane, tobacco, and coffee fields and told stories of the Taino Indians from the island of Boriken near Puerto Rico. My mother's side migrated to Hawaii from Spain and Puerto Rico to work in the pineapple and sugar cane fields. My mom and relatives were in Pearl Harbor and some served in WWII.

My mom's maternal grandmother was born near Ponce, Puerto Rico.

I knew that I had Spanish and heard there might be some Native American from my grandparents, but I did not know for sure. I always had a gut feeling I was Native American, but I did not know how to confirm this until I took the DNA Fingerprint Plus and your Native American DNA test. My Dad talked about having some Taino Indian, and I thought maybe I had a trace. I did not know. I was always very curious about my ancestry.

It was a big surprise to me what the tests showed! I have a Spanish name, but the Native American DNA test showed that I have Native American on both sides and have a match to Taino and possibly Cherokee. My Native

American haplogroup, C1, is relatively rare and corresponds to Taino lineage. I am assuming the Taino is on my Dad's side and the Cherokee is on my mom's side. The latter was especially surprising since I am from the Southwest. I have not done any other DNA testing, but my sister did. She did a DNA test from another company and was told said she had Cherokee which we thought odd, but this is just more confirmation. The Spanish and French enslaved and resettled many Native Americans to the highlands of Puerto Rico, so I imagine that is where I got Cherokee ancestry. Also, the DNA Fingerprint Plus showed I have top matches to Native American populations in my world and megapopulations. It was a big surprise to discover I have so much Native American. Oh, and I discovered I also have some Jewish in my ancestry which was quite a surprise.

I am hoping to now be able to connect with some of my ancestors online on my mom's side to discover even more from the Native American DNA test and to join the Dr. Yates' Cherokee Project with DNA Consultants. Dr. Yates believes my mother's line is Cherokee. I am very excited about that. You guys have my full support. I finally know who I am! This has helped me very much. It isn't that it was just useful to me. This is a useful tool that would help everyone find out who they are. God bless you and what you are doing. You are a dynamic duo and have given me a golden key. I always had a gut feeling that I was Native American, and it was such a relief to find out I have a strong line of it from my mother. I am usually a very quiet person, but I am so excited about this that I want to be recognized. This is me!

*52-year-old Cherokee DNA Project Phase II Participant No. 20, Jesse Montes of Richmond, Calif., was interviewed by Teresa Panther-Yates, Vice President of Communications, August 6, 2014.*

## Did Chinese Ships Transport the Cherokee to America?
*Thruston Tablet Revisited*

Our book *Old World Roots of the Cherokee* (McFarland, 2012) describes an expedition from Ptolemaic Egypt that brought the original nucleus of the Cherokee people across the Pacific to America. One of the key pieces of evidence is the Thruston Tablet, also known as the Rocky Creek Stone.

This engraved limestone tablet was exhumed in a Mississippian Period mound near Castalian Springs in Sumner County, Tennessee by archeologist Gates P. Thruston in 1870. It depicts scenes of warfare, a peace treaty, marriage and trade relations involving a Cherokee chief, dressed in a Greek hoplite's armor, and a local foe with a Mohawk hairdo, feathers and large square shield with "sky-serpent" design.

The obverse side shows how the two tribes sue for peace and smoke the calumet in a longhouse. The Cherokee chief, plainly identified by his topknot, sun-skirt and lunette around his neck, then gives his daughter in marriage to the opposing chief . She carries a wampum belt signifying peace, wears a plaid kilt and has a star of David on her breast (pp. 80-81).

Writing on the Thruston Stone includes ogam (a type of stick alphabet), Tifinagh (a North African script) and some pictograms that have not been identified . . . until now.

*Thruston Tablet (obverse).*

We recently sent scans of both the reverse and obverse to John Ruskamp, author of *Asiatic Echoes-The Identification of Ancient Chinese Pictograms in pre-Columbian North American Rock Writing* (Kluwer, 2013). The unidentified writing system turns out to be Chinese.

It appears to me that there could be three Chinese based symbols involved with this item," reports Ruskamp. "First, within the red outline the four horizontal lines may be for the number four 'Si.' If so, this is one of the oldest styles of Chinese script used for writing 4.

Second, within the green outline the stylized X-shaped stick-man could be a figure of 'Wen,' which in this case looks as if it is holding a fishing pole with a forked end of the line. Or it could just be a drawing of a stick-man, as this is a difficult image to work with because of its artistic nature.

Finally, within the blue outline there appears to be the Chinese symbol 'Mi' for thread or rope (a couple of twisted fibers). This may be a separate drawing, or it could relate to the larger depictions.

In addition, we note that there are similar pictograms on the front in the upper right, as well as a Chinese seal script mark in the upper left.

**b**

*Thruston Tablet (reverse, detail)*

Putting it all together, although much still remains to be elucidated, the Thruston Stone appears to record contracts between the Cherokee, Shawnee and a third party who used Chinese writing. Since the principal figure is shown wearing ceremonial attire appropriate for the ancient world (500 BCE to 500 CE,), and given the use of Chinese seal script and primitive pictograms, not to mention the ogam and Tifinagh, could the Thruston Tablet be a lot older than its archeological context suggests?

Could it in fact commemorate the original expedition of the 3rd century BCE in which Chinese ships helped transport the colonists to the New World? Were the Chinese pictograms made by the hand of a Chinese trade partner or simply by someone on these shores familiar with Chinese writing? Did the Algonquian tribes (to which the Shawnee belong) use Chinese writing? Does the pictogram of the rope (Mi) stand for the Twister Clan (Cherokee Haplogroup B), whose name, like that of Hilo, is derived from the twisted navigational ropes emblematic of Hawaiians? And finally, is the central symbol on the obverse really a rooster? If not, what is it?

## Where Do I Come From: Jim Stritzel

I live in Washington State, and grew up all over the Western United States, including Alaska. My dad, John Rolland Stritzel, was in the Army. His father, Albert Stritzel, was born in Austria, as was his mother, Marie Mauser. My mother and my maternal aunts said our ancestors were fur traders of both French and Native American ancestry (Metis, Mohawk, Cree), but I had no proof of my Native American ancestry until participating in the Cherokee DNA Project. I am now sixty-six and one of my earliest memories as a very young child is trying to do broom dancing to fiddle music. Recently, I have built on the base of family oral history I heard as a child concerning my American Indian heritage. I have taken DNA ancestry tests and started following a beginning paper trail. I have also begun making pipes with the permission of a sixth-generation Lakota Nation Pipe Maker. At his request, I spent part of the summer with him and learned a lot about carving pipes. In the picture on page 123, I am carving a Deer pipe from Minnesota red pipestone. I also carve animals and natural scenes using soapstone, alabaster, sandstone and limestone.

My mother was Kathleen Ena Walsh (her birth name). She was born in 1926 in Birmingham, Alabama. Her mother was Eunice Mabel Ahearn (born 1896/97 or 98) per Eunice's 1917 New York wedding license, and my maternal great grandmother was Anna Elizabeth. My family's oral history was that Eunice was adopted and either full or at least half Native

American, with Metis, Mohawk, Cree/French and Cherokee further back. Until I did DNA testing with the project, this was as far as I could get on the paper trail, as New York is a closed adoption record state. However, I found a proven relation from DNA testing that seems to confirm our oral history of her. Our oral history of this line is Metis in the fur trade, and this relation is not far from where I thought my great-grandmother was from in Montague, Massachusetts, so I now believe I have her name down and have found her line to either Tighe or Terry. Moreover, I am now starting to verify this with a paper trail as well. In sum, my family's oral history of the line has been confirmed as Native American through mitochondrial testing and some close matches.

My Native American DNA Ancestry Test from DNA Consultants shows that my maternal line is a unique form of J with no exact matches in Mitosearch though my mutations did closely match someone else in the Cherokee DNA Project. My mtdna haplotype J is unmatched in the world. Despite it generally being viewed as a type reflecting Jewish lineage, my particular line, according to the company's analysis, is Native American. The closest match to my mother's J line was a lady in Australia that I have emailed, but we found no common ancestors. I believe Dr. Yates said the match may be of ancient origin. The company report says my maternal line is American Indian despite being an unaccepted mitochondrial type:

Although not one of the classic Native American lineages (A, B, C, D, and X), J has been discovered in the Cherokee Indians (Schurr, Bolnick, and Smith). Most investigators attribute this to recent European admixture. But J haplotyes without Old World exact matches and with only New World exact matches or unique occurrences could just as well be considered Native American. Since this does appear to be the case with the subject's type, it probably is Native American.

I am continuing to learn more about my family history and would be interested in comparing the autosomal results of members of the Cherokee Study to each other on gedmatch.com. If anyone has uploaded their autosomal results there my gedmatch number is F301307.

DNA Consultants was also able to show I had Native American markers (I and II) which led me to further explore DNA testing. I further corroborated my Native American ancestry after Dr. Yates kindly referred me to the (now retired) Family Tree's Acadian Amerindian study. There I matched autosomally with people of Metis, Mohawk and French ancestry from near the Montreal area and possibly with Cree as well. This led to a beginning paper trail, and I now have the strength of knowledge of not only my family's oral history, but DNA and genealogical records. I now have some actual names. Thanks to DNA Consultants I possess a strong base to find more ancestors.

I believe there is a lot of resistance to admitting Native American haplotypes can go beyond the standard A, B, C, D and X haplotypes because a lot of professional people have their careers staked on perpetuating this dogma. However, it runs deeper than this. If you want to conquer a people, you've got to make them other than you, not as civilized as you; otherwise, you cannot call them savages and yourself superior.

What the study has done for me is this: through it, I have found my people on Mother Earth. I am thankful to all concerned for that.

# 10 EPILOG

These are the facts (and data) behind an extraordinary ten-year study of Cherokee DNA. Extraordinary in its findings, and potentially game-changing. But extraordinary also in the many wonderful and rewarding interactions we had in reporting the results and writing this book. What began as a scientific investigation has become for many a sort of social experiment.

Although it may run counter to conventional thinking, the Cherokees' 'differentness' has received a new definition through DNA. But what about the Cherokees' similarities, with white people and other Indians?

When we ended *Old World Roots of the Cherokee* (2012), the Cherokee anomaly was still somewhat disembodied and bloodless. We thought science might finally begin to give American Indians what society had so far denied them, equality of consideration and recognition. If the Cherokee had East Mediterranean roots were they not common heirs of Greco-Roman civilization and Judeo-Christian ideals? Acceptance of the Cherokee as an ancient people not unlike the Greeks, Egyptians, Romans, Jews, Persians, Turks and Arabs ought naturally to change one's view, shouldn't it? Were not some of the same qualities we admire in Greek philosophers and heroes of the Bible now to be glimpsed in American Indians and their descendants?

After hearing participants' stories, we are perhaps less optimistic about society and more hopeful than ever about individuals. Jim Stritzel, a participant in Phase II, seems to put his finger on the matter when he says, "If you want to conquer a people, you've got to make them other than you, not as civilized as you; otherwise, you cannot call them savages and yourself superior." We had not considered the ramifications of that thought before hearing it so innocently expressed.

It has long been maintained that A, B, C, D, and X were the only permissible haplotypes if someone claimed to have American Indian ancestry. Anything else was due only to admixture. This rule was considered sacrosanct, and all that followed from it ironclad. However, the recent finding of a 24,000 year old Siberian boy who had a "portion of [his] genome ...shared only by today's Native Americans and no other groups," and who also had European and West Asian roots but no affinity with East Asians, is shaking the world of science and beginning to alter public perception. The Siberian boy's analysis reveals a crack in the cherished theory that American Indians have no ancestral connections to Europeans (Schulz 2013).

Schulz writes that "the common assumption was that these genes were picked up, mixed into the gene pool from European colonists." In other words, when someone claims to have Native American ancestry but does not fall into the A, B, C, D, or X box, this is how it has been rationalized. But we now know from the genome of this Paleolithic boy, who wore "an ivory diadem, a bead necklace, and a bird-shaped pendant," that that is not always the case (Wade 2013). The mitochondrial and Y chromosome story is sometimes deep ancestry, not modern admixture. The first Americans have earlier ties to Europe. "About a third of Native Americans' ancestry can be traced to Western Eurasia" (Schulz). Schulz quotes Danish professor Eske Willerslev, who helped accomplish the Mal'ta skeleton's sequencing , as saying, "The West Eurasian signatures that we often find in today's Native Americans don't all come from postcolonial admixture...some of them are ancient."

The mitochondrial DNA haplogroup of the Siberian boy is U, customarily categorized as Eurasian. On the basis of this assignment, "some scientists have suggested that Native Americans descended from Europeans who sailed west across the Atlantic" since such haplotypes are not found in East Asia (Yong 2013). Yong points out that "the boy's nuclear DNA [autosomal] told the same story."

Additionally, the male haplotype of the Siberian skeleton is R, a type diagnostic of European ancestry, but one that has usually been attributed to admixture among Native Americans (Raghavan et al. 2014). Male haplotype R is also prominent in the Lakota Sioux, though this incidence has also been explained as coming from admixture).

No doubt the genetic profile of the Siberian boy stunned more than a few geneticists and anthropologists, to say nothing of the lay public. Yong writes that the project was shelved for a year because opponents assumed the samples had been contaminated. It was eventually vindicated as one of the most complete and accurate sequencings of ancient DNA, a technological marvel.

What can be further concluded? Since we now know that Native Americans have deep ancestry from Europe, isn't it logical that some would also have haplotypes before now only classified as European? Genes do not listen to borders. Should these European haplotypes still be attributed to recent admixture when scientists are now saying the European ancestral roots of Native Americans go very deep? Wouldn't the genes match the ancestry? We have many U's (as well as T's and other Middle Eastern types) in our Cherokee DNA Project that contradict received science, that are considered primarily European or Eurasian, never Native American.

It is interesting that the genetics establishment shelved the project concerning the archaic Siberian boy for a year. Surely contamination was a key consideration, but did something else drive them to take this step as well? Was it fear that the Native population was not as different as they had long claimed? Did alarm over the conclusions also contribute to their actions? It would not be the first time that anthropology and racism were bedfellows. Vine Deloria, American Indian author and professor of history, law, and religious studies, in his book *God is Red* sums up the only way the two have long been intertwined: 'People are not allowed to be Indians and cannot become white." It seems a paradox. Native Americans are expected to assimilate and be other at the same time. Can anyone pigeonholed as predominately white claim Native American as far as the government is concerned? No. Yet, if someone has a drop of Sub-Saharan African blood they are not only welcome to espouse this ethnicity, they are automatically consigned to it. What basis do these ideas have in science?

Could it be triumphalist thinking to place Native Americans in a few fixed haplotypes that Europeans do not share? Much like placing many of them on reservations? First, we conquer. Then we tell you who you are (you are not allowed to do this for yourself). You may not practice a religion that is not ours. You don't have a literature, only myths. On and on.

Of course, the crux of the problem may just be an all too common one. The danger in our copy-and-paste research world is that many too often just jump on the bandwagon of what someone else said without doing any actual research themselves. Anyone that does this commits the logical fallacy of begging the question (not citing sources).

All of Western Civilization considers Aristotle to be the father of logic. If we analyze the statement, "All American Indians must be A, B, C, D, or X," using Aristotelean logic, we run into several problems. First, logical arguments are not simple; they are complex. This statement has several fallacies. It is an over-generalization, as you have not qualified the argument to show possible exceptions. Another example would be to say, "Women are not good pilots because a female pilot just crashed a plane in London." This argument is based on too small a sample size and on bias.

Is there a problem with the sample size of Native Americans that have been used to identify haplotypes? Jones says there is: "One of the current limitations with the uses of haplogroups for inferring American Indian biological affiliation is that there is the possibility of discovering new haplotypes as more tribes are studied" (101). The argument is also an absolute argument, another fallacy, as it rules out any other conclusions before they are postulated. Finally, it falls into the category of the "either/or" fallacy, or false dilemma. You must have a haplotype considered European, OR you must have a haplotype that is Native American. Everything must neatly fit into this box or that box.

In conclusion, it is also a definition argument. How do we define Native American? Defining a people narrowly has never worked. As William James said, "A great many people think they are thinking when they are merely rearranging their prejudices." The stories of the hundred-plus project volunteers who listened to their instincts and defied the scientists suggest that they may have been enacting the original meaning of the tribal name ("Volunteer Settlers"). The United States of America is just a little over two hundred years old. That is about one-tenth the span of the Tsalagi Nation. Isn't it time government and universities stopped patronizing us?

# DATA

| Phase I | Hg | HVS1 |
|---|---|---|
| 1 | H | 16239A 16519C |
| 4 | H | 16183C 16189C 16193.1C 16362C 16519C |
| 6 | H | 16189C 16193.1C 16193.2C 16356C 16362C 16519C |
| 8 | H | 16519C |
| 3 | J* | 16069T 16126C 16311C 16519C |
| 9 | J* | 16069T 16126C 16162G |
| 44 | J* | 16069T 16126C 16172C |
| 45 | J* | 16069T 16126C 16311C 16366T 16368C 16519C |
| 46 | J* | 16069T 16126C 16172C |
| 30 | K | 16093C 16224C 16245T 16311C 16519C |
| 23 | K2 | 16093C 16192T 16224C 16311C 16519C |
| 38 | L1b1 | (16234T) |
| 42 | L1c2 | (African sequences) |
| 43 | L3 | 16223T 16258T 16320T 16519C |
| 28 | T* | 16126C 16189C 16193.1C 16278T 16294T 16296T 16519C |
| 35 | T* | 16126C 16172C 16185.1T 16189D 16294T16298C 16399G 16519C |
| 41 | T* | 16126C 16189C 16193.1C 16193.2C 16294T 16296T 16519C |
| 25 | T1* | 16126C 16163G 16185.1T 16189D 16294T 16519C |
| 26 | T1* | 16126C 16163G 16185.1T 16189D 16294T 16519C |
| 24 | T1a | 16126C 16163G 16185.1T 16189D 16294T 16519C |
| 32 | T1a | 16126C 16163G 16185.1T 16189D 16257T 16294T 16519C |
| 50 | T1a | 16126C 16163G 16185.1T 16189D 16294T 16324C 16519C |
| 29 | T2* | 16126C 16266T 16294T 16304C 16519C |
| 31 | T2* | 16126C 16187T 16294T 16296T 16304C 16519C |
| 51 | T2c | 16126C 16182C 16183C 16189C 16294T 16296T 16298C 16519C |
| 52 | T2c | 16126C 16182C 16183C 16189C 16294T 16296T 16298C 16519C |
| 34 | T2e | 16126C 16153A 16294T 16296T 16519C |
| 39 | T4 | 16126C 16256T 16294T 16296T 16519C |
| 11 | U2e* | 16051G 16129C 16145A 16182C 16183C 16189C 16362C 16519C |
| 12 | U2e* | 16051G 16075C 16092C 16129C 16183C 16189C 16362C 16519C |

| 13 | U2e* | 16051G 16092C 16129C 16183C 16189C 16362C 16519C 16525G |
|----|------|---------------------------------------------------------|
| 14 | U2e* | 16051G 16129C 16183C 16189C 16362C 16519C 16525G |
| 16 | U2e* | 16051G 16092C 16129C 16182C 16183C 16189C 16362C 16519C |
| 49 | U2e* | 16051G 16075C 16092C 160129C 160183C 160189C 160362C 160519C |
| 21 | U4* | 16342C 16343G 16356C 16390A 16519C |
| 18 | U5* | 16193T 16270T 16296T 16391A |
| 17 | U5a1a | 16231C 16256T 16270T 16399G |
| 19 | U5a1a* | 16114A 16192T 16256T 16270T 16294T 16526A |
| 20 | U5a1a* | 16192T 16249C 16256T 16270T 16399G |
| 15 | U5b* | 16189C 16193.1C 16193.2G 16270C 16519C |
| 22 | U5b2 | 16114T 16224C 16270T |
| 33 | Unknown | 16183C 16189C 16193.1C 16276A 16325C |
| 36 | Unknown | 16069T 16164G 16234T 16519C |
| 37 | Unknown | 16183C 16189C 16193.1C 16261T 16519C |
| 40 | Unknown | 16039A 16188D 16193.1C 16223T 16290T 16319C 16362C 16519C |
| 2 | X2 | 16182C 16183C 16189C 16223T 16248T 16278T 16519C |
| 5 | X2 | 16183C 16189C 16193.1C 16223T 16255A 16278T 16519C |
| 7 | X2 | 16129A 16183C 16189C 16193.1C 16223T 16255A 16278T 16519C |
| 10 | X2 | 16189C 16193.1C 16223T 16278T 16519C |
| 27 | X2 | 16189C16223T 16271C 16278T 51619C |
| 47 | X2 | 16189C 16192T 16223T 16278T 16519C 16528T |
| 48 | X2 | 16189C 16223T 16278T 16519C |

| Phase I | Hg | HVS2 |
|---------|------|------|
| 1 | H | 263G 315.1C |
| 4 | H | 73G 153G 195C 225A 263G 309.1C 309.2C 315.1C |
| 6 | H | 73G 185A 188G 228A 263G 295T 309.1C 315.1C |
| 8 | H | 257G 263G 309.1C 309.2C 315.1C |
| 3 | J* | 73G 153G 195C 225A 227G 263G 315.1C |
| 9 | J* | 93G 263G 315.1C |
| 44 | J* | 73G 153G 195C 225A 226C 263G 309.1C 315.1C |
| 45 | J* | 185A 263G 315.1C |
| 46 | J* | 73G 228A 263G 295T 309.1C 315.1C |
| 30 | K | 73G 153G 195C 225A 226C 227G 263G 309.1C 315.1C |
| 23 | K2 | 73G 152C 217C 263G |
| 38 | L1b1 | 73G 152C 217C 263G |

| 42 | L1c2 | 73G 152C 217C 263G 315.1C |
|---|---|---|
| 43 | L3 | 73G 152C 217C 263G 315.1C |
| 28 | T* | 73G 150T 185A 163G 309.1C 315.1C |
| 35 | T* | 73G 150T 185A 163G 309.1C 315.1C |
| 41 | T* | 73G 152C 263G 315.1C |
| 25 | T1* | 73G 150T 263G 315.1C |
| 26 | T1* | 73G 263G 315.1C |
| 24 | T1a | 73G 199C 263G 315.1C |
| 32 | T1a | 73G 150T 263G 309.1C 315.1C |
| 50 | T1a | 73G 150T 263G 279C 315.1C |
| 29 | T2* | 73G 194C 263G |
| 31 | T2* | 73G 152C 195C 263G 309.1C 315.1C |
| 51 | T2c | 73G 152C 195C 263G 309.1C 315.1C |
| 52 | T2c | 73G 152C 195C 263G 309.1C 315.1C |
| 34 | T2e | 73G (or 73.1G) 153G 195C 225A 226C 227G 263G 309.1C 315.1C |
| 39 | T4 | 73G 263G 309.1C 315.1C |
| 11 | U2e* | 73G 263G 309.1C 315.1C 385G |
| 12 | U2e* | 73G  263G 309.1C 309.2C 315.1C |
| 13 | U2e* | 73G 151D 152.1C 263G 309.1C 315.1C |
| 14 | U2e* | 73G 152C 183G 195C 263G 309.1C 315.1C |
| 16 | U2e* | 73G 149.1T 152D 263G 315.1C |
| 49 | U2e* | 73G 150T 263G 309.1C 315.1C |
| 21 | U4* | 73G 146C 263G 309.1C 315.1C |
| 18 | U5* | 73G 185A 188G 228A 263G 295T 309.1C 315.1C |
| 17 | U5a1a | 263G 309.1C 309.2C 315.1C |
| 19 | U5a1a* | (357G) |
| 20 | U5a1a* | 73G  263G 309.1C  315.1C |
| 15 | U5b* | 73G 152C 235G 263G 309.1C 315.1C |
| 22 | U5b2 | 73G 151D 152.1C 236C 263G 315.1C |
| 33 | Unknown | |
| 36 | Unknown | 73G 150T 189G 195C 263G 309.1C 315.1C |
| 37 | Unknown | |
| 40 | Unknown | 93G 185A 188G 228A 263G 295T 309.1C 315.1C 462T  489C 522D 523D |
| 2 | X2 | 73G 228A 263G 295T 315.1C 426T 482C 489C |
| 5 | X2 | |

|    |    |                                           |
|----|----|-------------------------------------------|
| 7  | X2 |                                           |
| 10 | X2 | 73G 152C 217C 263G                        |
| 27 | X2 | 73G 152C 183G 195C 263G 309.1C 315.1C     |
| 47 | X2 | 73G 195C 263G 315.1C                      |
| 48 | X2 | 73G 195C 263G 315.1C                      |

| Phase II | Hg   | HVS1 Mutations                                                                  |
|----------|------|---------------------------------------------------------------------------------|
| 17       | A    | 16111T 16223T 16290T 16319A 16362C                                              |
| 46       | A    | 16223T 16290T 16319A 16362C 16391A 16519C                                       |
| 61       | A    | 16111C 16129A 16187T 16189C 16209T16230G 16278T 16290C 16311C 16319G 16362T     |
| 38       | B    | 16183C 16189C 16193.1C 16217C 16519C                                            |
| 58       | B    | 16111T 16182C 16183C 16189C 16217C 16320T 16465T 16483A 16519C                  |
| 20       | C    | 16086C 16183C 16189C 16223T 16278T 16298C 16325C 16327T                         |
| 66       | C    | 16223T 16298C 16325C 16327T                                                     |
| 10       | D    | 16093C 16189C 16223T 16274A 16325C 16362C                                       |
| 25       | D    | 16192T 16223T 16325C 16362C                                                     |
| 9        | H    | 16183C 16189C 16519C                                                            |
| 11       | H    | 16319A 16519C                                                                   |
| 12       | H    | 16519C                                                                          |
| 15       | H    | 16519C                                                                          |
| 24       | H    | 16311C                                                                          |
| 26       | H    | 16092C 16362C 16482G                                                            |
| 27       | H    | 16093C 16104T 16265G 16519C                                                     |
| 43       | H    | 16357C 16519C                                                                   |
| 45       | H    | 16188G 16519C                                                                   |
| 62       | H    | none                                                                            |
| 33       | Unk. | 16051G 16162G 16343G 16519C                                                     |
| 54       | I    | 16129A 16223T 16311C 16391A 16519C                                              |
| 48       | I4   | 16129A 16223T 16304C 16391A 16519C                                              |
| 3        | J*   | 16069T 16126C                                                                   |
| 41       | J*   | 16069T 16126C 16319A                                                            |
| 35       | J1a  | 16069T 16093C 16126C 16145A 16231C 16261T                                       |
| 8        | J1b1 | 16069T 16126C 16145A 16172C 16222T 16261T                                       |
| 32       | J1b1 | 16069T 16126C 16519C                                                            |
| 63       | J1b1 | 16069T 16126C 16145A 16172C 16222T 16261T                                       |
| 13       | K    | 16224C 16311C 16320T 16519C                                                     |

| 29 | K | 16183C 16189C 16224C 16311C 16519C |
|----|---|------------------------------------|
| 34 | K | 16187T 16224C 16311C 16519C |
| 53 | K | 16145A 16224C 16311C 16325C 16519C |
| 64 | L2 | 16223T 16278T 16294T 16309G 16368C 16390A 16519C |
| 16 | L3 | 16163G 16223T 16320T 16399G 16519C |
| 52 | L3 | 16124C 16223T 16265R 16262C 16519C |
| 51 | L3* | 16051G 16086C 16189D 16192.1T 16223T 16293T 16311C 16316G 16355T 16362C 16399G 16519C |
| 50 | L3e* | 16179T 16223T 16237T 16519C |
| 47 | L3f | 16129A 16209C 16223T 16292T 16295T 16311C 16519C |
| 2 | N1a | 16147A 16154C 16172C 16223T 16248T 16320T 16355T 16519C |
| 1 | T* | 16126C 16292T 16294T 16296T 16324C 16519C |
| 18 | T* | 16126C 16294T 16296T 16519C |
| 21 | T* | 16069C 16188T 16257T 16294T 16296T 16519C |
| 49 | T* | 16126C 16294T 16296T 16519C |
| 59 | T* | 16126C 16188T 16257T 16294T 16519C |
| 5 | T1a | 16126C 16163G 16186T 16189C 16294T 16519C |
| 6 | T1a | 16126C 16163G 16186T 16189C 16294T 16519C |
| 19 | T2 | 16294T 16304C 16519C |
| 28 | T2 | 16126C 16184T 16189C 16294T 16304C 16519C |
| 37 | T2 | 16126C 16218T 16287T 16294T 16296T 16304C 16519C |
| 57 | T2 | 16126C 16294T 16296T 16304C 16519C |
| 56 | T2c | 16126C 16182C 16183C 16189C 16294T 16296T 16298C 16519C |
| 22 | T2e | 16126C 16153A 16294T 16519C |
| 14 | U | 16172C 16189C 16193.1C 16193.2C 16234T 16311C 16519C |
| 42 | U, T or H | 16189C 16193.1C 16193.2C 16356C 16362C 16519C |
| 55 | U2e | 16051G 16129C 16183C 16189C 16362C 16519C |
| 36 | U3 | 16343G 16390A 16519C |
| 7 | U5 | 16256T 16270T 16399G |
| 65 | U5a1 | 16192T 16256T 16270T 16278T 16362C 16526A |
| 60 | U5a1* | 16192T 16256T 16270T 16391A |
| 67 | U5a1* | 16256T 16270T 16291T 16399G 16519C |
| 44 | U5b | 16093C 16189C 16193.1C 16193.2C 16270T |
| 40 | U5b2 | 16258G 16270T 16292T 16362C |
| 39 | V | 16126C 16298C |
| 30 | W | 16166C 16189C 16192T 16223T 16292T 16325C 16519C |

| 31 | W | 16223T 16292T 16362C 16519C |
| 23 | X | 16104T 16145A 16182C 16183C 16189C 16223T 16519C |

| Phase II | Hg | HVS2 Mutations |
|---|---|---|
| 17 | A | 64T 73G 146C 153G 235G 263G 315.1C |
| 46 | A | 64T 73G 146C 153G 235G 263G 309.1C 315.1C |
| 61 | A | |
| 38 | B | 73G 263G 309.1C 309.2C 315.1C |
| 58 | B | 73G 263G 309.1C 315.1C |
| 20 | C | 73G 143A 249D 263G 290D 291D 315.1C |
| 66 | C | 73G 215G 249D 263G 290D 291D 315.1C |
| 10 | D | 73G 211G 263G 315.1C |
| 25 | D | 73G 194T 263G 315.1C |
| 9 | H | 263G 309.1C 315.1C |
| 11 | H | 72G 146C 195C 263G 315.1C |
| 12 | H | 189G 263G 309C 315.1C |
| 15 | H | 146C 263G 315.1C |
| 24 | H | 195C 214R 263G 315.1C |
| 26 | H | 239C 263G 309.1C 315.1C |
| 27 | H | 263G 309.1C 315.1C |
| 43 | H | 263G 315.1C |
| 45 | H | 263G 315.1C |
| 62 | H | 73G 194T 263G 315.1C |
| 33 | H, H1a, A or U3 | 73G 263G 315.1C |
| 54 | I | 73G 199C 204C 204C 207A 250C 263G 315.1C |
| 48 | I4 | 73G 199C 204C 236C 250C 263G 315.1C |
| 3 | J* | 73G 185A 228A 263G 295T 315.1C |
| 41 | J* | 73G 185A 228A 263G 295T 315.1C |
| 35 | J1a | 73G 149.1T 152D 195C 215G 263G 295T 310.1T 315.1C 319C |
| 8 | J1b1 | 73G 146C 207A 242T 263G 295T 315.1C |
| 32 | J1b1 | 73G 185A 188G 228A 234R 263G 295T 315.1C |
| 63 | J1b1 | 73G 189G 263G 315.1C |
| 13 | K | 73G 146C 152C 263G 315.1C |
| 29 | K | 73G 146C 195C 200G 263G 315.1C |
| 34 | K | 73G 195C 263G 315.1C |

228

| 53 | K | 73G 149.1T 152D 195C 203A 204C 263G 310.1T 315.1C |
|---|---|---|
| 64 | L2 | 73G 146C 152C 195C 263G 315.1C |
| 16 | L3 | |
| 52 | L3 | 73G 152C 195C 199C 263G 315.1C |
| 51 | L3* | 73G 146C 152C 195C 244G 263G 315.1C 340T |
| 50 | L3e* | 73G 149.1C 152C 195C 203A 204C 263G 309.1C 315.1C |
| 47 | L3f | 73G 189G 200G 263G 309.1C 315.1C |
| 2 | N1a | 73G 152C 199C 204C 263G 315.1C |
| 1 | T* | 73G 263G 309.1C 315.1C |
| 18 | T* | 73G 263G 309.1C 315.1C |
| 21 | T* | 73G 263G 309.1C 315.1C |
| 49 | T* | 73G 263G 315.1C |
| 59 | T* | 73G 263G 309.1C 315.1C |
| 5 | T1a | 73G 152C 195C 263G 309.1C 315.1C |
| 6 | T1a | |
| 19 | T2 | 73G 152C 263G 309.1C 315.1C |
| 28 | T2 | 73G 152C 263G 315.1C |
| 37 | T2 | 73G 146C 263G 309.1C 315.1C |
| 57 | T2 | 73G 263G 309.1C 315.1C |
| 56 | T2c | 73G 195C 263G 315.1C |
| 22 | T2e | 73G 150T 263G 309.1C 315.1C |
| 14 | U | 73G 195C 263G 315.1C |
| 42 | U, T or H | 140T 263G 315.1C |
| 55 | U2e | 73G, 152C, 217C, 263G, 309.1C, 315.1C, 340T |
| 36 | U3 | 73G 150T 263G 309.1C 315.1C |
| 7 | U5 | 73G 263G 309.1C 315.1C |
| 65 | U5a1 | 73G 263G 315.1C |
| 60 | U5a1* | 73G 263G 315.1C |
| 67 | U5a1* | 73G 263G 272G 315.1C |
| 44 | U5b | 73G 150T 263G 315.1C |
| 40 | U5b2 | 73G 150T 263G 309.1C 315.1C |
| 39 | V | 72C 263G 315.1C |
| 30 | W | 73G 189G 194T 195C 204C 207A 263G 315.1C |
| 31 | W | 73G 189G 194T 195C 204C 207A 263G 309.1C 315.1C |
| 23 | X | 73G 146C 153G 309.1C 315.1C |

# BIBLIOGRAPHY

Abu-Amero, Khaled K. et al. (2008). "Mitochondrial DNA Structure in the Arabian Peninsula." *BMC Evolutionary Biology* 8:45, doi:10.1186/1471-2148-8-45.

Achilli, A. et al. (2004). "The Molecular Dissection of mtDNA Haplogroup H Confirms That the Franco-Cantabrian Glacial Refuge Was a Major Source for the European Gene Pool." *American Journal of Human Genetics* 75(5):910-8.

---------- (2008). "The Phylogeny of the Four Pan-American mtDNA Haplogroups: Implications for Evolutionary and Disease Studies." *PLoS ONE* 3(3).

Adair, James (1930). *Adair's History of the American Indians*, ed. by Samuel Cole Williams, originally published London, 1775. Johnson City: Watauga.

Adovasio, James and Jake Page (2003). *The First Americans*. New York: Modern Library.

Arden, Harvey and Steve Wall (n.d.). *Wisdomkeepers. Meetings with Native American Spiritual Elders*. Hillsboro: Beyond Words.

Andersen, Johannes C. (1969). *Myths and Legends of the Polynesians*. Tokyo: Tuttle.

Anderson, S. et al. (1981). "Sequence and Organization of the Human Mitochondrial Genomes." *Nature* 290:457-65.

Anderson, William L. et al., eds. (2010). *The Payne-Butrick Papers*. 6 vols. in 2. Lincoln: U of Nebraska P.

Andrews, R. M. et al. (1999). "Reanalysis and Revision of the Cambridge Reference Sequence for Human Mitochondrial DNA." *Nature Genetics* 23:147.

Arnaiz-Villena, A. et al. (2010). "The Origin of Amerindians and the Peopling of the Americas." *Current Genomics* 11(2):103-14.

Aubet, Maria Eugenia (2001). *The Phoenicians and the West: Politics, Colonies and Trade*. Cambridge: Cambridge UP.

Bailliet, G et al. (1994) "Founder Mitochondrial Haplotypes in Amerindian Populations. "*Am J Hum Genet.* 55(1):27-33.

Bancroft, Hubert H. (2012). *History of Arizona and New Mexico, 1530-1888*. In: *The Works of Hubert Howe Bancroft*. N.p: Classic Reprint.

---------- (2006). *History of Mexico, Being a History of the Mexican People from the Earliest Primitive Civilization to Present*. In: *The Works of Hubert Howe Bancroft*. N.p: Classic Reprint.

---------- (1884). *History of the North Mexican States*. Vol. 1, *The Works of Hubert Howe Bancroft*. San Francisco: A.L. Bancroft.

---------- (1884). *The Native Races*. Vol. 5, *The Works of Hubert Howe Bancroft*. San Francisco: A.L. Bancroft, 1884.

Bardill, Jessica (2013). Review of *Old World Roots of the Cherokee: How DNA, Ancient*

*Alphabets, and Religion Explain the Origins of America's Largest Indian Nation,* by Donald N. Yates. *American Indian Culture and Research Journal* 37/4: 199-202.

Bedford, Felice L. (2012). "Sephardic Signature in Haplogroup T Mitochondrial DNA." *Eur J Hum Genet* 20(4):441-48.

Beinlich, Horst and Friedhelm Hoffmann (1994). "Ancient Egyptian Word-list," database, see *Göttinger Miszellen* 140:101-3. URL: www.fitzmuseum.cam.ac.uk/er/beinlich/beinlich.html.

Bolnick, D. A. and D. G. Smith (2003). "Unexpected Patterns of Mitochondrial DNA Variation among Native Americans from the Southeastern United States." *American Journal of Physical Anthropology* 122(4):336-54.

Boorstin, Daniel J. (1993). *The Lost World of Thomas Jefferson.* Chicago: U of Chicago P.

Brandt, G. et al. (2013). "Ancient DNA Reveals Key Stages in the Formation of Central European Mitochondrial Genetic Diversity." *Science* 342(6155):257-61.

Butler, John M. (2010). *Fundamentals of Forensic DNA Typing.* Amsterdam: Elsevier.

Cann, R. L. (1994) "mtDNA and Native Americans: a Southern Perspective." *Am J Hum Genet.* 55(1):7-11.

Caramelli D. et al. (2008). "A 28,000 Years Old Cro-Magnon mtDNA Sequence Differs from All Potentially Contaminating Modern Sequences." *PLoS ONE* 3(7): e2700, doi:10.1371/journal.pone.0002700.

Cavalli-Sforza, L. L. et al. (1994). *History and Geography of Human Genes.* Princeton: Princeton UP.

Churchill, Ward (1998). *A Little Matter of Genocide: Holocaust and Denial in the Americas 1492 to the Present.* San Francisco: City Lights.

Childress, David Hatcher (2009). *Lost Cities & Ancient Mysteries of the Southwest.* Lost Cities Series. Kempton: Adventures Unlimited.

Cohen, Felix S. (1942). *Handbook of Federal Indian Law.* Washington: GPO.

Comas, D. et al. (1996). "Geographic Variation in Human Mitochondrial DNA Control Region Sequence: The Population History of Turkey and Its Relationship to the European Populations. *Molecular Biology and Evolution* 13:1067-1077.

Cooper, John H. (2001). "Ancient Greek Cultural and Linguistic Influences in Atlantic North America." *NEARA Journal* 35/2:81-91.

Cox, Brent Alan Yanusdi (1999). *Heart of the Eagle. Dragging Canoe and the Emergence of the Chickamauga Confederacy.* Milan: Chenanee.

Crawford, Michael H. (1998). *Origins of the Native Americans. Evidence from Anthropological Genetics.* Cambridge: Cambridge UP.

Crutchfield, James (1976). *Early Times in the Cumberland Valley.* Nashville: First American National Bank.

Debo, Angie (2000) *A History of the Indians of the United States.* London: Folio Society.

Decker, Geoffrey (2011). "Hispanics Identifying Themselves as Indians." *The New York Times*, July 4, 2011: N.Y./Region section.

Del Mar, Alexander (1902). *A History of the Precious Metals*. New York: Burt Franklin.

Deloria, Vine, Jr. (1988),. *Custer Died for Your Sins*. With a new preface by the author. Norman: U of Oklahoma P.

---------- (1992). *God Is Red. A Native View of Religion. The Classic Work Updated*. Golden: Fulcrum.

Diaz-Granadox, Carol and James R. Duncan, ed. (2004). *The Rock-Art of Eastern North America*. Tuscaloosa: U of Alabama P.

Driver, Harold E. (1961). *Indians of North America*. Chicago: U of Chicago P.

Dulike, Matthew C. et al. (2012). "Mitochondrial DNA and Y Chromosome Variation Provides Evidence for a Recent Common Ancestry between Native Americans and Indigenous Altaians." *AJHG* 90/2, 229-246.

Estes, Roberta (2009). "Where Have All the Indians Gone? Native American Eastern Seaboard Dispersal, Genealogy and DNA in Relation to Sir Walter Raleigh's Lost Colony of Roanoke. *Journal of Genetic Genealogy* 5(2):96-130. Online journal.

Farley, Gloria (1994). *In Plain Sight*. Columbus, Ga.: ISAC Press, 1994.

Fell, Barry (1989). *America B.C.* Rev. ed. New York: Pocket.

----------- (1980). *Saga America*. New York: Times.

Fewkes, Jesse Walter (1923). *Designs on Prehistoric Pottery from the Mimbres Valley, New Mexico." Smithsonian Miscellaneous Collections 74(6)*. Washington: GPO.

Fogelson, Raymond D. (2003). "Cherokee in the East," in *Handbook* 337-53.

Garcia, Gregorio de (2005). *Origen de los indios del nuevo mundo e indias occidentales*. Madrid: Consejo Superior de Investigaciones Científicas.

Gatschet, Albert S. (n.d.). "Notes on Six Cherokee Gentes" [card files in the Smithsonian Institution], including notations by James Mooney and J.N.B. Hewitt recording information from Cherokee medicine man John Ax among others, together with manuscript materials by J.T. Garrett, interpreted by John D. Strange, Allogan Slagle and Richard Mack Bettis.

Gimbutas, Marija (2006). *The Language of the Goddess*. London: Thames and Hudson.

Gladwin, Harold Sterling (1947). *Men Out of Asia*. New York: Whittlesey House.

González-Oliver, A. et al. (2001). "Founding Amerindian Mitochondrial DNA Lineages in Ancient Maya from Xcaret, Quintana Roo. *American Journal of Physical Anthropology* 116/3: 230-235.

Goodman, Jeffrey (1981). *American Genesis: The American Indian and the Origin of Modern Man*. New York: Summit.

Green, L. D. et al. (2000). "MtDNA Affinities of the Peoples of North-Central Mexico." *American Journal of Human Genetics* 66:989-98.

Greenberg, Joseph H. (1987). *Language in the Americas*. Stanford: Stanford UP.

Guthrie, James L. (2001). "Human Lymphocyte Antigens: Apparent Afro-Asiatic, Southern Asian, and European HLAS in Indigenous American Populations." *Pre-Columbiana* 2.2-3:90-163.

Harris, Hendon M., Jr. (2006). *The Asiatic Fathers of America. Chinese Discovery and Colonization of America*, ed. and abridged by Charlotte Harris Rees. Lynchburg: Warwick House.

Herm, Gerhard (1975). *The Phoenicians. The Purple Empire of the Ancient World*, trans. Caroline Hillier. New York: Morrow.

Herodotus. *The Histories*, trans. Aubrey de Sélincourt. London: Folio Society, 2006.

Hicks, Theresa M. (1998). *South Carolina Indians, Indian Traders and Other Ethnic Connections Beginning in 1670*. Spartanburg: Reprint.

Hirschman, Elizabeth Caldwell and Donald N. Yates (2012). *Jews and Muslims in British Colonial History: A Genealogical History*. Jefferson: McFarland.

Hodgkinson, H.L., J.H. Outtz & A.M. Obarakpor (1990). *The Demographics of American Indians: One percent of the people: Fifty percent of the Diversity*. Report prepared for the Institute for Educational Leadership, Inc. and Center for Demographic Policy. Washington: U.S. Government Printing Office.

Horai, S. et al. (1993) "Peopling of the Americas, Founded by Four Major Lineages of Mitochondrial DNA." *Mol Biol Evol.* 10(1):23-47.

Hornblower, Simon and Anthony Spawforth, ed. (2003). *The Oxford Classical Dictionary*. 3rd ed. Oxford: Oxford UP.

Jett, Stephen C. (2009). "Genetics Geography Implies a Minimum of Four Major Late Pleistocene Movements and Four Major Early to Middle Holocene Movements of Modern Humans into the Americas." International Science Conf., Los Angeles, May 2009.

---------- (1999). "The Jomon of Neolithic Japan: Early Ocean-Goers." *Pre-Columbiana: A Journal of Long-Distance Contacts* 1/3-4:158-63.

---------- (1968). Malaysia and Tropical America: Some Racial, Cultural, and Ethnobotanical Comparisons.. *Congress of Americanists* 37/4:133-77.

---------- (2003). "Pre-Columbian Transoceanic Contacts: The Present State of the Evidence." New England Antiquities Research Assn. *NEARA Journal* 36/2:4-8.

Johansen, Bruce E. (n.d.). "Individual Indian Monies: American Indian Heritage Month: Commemoration vs. Exploitation," article in ABC-CLIO series *History and the Headlines*. Available at http://www.historyandtheheadlines.abc-clio.com.

Jones, Peter N. (2002). *American Indian Demographic History and Cultural Affiliation: A Discussion of Certain Limitations on the Use of mtDNA and Y Chromosome Testing*. Boulder: Bäuu Institute. Published in *AnthroGlobe Journal*. Online: http://www.bauuinstitute.com/Articles/JonesmtDNA.pdf.

Jordan, Jerry Wright (2009). *Cherokee by Blood: Records of Eastern Cherokee Ancestry in the U.S. Court of Claims 1906-1910*. Vol. 1: *Applications: 10171-13260*. Baltimore: Heritage.

Josephy, Alvin M., Jr. (2001). *500 Nations : An Illustrated History of North American Indians*. New York: Gramercy.

Kehoe, Alice B. (1981). *North American Indians: A Comprehensive Account*. New York: Prentice Hall.

Kemp, Brian M. and Theodore G. Schurr (2010). "Ancient and Modern Genetic Variation in the Americas." In: *Human Variation in the Americas: The Integration of Archaeology and Biological Anthropology*, ed. Benjamin M. Auerbach, pp. 12-50. Carbondale: Southern Illinois UP.

King, Turi E. and Mark A. Jobling (2009). " Founders, Drift, and Infidelity: The Relationship between Y Chromosome Diversity and Patrilineal Surnames." *Mol Biol Evol.* 26(5):1093–1102.

Kivisild et al. (2002). "The Emerging Limbs and Twigs of the East Asian mtDNA Tree." *Mol Biol Evol.* 19(10):1737-51.

Klein, Barry T., ed. (2003). *Reference Encyclopedia of the American Indian*. 10th ed. Nyack, N.Y.: Todd Publications.

Krings, M. et al. (1999). "mtDNA Analysis of Nile River Valley Populations: A Genetic Corridor or a Barrier to Migration?" *Am J Hum Genet* 64:1166–1176.

Lalueza, C. et al. (1997). "Lack of Founding Amerindian Mitochondrial DNA Lineages in Extinct Aborigines from Tierra del Fuego-Patagonia." *Hum Mol Genet* 6:41-46.

Lalueza, C. et al. (1996). "Mitochondrial DNA Haplogroups in Four Tribes from Tierra del Fuego-Patagonia: Inferences about the Peopling of the Americas. *Hum Biol* 68:855-71.

Las Casas, Bartolomé de (1974). *In defense of the Indians; the defense of the Most Reverend Lord, Don Fray Bartolomé de las Casas, of the Order of Preachers, late Bishop of Chiapa, against the persecutors and slanderers of the peoples of the New World discovered across the seas*. Ed. Stafford Poole. DeKalb: Northern Illlinois UP.

Lazaridis, I. et al. (2014). "Ancient Human Genomes Suggest Three Ancestral Populations for the Present-day Europeans." *Nature* 513(7518):409-13.

Lawson, John (1709). *A New Voyage to Carolina; Containing the Exact Description and Natural History of That Country: Together with the Present State Thereof. And A Journal of a Thousand Miles, Travel'd Thro' Several Nations of Indians. Giving a Particular Account of Their Customs, Manners, &c*. London:   1709. Available online at http://docsouth.unc.edu/nc/lawson/menu.html.

Logan, J. (2008). "The Subclades of mtDNA Haplogroup J and Proposed Motifs for Assigning Control-Region Sequences into These Clades." *Journal of Genetic Genealogy* 4:12-26.

Lorenz, J.G. and D.G. Smith (1996). "Distribution of Four Founding mtDNA Haplogroups among Native North Americans." *Am J Phys Anthropol* 101:307-23.

---------- (1997). "Distribution of Sequence Variation in the mtDNA Control

Region of Native North Americans." *Human Biology* 69:749-76.

Lounsbury, Floyd G. (1961). "Iroquois-Cherokee Linguistic Relations." In: William Fenton and John Gulick, eds. *Symposium on Cherokee and Iroquois Culture*. Bureau of American Ethnology Bulletin 180, 11-17.

Maca-Meyer, N. et al. (2001). "Major Genomic Mitochondrial Lineages Delineate Early Human Expansions." *BMC Genetics* 2:13.

Macaulay, V. et al. (1999). "The Emerging Tree of West Eurasian mtDNAs: A Synthesis of Control-Region Sequences and RFLPs." *American Journal of Human Genetics* 64:232-49.

Mainfort, Robert C. and Mary L. Kwas (2004). "The Bat Creek Stone Revisited: A Fraud Exposed." *American Antiquity* 64 (Oct. 2004) 761-69. Anonymous review, *American Antiquity* 69(4):761-69, in *Pre-Columbiana. A Journal of Long-Distance Contacts* 3/4 and 4/1 & 2 (2005/2006/2007): 259-60.

Malhi, R. S., et al. (2006). "Demystifying Native American Genetic Opposition to Research." *Evolutionary Anthropology* 15:88-92.

---------- (2001). "Distribution of Mitochondrial DNA Lineages among Native American Tribes of Northeastern North America. *Hum Biol* 73:17-55.

---------- (2006). "Mitochondrial Haplogroup M Discovered in Prehistoric North Americans." *J. Archaeological Sc. I20:1-7.*

---------- (2003). "Native American mtDNA Prehistory in the American Southwest." *Am J of Phys Anthropol* 120:108-24.

---------- (2001). "The Structure of Diversity within New World Mitochondrial DNA Haplogroups: Implications for the Prehistory of North America." *Am. J. Hum. Genet.* 70:905-919.

Malhi, R. S. and Smith, D. G. (2002) "Haplogroup X Confirmed in Prehistoric America. Brief Communication. *Am. J. of Phys. Anthrop.* 119:84-86.

Malhi, Ripan S. and Jason A. Eshleman (2004). "The Uses and Limitations of DNA Ancestry Tests for Native Americans." Online: http://www.tracegenetics.com/newsevents.html.

McIntosh, John (1843). *The Origin of the North American Indians*. New York: Nafis & Cornish.

McNickle, D'Arcy (1993) *Native American Tribalism*. New York: Oxford.

Brad Montgomery-Anderson (2008). *A Reference Grammar of Oklahoma Cherokee*. Ph.D. Dissertation, U of Kansas.

Martin, Joel W. (1996). "'My Grandmother Was a Cherokee Princess': Representations of Indians in Southern History." In: *Dressing in Feathers: The Construction of the Indian in American Popular Culture*, ed. S. Elizabeth Bird, pp. 130-41. Boulder: Westview.

Malyarchuk, B. et al. (2010). "The Peopling of Europe from the Mitochondrial Haplogroup U5 Perspective." *PLoS One* 5(4):e10285.

Merriwether, D. A., F. Rothhammer and R. E. Ferrell (1995). "Distribution of the

Four Founding Lineage Haplotypes in Native Americans Suggests a Single Wave of Migration for the New World." *American Journal of Physical Anthropology* 98(4):411-430.

Mertz, Henriette (1972). *Pale Ink: Two Ancient Records of Chinese Exploration in America*. 2nd ed. Chicago: Swallow.

Miller, K. W. P. and J. L. Dawson. *The Concordance of Nucleotide Substitutions in the Human mtDNA Control Region*. Online database made available by the Department of Biological Anthropology of the University of Cambridge. URL: http://www.bioanth.cam.ac.uk/mtDNA/toc.html.

Mitosearch. Online database made available by Family Tree DNA, Houston. URL: http://mitosearch.org./

Monson, K. et al. (2002). "The mtDNA Population Database: An Integrated Software and Database Resource for Forensic Comparison." *Forensic Science Communications* 4/2.

Montgomery-Anderson, Brad (2008). *A Reference Grammar of Oklahoma Cherokee*. Ph.D. Diss., U of Kansas.

Mowat, Farley (2002). *The Farfarers. A New History of North America*. New York: Skyhorse.

Mooney, James (1975). *Historical Sketch of the Cherokee*, with a foreword by W.W. Keeler, intro. by Richard Mack Bettis. Chicago: Aldine.

---------- (1982). *Myths of the Cherokee and Sacred Formulas of the Cherokees*. Nashville: Cherokee Heritage.

Moreau, C. et al. (2011). "Deep Human Genealogies Reveal a Selective Advantage to Be on an Expanding Wave Front." *Science* 334(6059):1148-50.

Mulligan, C. J., K. Hunley, S. Cole and J. C. Long (2004). "Population Genetics, History, and Health Patterns in Native Americans." *Annual Review of Genomics and Human Genetics* 5(1):295-315.

O'Fallon, Brendan D. and Lars Fehren-Schmitz (2011). "Native Americans Experienced a Strong Population Bottleneck Coincident with European Contact," *Proceedings of the National Academy of Science* 108(51):20444-20448. .

Pääbo, Svante et al. (1988). "Mitochondrial DNA Sequences from a 7000-year-old Brain," *Nucleic Acids Research* 16.20:9775-87. Pauketat, Timothy R. and Diana DiPaolo Loren, eds. (2005). *North American Archaeology*. Oxford: Blackwell.

Panther-Yates, Donald N. (2001). "A Portrait of Cherokee Chief Attakullakulla from the 1730s? A Discussion of William Verelst's 'Trustees of Georgia' Painting." *Journal of Cherokee Studies* 22:5-20.

---------- (2013). *Cherokee Clans: An Informal History*. Cherokee Chapbooks 4. Phoenix: Panther's Lodge.

Patterson-Rudolph, Carol (1997). *On the Trail of Spider Woman: Petroglyphs and Myths of the Southwest*. Santa Fe: Ancient City.

Pena, S.D.J. et al. (1995). "A Major Founder Y-chromosome Haplotype in

Amerindians." *Nature Genet* 11:15-16.

Perego, Ugo A. et al. (2009). "Distinctive Paleo-Indian Migration Routes from Beringia Marked by Two Rare mtDNA Haplogroups." *Current Biology* 19(1):1-8.

Pevar, Stephen L. (1992). *The Right of Indians and Tribes. The Basic ACLU Guide to Indian and Tribal Rights.* Carbondale: Southern Illinois UP.

Pike, D. A. et al. (2010). "mtDNA Haplogroup T Philogeny Based on Full Mitochondrial Sequences." *J Genet Geneal.* 6(1):1-24.

Pocahontas Foundation (1994-1997). *Pocahontas' Descendants.* 3 vols. Baltimore: Genealogical.

Popper, Karl (2005). *The Logic of Scientific Discovery.* New York: Routledge.

Pynes, Patrick (2003). "Cherokee Traditions among the Talleys, Gentrys and Associated Families of Texas and Arkansas: A Genealogical and Historical Exploration." *Journal of Gentry Genealogy* 3(6)

Quinn, William W., Jr. (1990). "The Southeast Syndrome: Notes on Indian Descendant Recruitment Organizations and Their Perceptions of Native American Culture." *American Indian Quarterly* 14/2:147-54.

Rafinesque, Constantine Samuel (1836). *The American Nations, or, Outlines of Their General History, Ancient and Modern: Including the Whole History of the Earth and Mankind in the Western Hemisphere: the Philosophy of American History: the Annals, Traditions, Civilization, Languages, &c., of All the American Nations, Empires, and States...* Philadelphia: Printed for the Author.

---------- (1824). *Ancient History, or Annals of Kentucky: with a Survey of the Ancient Monuments of North America, and a Tabular View of the Principal Languages and Primitive Nations of the Whole Earth.* Frankfort: Printed for the author. Available online courtesy of the Filson Historical Society and University of Chicago Press at http://memory.loc.gov/

---------- (1836). *A Life of Travels and Researches in North America and South Europe, or Outline of the Life, Travels and Researches of C. S. Rafinesque...* Philadelphia: Printed for the Author. Available online courtesy of the Filson Historical Society and University of Chicago Press at http://memory.loc.gov/

Raghavan, M. et al. (2014). "Upper Palaeolithic Siberian Genome Reveals Dual Ancestry of Native Americans." *Nature* 2/505(7481):87-91.

Reese, Charlotte Harris (2013). *Did the Ancient Chinese Explore America?* N.p.: Torchflame.

Reich, David et al. (2012). "Reconstructing Native American Population History." *Nature* 488:370–374.

Richards, Martin et al. (2000). "Tracing European Founder Lineages in the Near Eastern mtDNA Pool." American Journal of Human Genetics 67:1251-76. Supplementary Data. URL: http://www.stats.gla.ac.uk/ ~vincent/ founder2000/index.html

Richards, Martin and Vincent Macaulay (2000). "The Mitochondrial Gene Tree

Comes of Age." *American Journal of Human Genetics* 68:1315-20.

Robinson, Andrew (2010). "History: How to Behave beyond the Grave." *Nature* 468:632-33.

Rogers, Edward Andrew and Mary Evelyn Rogers (1986, 1988). *A Brief History of the Cherokees 1540-1906.*

Roth, Wendy D. (2012). *Race Migrations. Latinos and the Cultural Transformation of Race.* Stanford: Stanford UP.

Rountree, Helen C. (1996). *Pocahontas's People: The Powhatan Indians of Virginia Through Four Centuries.* Norman: U of Oklahoma P.

Royce, Charles (1975). *The Cherokee Nation of Indians*, intro. by Richard Mack Bettis. Chicago: Aldine.

Ruskamp, John (2013). *Asiatic Echoes-The Identification of Ancient Chinese Pictograms in pre-Columbian North American Rock Writing.* 2nd ed. Boston: Kluwer Academic.

Salzano, F. M. (2002). "Molecular Variability in Amerindians: Widespread but Uneven Information." *An. Acad. Bras. Ciênc.* 74/2. Available online at http://www.scielo.br/.

Schroeder, Kari et al. (2009). "Haplotypic Background of a Private Allele at High Frequency in the Americas," *Mol. Biol. Evol.* 26/5:995-1016.

Schroedl, Gerald F. (2001). "Cherokee Archaeology since the 1970s." *Archaeology of the Appalachian Highlands*, ed. L. P. Sullivan and S.C. Prezzano, 278-97. Knoxville: U of Tennessee P.

Shlush, L. I. et al. (2009) "The Druze: A Population Genetic Refugium of the Near East." *PLoS ONE* 3(5): e2105.

Schulz, Colin (2013)."The Very First Americans May Have Had European Roots." *Smithsonian.com.* Available: http:// www. smithsonianmag.com/ smart- news/5517714/.

Schurr, Theodore G. (2000). "Mitochondrial DNA and the Peopling of the New World," *American Scientist* 88:246-53.

Smith, D. G., et al. (1999). Distribution of mtDNA Haplogroup X among Native North Americans. *Am J Phys Anthropol* 110:271-84.

Smith, Linda Tuhiwai (1999). *Decolonizing Indigenous Methodologies. Research and Indigenous Peoples.* London: Zed.

Sorenson, John L. and Carl L. Johannessen (2009). *World Trade and Biological Exchanges before 1492.* New York: iUniverse.

Starr, Emmet (1977). *History of the Cherokee Indians and Their Legends and Folk Lore.* Millwood: Kraus Reprint. Originally published in Oklahoma City by The Warden Company, 1921.

Steiner, Stan (1979). *Fusang: The Chinese Who Built America.* New York: Harper.

---------- (1967). *The New Indians.* Harper & Row.

Sterkx, Henry Eugene and Brooks Thompson (1961). "Philemon Thomas and the West Florida Revolution." *Florida Historical Quarterly* 39(2):378-86.

Stone, A. C. and M. Stoneking (1993). "Ancient DNA from a Pre-Columbian Amerindian Population." *Am J Phys Anthropol.* 1993 Dec;92(4):463-71.

Stone, A. C. and Stoneking, M. (1999). "Analysis of Ancient DNA from a Prehistoric Amerindian Cemetery." *Philos Trans R Soc Lond B Biol Sci* 354:153-59.

Stoneking, M. et al. (1990). "Geographic Variation in Human Mitochondrial DNA from Papua New Guinea." *Genetics* 124:717-33.

Sturtevant, William C., gen. ed. (2004). *Handbook of North American Indians*, vol. 14: *Southeast*, ed. Raymond D. Fogelson. Washington: Smithsonian Institution.

Swaminathan, Nikhil (2014). "America, in the Beginning." *Archaeology* 67/5:22-29.

Sykes, Brian (2001). *The Seven Daughters of Eve. The Science that Reveals Our Genetic Ancestry*. New York: Norton.

Ten Kate, Herman (2004). *Travels and Researches in Native North America, 1882-1883*, ed. Pieter Hovens et al. Albuquerque: U of New Mexico P.

Thomas, M. et al. (2002). "Founding Mothers of Jewish Communities: Geographically Separated Jewish Groups Were Independently Founded by Very Few Female Ancestors." *American Journal of Human Genetics* 70:1411-20.
Thompson, Gunnar (1994). *American Discovery. Our Multicultural Heritage*. Seattle:
Argonauts Misty Isles.

---------- (2010). *Ancient Egyptian Maize*. Seattle: New World Discovery Institute.

Thornton, Russell (1992). *The Cherokees: A Population History*. Omaha: U of Nebraska P.

Torroni, A. et al. (1993). "Asian Affinities and Continental Radiation of the Four Founding Native American mtDNAs." *Am J Hum Genet*. Sep 1993; 53(3): 563–590.

---------- (1996). "Classification of European mtDNAs from an Analysis of Three European Populations." *Genetics* 144:1835-50.

---------- (2006). "Harvesting the Fruit of the Human mtDNA Tree." *Trends Genet* 22(6):339-45.

Torroni, A. and D. C. Wallace (1995). "Mitochondrial Haplogroups in Native Americans." *Am J Hum Genet*. 56(5):1234–1238

Thurston, Gates P. (1890). *The Antiquities of Tennessee and the Adjacent States*. Cincinnati: Clarke.

Van Oven, Mannis and Manfred Kayser (2008)."Updated Comprehensive Phylogenetic Tree of Global Human Mitochondrial DNA Variation." *Human Mutation* 30(2): E386-E394.

Vining, Edward P. (1885). *Inglorious Columbus, or, Evidence that Hwui Shen and a Party of Buddhist Priests from Afganistan Discovered America*. New York: Appleton.

Wade, Nicholas (2013). "24,000 Year Old Body Shows Kinship to Europeans and American Indians." *NY Times* (Nov. 21, 2013):A8.

Wallace D. C. and A. Torroni (1992). "American Indian Prehistory as Written in the Mitochondrial DNA: a Review. *Hum Biol.* 64(3):403-16.

Wallace, D. C. et al. (1985). "Dramatic Founder Effects in Amerindian Mitochondrial DNAs." *Am J Phys Anthropol* 68:149-55.

Waldman, Karl (2000). *Atlas of the North American Indian.* Rev. ed. New York: Checkmark.

Wang, S. et al. (2007). "Genetic Variation and Population Structure in Native Americans." *PLoS Genetics* 3/11.

Warrior, Robert Allen (1994). *Tribal Secrets. Recovering American Indian Intellectual Traditions.* Minneapolis: U of Minnesota P.

Waters, Frank (1963). *Book of the Hopi*, drawings and source material recorded by Oswald White Bear Fredericks. New York: Viking.

Wauchope, Robert (1962). *Lost Tribes & Sunken Continents.* Chicago: U of Chicago P.

Wilson, Joseph Andrew Park (2011). *Material Cultural Correlates of the Athapaskan Expansion: A Cross-Disciplinary Approach.* Ph.D. Dissertation, University of Florida.

Wolter, Scott F. (2013). *Akhenaten to the Founding Fathers: The Mysteries of the Hooked X.* St. Cloud: North Star.

Xiao, Feng-Xia et al. (2002). "Diversity at Eight Polymorphic Alu Insertion Loci in Chinese Populations Shows Evidence for European Admixture in an Ethnic Minority Population from Northwest China," *Human Biology* 4:555-568.

Yates, Donald N. (1995). *The Bear Went Over the Mountain. Genealogy and Social History of a Southern U.S. Family; the Story of the Native American-English Yates Family, from Colonial Virginia to Twentieth-century Florida.* Princeton: Cherokee.

---------- (2014). *Old Souls in a New World: The Secret History of the Cherokee Indians.* Phoenix: Panther's Lodge.

---------- (2012). *Old World Roots of the Cherokee: How DNA, Ancient Alphabets and Religion Explain the Origins of America's Largest Indian Nation.* Jefferson: McFarland.

Yong, Ed (2013). "Americas' Natives Have European Roots." *Nature* (20 November 2013) doi:10.1038/nature.2013.14213.

# INDEX

Numbers in **boldface** indicate pages with photographs.

(Little) 119, 185; Tyre 119

George I 68

Gibson, Gayl A. 54, 110

Gilbert, Michael 66

Gillette, Rusty 190

Gimbutas, Marija 197

Ginn, Olivia McCorkle Walker 63

Gladwin, Harold Sterling 181

Glass, Thomas (The Glass), chief 51

Glover, Emily 64

Goble 131; Lucinda (Shankles) 134; Dovie Palestine (Cooper) **143**, 144, 177

Goodman, Jeffrey 183

Gorman, Brent 95

Graben, Louis 131

Grant, Campbell 182

Grant, Ludovic 49, 52, 77

Greeks 64, 72-94, 122, 150, 156-57, 179, 196, 218

Green, Clarissa 65

Greenberg, Joseph H. 14, 181

Greene, Dorcas 148

Guignes, Joseph de 201

Guion Miller Rolls 23-24, 132, 136-37, 144-47

Gurule, Patricia 110

H (lineage, haplogroup) 61-62, 103, 111-12, 210

Haak, Wolfgang 162

Hand, George and Mary 68; Zella 68

*Handbook of American Indians* 27

Harris, Hendon M., Jr. 199; Joel E. 101, 111

Hart, Annie Elizabeth Aruna 148; Bear 148

Haston, Mary Lackey **143**

Hawaii 77, 102, 162-67, 211, 215

Haynes, Gregory Damon 125

Henry I 7

Herodotus 71

Hewitt, J. N. B. 75

Hispanics 4, 53, 109, 127, 205-7

Hohokam 87, 91, 159-62, 166, 182, 203-4

Holman, Tony 154

Homastubbee, Chief 31

Hooton, Earnest 182

Hopi Indians 77, 84-89, 91-96, 159-62, 166; Egyptian words and 87-88; reservation 2; sun clan tablet **94**

Horai, Satoshi 97

Huichol Indians 203, 207

Hurd, June 104

Hurst, Raymond 35

Hyde, Betsy Walker 50-51, 64

Hynson, Johnny 42; Pamela 36, 42

I (lineage, haplogroup) 97, 123

Incas 77

Indian Gallery 19

Indian Territory 3, 17, 29-30, 35-36, 63, 65, 118, 121, 132, 136-37, 145, 147

Indian Tribes Southeast e-mail discussion group 130

Individual Indian Monies 9-10, 46-47

Inman, Henry 154

*International Newsletter on Rock Art* 167

Ironwood National Forest 200, 203

Iroquois 18-19; *see also* Mohawk Indians

Israel 56, 62-63, 70, 72, 78, 96, 152, 170

J (lineage, haplogroup) 64-65, 216

Jackson, Andrew 30; Elizabeth 148

James I 2

James, William 221

Jefferson, Thomas 177

Jett, Stephen 10, 196

Jews 29, 32, 43, 48-55; ancestry 115, 119-20, 130, 138, 145-53, 176, 152; Ashkenazic 50, 52, 69, 114, 122-23, 186; crypto 51-55, 147, 149, 151, 184; diseases 171; holocaust 43, 153; Sephardic 50, 54, 67, 114-15, 126, 138, 145, 177, 188, 192, 200

Johannessen, Carl L. 197

Johansen, Bruce E. 46-47

Jones, Peter N. 14-15, 50, 100, 221

Jordan, Enoch 67, 138

*The Journal of Cherokee Studies* 26

17952943R10145

Made in the USA
San Bernardino, CA
22 December 2014